THE
Economics
OF Ethnic
Conflict

THE
Economics
OF Ethnic
Conflict
THE CASE OF BURKINA FASO

Andreas Dafinger

Associate Professor of Social Anthropology
Central European University, Budapest

JAMES CURREY

James Currey
is an imprint of
Boydell & Brewer Ltd
PO Box 9, Woodbridge
Suffolk IP12 3DF (GB)
www.jamescurrey.com
and of
Boydell & Brewer Inc.
668 Mt Hope Avenue
Rochester, NY 14620-2731 (US)
www.boydellandbrewer.com

© Andreas Dafinger 2013

First published 2013

1 2 3 4 5 16 15 14 13

British Library Cataloguing in Publication Data
A catalogue record for this book is available on request from the British Library

ISBN 978-1-84701-068-1 (James Currey cloth)

The publisher has no responsibility for the continued existence or accuracy of URLs for
external or third-party internet websites referred to in this book, and does not guarantee
that any content on such websites is, or will remain, accurate or appropriate.

Papers used by Boydell & Brewer are natural, recycled products
made from wood grown from sustainable forests.

Typeset in 12/13 Bembo with Albertus MT display
by Avocet Typeset, Somerton, Somerset
Printed and bound in Great Britain
by CPI Group (UK) Ltd, Croydon, CR0 4YY

Contents

List of Maps

List of Figures

List of Tables

Acronyms

AVV	Aménagements des Vallées des Voltas (Volta Valley Improvement Scheme) Resettlement Programme in the 1970s
DANIDA	Danish development organization. Major financer of PDR and PIHVES
IGB	Institut Géographique du Burkina
IMF	The International Monetary Fund
MEE	Ministère de l'environnement et de l'eau
MVVN	Programme de mise en valeur de la vallée de Nouhao (Pastoral Zone). Development organization
PDR	Projet du développement rural. Development organization
PIHVES	Projet Hydraulique. Built 800 wells in the province over the past 10 years. Development organization
RAF	Réorganisation Agraire et Foncière. (Land reforms of 1984, 1991 and 1994 allowing private ownership in land)

Vernacular Expressions
(in Bisa)

bagotodo	Diviner
djatigi (Dyoula)	Non-Fulbe host, often in town
kiri	Village chief
kje	An individual's hut within a compound
naba	King or chief. Head of a cluster of villages
parza	Household head
tarabale	(annual) sacrifice to the earth, carried out by the earthpriest, *taraza*
taraza	Earthpriest, descendant of the firstcomers
zirobalen	Sacrifice to the ancestors

Acknowledgements

This book would not have been possible without the help and support of many people and academic institutions.

My first thanks go to people in Boulgou and Burkina Faso, with whom I had the pleasure of living and working, especially Abdoulaye Diallo and Issaka Bangagne, field assistants and friends over many years. I thank them and many other people for their commitment and hospitality. They helped make Burkina Faso my second home and I dedicate this book to them in gratitude.

Academically, I am indebted to Günter Schlee as the director of the Max Planck Institute for Social Anthropology in Halle for providing a most stimulating academic environment. The Institute has been my intellectual home for several years, and its financial and logistical support helped realize most of the studies presented in this book. My special thanks go to all my colleagues there for creating a wonderful, productive and enjoyable atmosphere. At the University of Leipzig, Bernhard Streck has been a generous supporter of my work. Stephen Reyna and Nina Glick Schiller have also been there for me over many years.

This work has also profited from the research I carried out at the Department of Anthropology at the University of Manchester as a Fellow of the Leverhulme Trust. My sincere thanks go to both institutions. The Central European University in Budapest provided important support in the concluding phases of this book.

My most heartfelt thanks go to Ana Carden Coyne for being a critical and most encouraging reader and my strongest moral support.

Dedication

To Aysher

1

Introduction

In the two decades since the end of the cold war the world has seen a profound change in the way conflicts are perceived. Conflicts appear smaller in scale, larger in number, and more local in scope. Having lost the support of a clear-cut world order, public perception and the media have had to find ways of explaining and categorizing these new conflicts, which were often no longer wars between nation states or national alliances. Conflicts are often perceived as directed against the state and most violence as insurgencies against the state's monopoly of warfare, power and jurisdiction. Wars are led by groups that are often, despite more appropriate terms, considered 'ethnic', and the new category, 'ethnic conflicts', has become a catch-all term to include most clashes on sub-national levels.

This book presents a series of case studies from Burkina Faso to show that this is not merely a process of global (re-)classification, but that the change of rhetoric has begun to reshape social relations on the ground, impact upon political strategies and affect local production patterns. As national and developmental organizations refute ethnic criteria, 'non-ethnicity' has become a key factor in defining civic entitlements and political participation. Ethnic groups, ethnically defined tensions and resource competition stand as synonyms for the pre-modern, under-developed and unruly and offer legitimate frames for political and judicial intervention. At the same time, local groups, elites and individuals appropriate the discourse over ethnicity when dealing with the state (and with development and other NGOs) in order to secure scarce resources under pressure from population growth and climate change.

The increased focus on ethnic conflicts, or rather, 'ethnicized' conflicts, is also indicative of wider interest in local systems of political and economic production. Ethnicity is often seen as an impermeable barrier between open global networks and local relations (Chapters 2 and 4). The neoliberal turn in world economics since the 1980s has emphasized direct access of global economic networks to local resources, especially through the privatization of essential infrastructure, such as health, education and communication. States now increasingly draw their raison d'être from being agents of a global economic community, safeguarding principles of free trade and enterprise. Paradoxically, while the state is expected to withdraw from the public sector and give up its economic stakes in the former first and second world, it is, in most African countries, only now making its appearance on the local level as a political and legal authority, replacing local political systems.

It was only after the implementation of the new liberal agenda that many African states effectively pursued land privatization (Chapter 2) and conflict prevention (Chapter 5), and in the process they have, eventually, become significant actors at local level. None of the conflicts and local economic and social relations with which this book engages can be seen independently of the 'arriving state' and the process of global economic integration. Although defined by local practice and specific historical conditions, the processes described are the result of both national and international developments. A large number of the institutions which regenerate ethnic boundaries are the outcome of colonial and post-colonial politics and economics. World market prices affect local production and have an immediate effect on how conflicts are negotiated: damage involving cash crops, for example, is less likely to be tolerated than damage in the millet fields. The same is true for many other contested resources, such as education, health or political recognition, which had only been created or supplied by state and development organizations. In supplying these resources, organizations define legitimate user groups and modes of appropriation and also control any conflicts over these assets.

Struggles in the local arena are also exploited by local elites in their attempts to re-appropriate ethnicity and ethnicized conflicts. Social groups set up ethnic boundaries through local practice, build local economies on the ethnic division of labour and lead conflicts that are defined through the ethnic boundary. In almost all cases, these ethnic conflicts lack the violence that shapes public perception: ethnicity is foremost a means of controlling local political, social and economic relations and conflicts are an essential part of a local agropastoral economy. That is, however, no reason to underrate these conflicts or to romanticize ethnicity as a means of anti-state resistance.

The chapters that follow reveal the injustices inherent in this system and name the winners and the losers – and this book has not been written in defence of local practice. In fact, the ethnic division of labour and political authority – just as that along gender lines or the uneven distribution of authority according to age – is a source of profound injustice. Nor have local resource regimes delivered proof that they might master the imminent demographic and ecological changes.

The state's approach of turning a blind eye and officially disregarding and delegitimizing ethnicity is, however, not a real alternative, as I will argue. The discrimination that is produced in the local ethnicized discourse works its way into state and development organizations. As a result, we see local elites continuing to dominate the process of resource allocation through these institutions: ethnic criteria are concealed by formal parameters. The 'ethnicization of bureaucracy' (Chapter 5) turns out to be a more complex phenomenon than anthropological approaches to ethnicity and ethnic conflicts have previously assumed. Development organizations that draw on principles of civil society and states that pursue explicitly non-ethnic politics do not exclude certain marginal groups as a result of ethnically selective recruitment – the exclusion of marginal groups and positive discrimination of others.

The bureaucratic elites in fact think less along ethnic lines and define themselves more through an ideology of modernism. In their shared view they see themselves as spearheading the transformation process and tend to dissociate themselves from members of their own home communities, which are often constituted along ethnic criteria.

Still, most current models on ethnic politics – or politicized ethnicity – presume an implicit preference for members of the same ethnic group. They do not explain, however, *why* the administrative elites should privilege members of their own ethnic groups. Many of these theories explicitly argue within a constructivist framework; building on the premise that ethnicity is exploited in the struggle over collective goods and infrastructural resources supplied by the state (Cohen, 1974). However, this still risks letting primordialist assumptions in through the back door, when those same models invoke shared language, shared culture, sentiments of common origin, kinship and trust as presumed motives of ethnic nepotism (Geertz, 1963; 1994; Wimmer, 2004).

The reasons why some ethnic groups, such as the Fulbe herders in this book, often are (or perceive themselves to be) disadvantaged by the administration in terms of access to basic infrastructure are found elsewhere, as the following cases suggest. While the administration does not necessarily perceive itself as representative of any ethnic group and rather tends to dissociate itself from ethnic fellowship, the state and its related agents ignore the fact that ethnic ascriptions are still viable categories in public discourse and local politics, and so allow for their continued, but concealed, persistence. In the local arena, ethnic relations remain strongly defined by criteria that have their roots in colonial practice: ethnic groups are ranked according to their degree of 'civilization', putting sedentary farmers over allegedly 'semi-nomadic' herders, principles of territorial organization over systems of selected resource control. Local perceptions of groups and practices as 'less or more civilized' show how the colonial rhetoric of ethnicity has entered the vernacular. While the administration may have established new ways of defining entitlement in accordance with a new global discourse of economic self-determination, such delineation persists as a means of inclusion and exclusion, of controlling access to economic, social and political resources between local groups.

This book approaches ethnically framed conflicts as occurrences of everyday life. It traces how ethnicity and ethnically framed conflict are at the heart of the local economy and analyses how these local conflicts are perceived and dealt with by national politics and international development practice. While state and development organizations tend to identify these tensions and conflicts as a competition over limited resources between socio-economic user groups, and regard them as obstacles to sustainable development and civil society formation, this book will take a different perspective and argue that the fight is less about the typical resources of an agropastoral economy, such as land and water, nor about modern state-supplied resources as others have argued (Asche, 1994; Cohen, 1981; Olivier de Sardan, 1988; Wimmer, 2004), but rather about political and social authority and control. Berry has already suggested that historically people, not land, were the scarce resource in Africa (Berry, 1993: 181). This book will show that despite the increasing pressure on the land, this claim still holds true in most local, national and global political contexts. At the same time, it becomes apparent that competition happens less between the groups than within the respective communities. The framing of conflicts as ethnic helps to conceal personal inter-ethnic ties, which, however, constitute an important resource. The concept of concealment of these political and economic relations across the ethnic divide is the central model and main argument of this book.

Scarce resources and scarcity as a resource

> '…les colonisateurs se sont transformés en assistants techniques;
> en fait, nous devrions dire qu'ils se sont transformés
> en assassins techniques'
> *Thomas Sankara*[1]

The small province of Boulgou, which is at the heart of this book, faces a chronic scarcity of resources. For its rural population, water and land are the most important concerns; during the dry season people in some remote settlements need to walk for hours to fetch water and the agricultural production constantly falls short of people's demands: in dire years, the land barely yields half of what is considered a minimum. In response, Boulgou has seen an increasing number of national and international development projects over the past decades, attempting to improve access to existing resources and to provide new ones. This, needless to say, has strongly affected local resource use patterns and resource control regimes. The new agents have established themselves as major actors with vested political and economic interests.

Consequently, anthropology also finds itself operating in a field that is shaped by the interaction of local groups with state and development organizations and their respective ecological, economic and political trajectories. The fight over modern resources, as supplied by these new agents, is just as fierce as the struggle over natural resources. The cases reported in this book reveal that skills in dealing with administration and bureaucracy are as vital as knowledge about agricultural or pastoral production.

One line of anthropological reasoning argues that modern conflicts are largely about competition over these new pools of collective goods as supplied by the state. While this cannot be denied, approaches that focus on modern resources as causes for conflict largely tend to overlook the agency of local actors and local social institutions. Local populations are not simply users of natural resources and recipients of modern infrastructural resources; they constitute a source of political legitimacy and economic power. Even critical models in development anthropology often disregard the fact that the state and the development machine are competitors over social and political resources and

---

[1] 'The colonizers have turned into technical assistants; actually, we should say that they have turned into technical assassins.' At the 25th meeting of the Organization of African Unity, Addis Ababa, July 1987.

at the same time equitable actors in the local arena. The field we are looking at is equally defined by local elites, marginalized groups and members of the administrative and development complex alike.

Scarcity is Boulgou's Achilles' heel in more ways than one. On the one hand, it is an obvious source of constant hardship and insecurity, yet it is also the gateway for the array of interventionist projects and organizations on which the precarious local economy depends (Bierschenk and Elwert, 1988; Olivier de Sardan, 1988; Kremling, 2004: 224–79). Most organizations have focused on resource scarcity in the fight against poverty, or 'la lutte contre la pauvreté' (UNDP, 2009), which they often see as the result of limited natural resources in combination with increasing population, inefficient resource use and inefficient management systems.

At the same time, resource scarcity has been identified as a principal cause of conflict. Most state-run programmes, development organizations and modernization projects operate on these or similar neo-Malthusian assumptions: that resources are objectively scarce and that they are becoming continuously sparser as populations increase. It is indeed hard to deny this argument's logic: when I arrived in Boulgou for the first time in fall 1994, the province had 350,000 people; as I write these lines, Boulgou is home to twice as many. Everybody I talk to readily confirms that access to land was so much easier 'then' and bush fields used to be 'so much closer'. There is always some lamenting when people reminisce about the past, but this one holds a grain of truth: people are running out of the land and the resources on which they depend.

Scarcity, however, is not merely a recent phenomenon, and not only an 'objective' problem, the consequence of a growing population running short of arable land. Scarcity is also politically induced and a prerequisite of political control: those who control access to land and other resources derive their power from precisely the fact that these resources are not abundant: controlling scarcity is a source of political and economic power. Interventionist 'relief' programmes which bring in (and consequently control) resources such as safe water, wells or educational, hygienic and health provisions, also 'restructure' local production systems in order to increase agricultural or pastoral output and to integrate local systems into a national and international framework. Privatization and economic restructuring invariably rank in the top five of international cure-all remedies (ibid.).

Are NGOs, in other words, Trojan horses (or technological assassins, in Sankara's more revolutionary terms, above)? Over-emphasizing the vested interests of development organizations in such a way may sound objectionable in the light of the factual shortage of and demand for water and food – and neither would it do justice to the agency of the people. Moreover, as this book also shows, there is no reason to believe that current resource use patterns could have kept up with the imminent demographic and economic changes. Local practice may have been able to deal with resource distribution and provide social order over the past hundred years or more. It might well do so for a number of years to come. But there is no indication that the current arrangements will be able to tackle the challenges of the next generations. Land is running out, based on current population growth and present cultivation techniques. Moreover, the state and international development organizations have made their appearance, and the impact of global market forces on the local economy cannot be simply wished away. The question is how this imminent change is negotiated between the various stakeholders.

Anthropological research needs to acknowledge and scrutinize the fact that the state and its agents have not come to distribute free gifts, but appear on the scene as competitors over political, social, judicial and economic power. On the local level, the new agents hide their agenda of political, economic and social restructuring behind a screen of material relief (while, on a global stage, the political ambitions are openly discussed). With new competitors in the scramble for economic assets and political power, we also witness competition over new definitions of groups and over defining the nature of social relations: a new meta-conflict (Horowitz, 1991: 27). Local elites (landowners, religious and political authorities, land-holding household heads) and new agents (members of state bureaucracy and development administration) draw on different principles of group formation to secure followers, legitimize authority and to contest their rivals' claims, by devaluating other criteria of inclusion and exclusion. On the one hand, infrastructural resources respond to the immediate needs of the local population, but on the other they are part and parcel of a redefinition of entitlements, which are no longer controlled by the local elites.

Before turning to questions of how local elites compete with national and international organizations in this field, we need to look at how resources are negotiated between the local elites and how resource conflicts are exploited by dominant local groups pursuing their own vested political and social interests. From the actors' point of view, most of these conflicts are framed in ethnic terms and the production and reproduction of ethnicity is a key element in this process. As this study will reveal, competition happens much less between the respective communities than within these groups. In the following sections, I will ask what issues are at stake and look at the way rights and obligations are negotiated within each of the groups.

Land rights, resources and ethnic conflict

In answering these questions, this book does not have to venture into uncharted territory. Major scholars have explored land use patterns and described their relation to changing global conditions. Several authors (Bassett and Crummey, 1993; Berry, 1993; 2002; Downs and Reyna, 1988, and Moore, 1998) have elaborated extensively on the complexity of West African land rights and their social implications. They have contributed to what has become canonical knowledge in legal and developmental anthropology: the fact that land is the substance and language of social and political relations in agricultural African societies. Their works have furnished us with an anthropological toolbox, allowing us to show the impact (and often the inadequacy) of state-run 'restructuring programmes' and the resilience of local land regimes. They have also helped to emphasize the agency of individuals in manoeuvring between the spheres of local and national property regimes. The description of land rights in this book will confirm the complexity of local land tenure regimes, and the political ordering of social groups according to their differential degrees of relatedness, and access rights, to land. At the same time, however, the study highlights the fundamental dichotomy of landed and landless groups, which coincides with socio-economic and – most importantly in the present case – ethnic delineations.

This is where we need to go beyond the debate over changing land rights and look at the nexus of land and ethnicity. Ethnicity is not merely seen as a marker of differential access to landed resources; more importantly, ethnicity and ethnically framed conflicts are used to delineate a distinct social and economic sphere that is largely hidden from members of the ethnic group itself and helps to overcome the major restrictions that are part of kinship, i.e. intra-group economy.

A work that focuses on resource competition, conflicts and ethnicity, examining the question of how resource use is negotiated and shared along ethnically defined criteria, will eventually find itself in the company of a broad range of contributions to 'ethnic conflict'. The sheer number of publications on the topic is almost insurmountable as is the scope of conflicts that are more or less systematically labelled as 'ethnic'. Virtually unused in both the academic and non-academic world before the 1960s, the term 'ethnic conflict' has become synony-

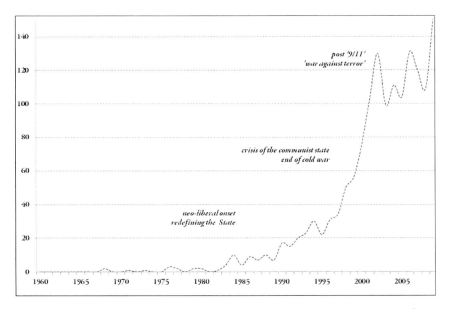

Figure 1 Books published on ethnic conflict by year of publication[2]

mous with almost any violent or non-violent clash below the nation state level – too broad to be of analytical value.

The Library of Congress Catalogue, the major repository of publications in the Anglophone world, lists fewer than 70 books on ethnic conflicts in the three decades before the end of the cold war, compared to almost 1,600 published in the 20 years after 1989. The social sciences were not alone in the field: in fact, only a small number of the books are scholarly works. Academic analysis of ethnic relations competes with diverging interpretations by public media and policy makers. Any anthropological study thus needs to delineate itself from common sense notions of ethnicity and ethnic conflict, but at the same time needs to incorporate these images into its analysis.

Global, mass-mediated notions of ethnicity, resource competition and conflict shape local relations and open new options for actors on the ground. In its analysis, this book leans on a tradition of critical development studies, reaching from Immanuel Wallerstein's world system model (e.g. Wallerstein; 1974; 2004a and b), James Scott's critical views of the homogenizing state machinery (Scott; 1998), to explicit criticism of development schemes as put forward by Ferguson

[2] Source: Library of Congress electronic catalogue. The search was carried out using the voyager database (z3950.loc.gov, Sep 06, 2011). Search for 'ethnic' + 'conflict' in book title or abstract. Search returned a total of 1641 titles published between 1900 and 2008. Wimmer (2004) has compiled and published a similar list, drawing on different sources and using a smaller dataset, however showing the same trajectory, with a pronounced increase on publications after the end of the cold war.

and Gupta (Ferguson and Gupta 1992; Gupta 1995). Tim Allen's works on the media's role in shaping a common sense understanding of local politics are a constant reminder that nothing in the periphery can be regarded independently of political processes in the centres of global power (Allen, Hudson and Seaton, 1996; Allen and Seaton, 1999).

I aim to answer to what extent the conflicts between Bisa farmers and Fulbe herders, described in this book, are ethnic conflicts in the sense of the politicized and mediatized image in global discourse. In doing so, I will address two distinct levels: on a local scale, conflicts are an integral part of social, political and economic relations. Relations between ethnic groups are marked by high intensity low-level conflicts, which are generally non-violent. Most of these tensions are an integral part of everyday relations and a number of social and economic institutions are located on the ethnic boundary building on these tensions; local elites often have a vested interest in maintaining a high frequency of these embedded low intensity conflicts.

On a second level, from the point of view of the nation state and international organizations, the 'ethnic' dimension of local relations and conflicts is a major obstacle to tenure security, state rule and the implementation of formal economic principles. Conflict avoidance, accordingly, is a major issue on the agenda of restructuring pro-grammes. At the same time, administration and many development organizations attempt to establish a different reading of local relations and conflicts. Rather than viewing local relations as primarily ethnic, local tensions are seen as outcomes of resource competition. This enables governmental and non-governmental organizations to address the problem through relief programmes, delivering resources and redefining the boundaries of conflict parties as user groups – a process Ferguson (1990; 2006) identified as the 'anti-politics machine' of inter-national development. In the end, all parties, the local elites and the new agents, emissaries of state and post-state led development compete over the nature of the conflict (Horowitz, 1991: 27).

The study of conflict

In current anthropological literature and beyond, 'conflict' is largely synonymous with violent conflict. This view marks a turn from earlier anthropological models of conflict from the 1950s onward that followed a more inclusive understanding (Aronoff, 1976; Gluckman, 1964; Goody, 1957; LeVine, 1961; Sahlins, 1961). Subsequent approaches became increasingly concerned with the causes and dynamics of violence in conflict (Chagnon, 1968; Ferguson and

Whitehead, 1992; Hallpike, 1973; Horowitz, 1985; Kapferer, 1988; Spencer, 1990), rather than looking at conflict in more general terms. There is certainly much to be gained from differentiating between peaceful disputes among violent and systematic persecutions of groups; motives and actors in violent conflicts are often not identical, expectations of outcome are likely to differ and processes of conflict settlement are different (Esman and Telhami, 1995; Hill, 1987). Over the past decades, a rising number of ethnic conflicts have made issues of organized violence an increasingly important issue globally (Ferguson, 2003; Gurr, 1993; Gurr and Harff, 2003). Recent works, however, also indicate a shift back to a broader understanding of conflict, underscoring its social embeddedness and interpreting conflict as part of a wider field of social options (Elwert, 2001; Elwert, Feuchtwang and Neubert, 1999; Esman, 2004; Schlee, 2006; Spencer, 1990). Eriksen insists that some types of conflict need to be predominantly non-violent by definition, such as struggles for recognition of ethnic groups within the nation state, which holds the monopoly of power and use of violence (Eriksen, 2002: 2).

Proponents of later approaches criticize violence-focused models for neglecting the role of individual agency; anthropological approaches need to consider participants as social actors and take violence and war as processes rather than as events (e.g. Schmidt, 1999: 211). Along the same line, Richards came to the conclusion that war is just 'one social project among many competing social projects' (Richards and Helander, 2005: 3). 'The danger of analyzing war as a disorderly 'bad' is that it tends to take war out of its social context' (ibid.). By discarding assumptions of conflict as 'disorderly' and dysfunctional, he emphasizes that any violent conflict is embedded in a field of social actions and thus cannot be 'bad' per se.

Ethnicity

The boundaries between the major ethnic groups draw on a number of culturally embedded practices and ideologies. Views of ideal social orders based on kinship and marriage rules differ clearly between Fulbe and Bisa, the two major ethnic groups in this study. Fulbe are almost all cattle herders and share a worldview that gravitates around cattle and mobility. Bisa, who are almost as exclusively farmers, feel deeply rooted in the land; their social, political and religious institutions are intricately connected to concepts of locality and autochthony. The different importance of land between the two groups – a non-territorial as opposed to a territorial view of the environment – is also a major obstacle in achieving a shared communal identity.

Perceived and factual differences are cause for the legitimacy of institutions' interventions and of the on-going processes that generate and regenerate the ethnic divide. The religious division of labour is based on the belief that Fulbe are specialists in dealing with spirits; economic division rests on the presumption that Fulbe are more skilful and trained in dealing with cattle; and the division of political authority is rooted in territorial vs. non-territorial forms of group formation. This division of rights and obligations underlines the mutual dependency and integration of groups on both sides of the ethnic divide into an overarching, 'meta'-society. Each interaction that draws on the division of labour at the same time legitimizes and regenerates the ethnic boundary.

This ethnic divide is highly ambiguous: the protagonists on both sides seem determined to maintain the image of an impermeable and often antagonistic and irreconcilable division of groups and individuals grounded in ethnic stereotypes. The public image of these interethnic relations is dominated by mutual accusations of fraud and embezzlement, violation of laws and conventions, by the high frequency of conflicts between members of either group and other social frictions.

However, manifold relations between individuals exist across the boundaries. Friendship ties, economic exchange based on trust, senses of shared locality and middlemen services build bridges across the ethnic divide. This, in itself, is hardly surprising. An entire school of anthropological conflict studies was built around the existence of these cross-cutting ties (Aronoff 1976; Gluckman 1964), convinced of their function in containing conflict and building paths of reconciliation. Gluckman's model was later modified, extended and eventually downgraded to explain cross-cutting ties in certain contexts; in Chapter IV, I will engage with these approaches in more detail. In other cases, bonds across ethnic boundaries can actually aggravate or be the cause of conflict.

The ethnic divide and the concealed economy

The cases in this book will propose yet another interpretation of cross-cutting ties. Relations between Bisa farmers and Fulbe herders suggest that such ties provide a scarce resource, which is produced through ethnic division and tensions: along with a number of social and economic institutions, they are located on the ethnic border and draw on its negative connotation, its alleged impermeability and opacity. By maintaining the ethnic boundary, actors create and recreate an opaque screen behind which they can carry out economic and political operations that cannot be performed in the public eye. In my analysis, I refer to these practices as a 'concealed economy', to account for the fact that social and economic assets are hidden behind an opaque screen erected on the ethnic boundary and to stress the rationality of these hidden forms of exchange.

One such example of a concealed economy is the practice of cattle entrustment that allows farmers to hide their wealth (in animals) from the prying eyes of their fellow kin by pasturing them with Fulbe herders. Many farmers keep cattle as an investment and as a buffer against harvest failures. Redistribution rules within the kin groups, however, make it almost impossible to accumulate any form of wealth openly. As a result, most farmers decide to 'hide' their cattle by entrusting them to Fulbe herders – to reclaim them in times of need. Entrusting cattle is a highly complex procedure that requires a high degree of trust. Given the secrecy of the operation, these transactions have no middlemen to vouch for the exchange. Given the material value of the animals entrusted (a single cow may be worth up to one year's harvest), and the otherwise negative representation of the ethnic other in the public discourse, this is most remarkable. The 'over-communication' of conflicts and ethnic tensions mainly provides the actors with a means of keeping the boundary opaque.

On the other side of the opaque screen, local Fulbe communities exploit the ethnic divide to ward off transhumant herders, who are their major competitors over pasture and other pastoral resources. Fulbe are generally in an underprivileged position as they depend on resources which are largely controlled by the dominant farmers' clans with whom they compete over the local resources – a fact that is incessantly stressed in public conversations. Despite this inequality in resource access and the public rhetoric around it, fellow herders in fact pose a much greater threat: resource use between pastoralists and agriculturalists can often be staggered along temporal and spatial lines; resources relevant to the herders (pasture, waterholes) on the contrary are less easily shared.

A dilemma which Fulbe communities consequently face is the need to keep away other herders, while simultaneously maintaining the rhetoric of ethnic solidarity. The resident Fulbe communities have found a solution to this problem by delegating resource control to neighbouring farmers, while they themselves tap into resources on the other side of the ethnic divide and ensure privileged access to pasture and water by exploiting their (hidden) inter-ethnic friendship ties.

Yet the ethnic border does not only depend on the permanence of conflicts. Any movement across the ethnic divide is also marked by a transition between different economic spheres and by different types of social relations (e.g. confidence vs. trust based, permanent vs. performative). The ethnic boundary not only helps to conceal social and economic relations from members of the ethnic group, it also prevents the state and other institutions from accessing local resources. From the point of view of formal economic institutions, the concealed economy can only appear as a shadow economy: the agents of modernization have a stake in revealing and formalizing economic transactions; make them taxable and impose political and judicial authority on local relations.

Friendship and the informality of exchange

Cattle, goods and services that are moved between the ethnic groups also oscillate between different spheres of exchange: farmers' cattle which are put into the custody of a Fulbe herder can no longer simply be sold or exchanged. This inexchangeability of certain goods was at the heart of Paul and Laura Bohannan's argument when they established the concept of spheres of exchange in anthropology (P. Bohannan, 1959; P. Bohannan and L. Bohannan, 1968) and a range of later studies that have shown its relevance throughout major parts of sub-Saharan Africa (e.g. P. Bohannan and Dalton, 1965; Gudeman, 1986; Hutchinson, 1992; I. Kopytoff, 1986; Piot, 1991; Shipton, 1989). When exchange between spheres occurs, so the argument goes, this was mainly the outcome of corrosion of the local economy through the colonial impact and through universal money. Piot, some 30 years later, however, proposed inverting the argument, suggesting that boundaries between the spheres exist 'precisely to be transgressed' (Piot, 1991: 409). It is this imbalanced exchange that establishes complex – and lasting – sets of social relationships. As exchange between the spheres can never be entirely level, it establishes and recreates complex and lasting social relationships. Piot's model is especially helpful in considering the exchange of cattle and herding labour. While the goods and services that are exchanged are the same across the spheres – cattle, herding labour, access rights, institutional favours – their meaning and the type of value that is transformed changes: gifts turn into commodities and cultural values become monetized. Gudeman suggested that separate spheres of exchange should be viewed as distinct cultural domains that are reified through complex cultural practices and expressed in cultural dichotomies, such as pastoral vs. agricultural production (Gudeman, 1986: 110–28).

Much of this reverberates in the opposition between Bisa farmers and Fulbe herders in Burkina Faso. In this case, the ethnic divide between the groups is maintained and reproduced through religious and economic practices, marked, as will be seen, by different production systems and by the emphasis of cultural and linguistic difference. Social, economic and political incompatibility is also at the heart of the narrative of perennial conflict, while – much as Piot predicted – the transition between the domains creates intense and complex social relations, an amalgam of conflict and friendship.

Unlike conflict, however, friendship still appears under-studied and under-conceptualized. This may be partly because friendship does not generate corporate groups and as a result has long failed to attract systematic sociological attention outside network analysis (Dafinger, 2004a; 2011; Gulliver, 1971). Nor does friendship constitute an exclusive category that can meaningfully be juxtaposed to other forms of social relations, such as socio-economic or local groups. Friendship ties rather tend to exist within and interact with kinship and other social webs.

Friendship studies were also confronted with the fluidity and polysemic nature of the concept (Bell and Coleman, 1999: ibid.; Desai and Killick, 2010; Firth, 1967). To Schmidt and Rexroth, however, 'the amorphous character of friendship' also suggested 'that friendship relations often carry much of a society's structural weight' (Schmidt et al., 2007: 9). African studies underscored friendship as an essential of the social fabric – which they often considered equally important as kinship ties (Bollig, 1998; Grätz, 2004; Grätz, Meier and Pelican, 2004; Gulliver, 1971; Schmidt et al., 2007). In particular, pastoral groups and inter-ethnic relations conceptualized friendship as an integral part of intra- and inter-group social and economic relations. Given the uncertainty of the pastoral lifestyle, such friendship ties helped to provide material security (Bollig, 1998; Gulliver, 1971; Moritz, 2011 [2003]; Schneider, 1979). This book confirms this observation. Friendship is often manifested through exchange relations and takes on a very pragmatic shape, even when the rhetoric in some of the accounts also stresses the emotional aspects and the pride of maintaining friendship across existing divides, as in the rural-urban 'djatigi' relations (Boesen, 2007; Dupire, 1996; Moritz, 2011 [2003]; van Dijk, 2000). Friendship often exists within other types of social relations: it may gradually morph into or out of patron-client (Du Toit, 1978; Klute, 2011) or host-newcomer relations (Lentz, 1995), may overlap with neighbourhood groups (Dafinger, 1999; 2004a), or cut straight across mutually exclusive divides such as class, ethnicity or different socio-economic systems.

Even though not mutually exclusive, friendship and kinship often belong to different cultural domains. Seligman has pointed to the distinction between confidence (the belief in the structural reliability of kinship webs) and trust (in individual partners) in this regard, whereby kinship ties are part of a persistent social order and can be drawn upon even after long periods of social inactivity (Grätz, Meier and Pelican, 2004; Seligman, 1997), while friendship ties generally need to be maintained and require continuous reaffirmation of trust through performance, exchange, mutual advice or general sociability, and that while it may well be true that a friend is often simply 'someone in whose company one feels at ease', as Gulliver described the essence of friendship, this needs to be nurtured and reaffirmed (ibid.: 17). The importance of exchange, gifts and counter-gifts cannot only be seen as having aspects of pragmatism but also appears to be constitutive parts of friendship itself: the exchange of goods and services are as much a token of friendship, as friendship emerges out of services rendered and gifts exchanged. Unsurprisingly, friendship is the dominant idiom that describes the relations that tie individuals across the ethnic and economic boundaries in the following chapters. It simultaneously creates social ties that help contain and mitigate conflict, and provides economic avenues that help people cope with the uncertainties of agro-pastoral production.

For Beer this liquidity is one of the essences of friendship, which she defines as 'an informal social relationship' (Beer, 2001: 5805). While this certainly grasps the difference between the rigid patterns that exist within the kin groups and the much looser personal ties between friends, however, this definition bears its own problems for its implicit assumption of informality as an exclusive category. The cases in the following chapters make it clear that friendship is never without its own behavioural codes and never without social expectations either. Informality, as much as it helps describe the social and economic goings-on outside the kin groups and beyond the state's controlling bureaucracy, can always only be relative. Some modes of transaction may simply be more informal than others, but still more regulated than others. Mostly we need to concur with Keith Hart's observation that informality lies in the eye of the beholder (Hart, 2011).

Local elites, state and development

Friendship transcends the constraints of ethnic categories in a local context, while administrative institutions propagate non-ethnic organization on a national level. By establishing bureaucratic, that is non-ethnic institutions, the state itself, almost paradoxically, has been midwife to a new powerful quasi-ethnic group. The members of state administration distinguish themselves through criteria which in fact are not unlike those of other, ethnically defined groups: language, marriage relations, shared belief, patterns of consumption and even a shared ideology of descent – that roots its ethnogenesis in the foundation of the state, as mentioned before. Functionaries and development officials converse in French (as opposed to the majority of the rural population); they share typical middle-class patterns of consumption, which most of their members perceive in terms of modernity as distinct from local rural livelihoods. As an educated and intellectual elite, they hold in common an ideology that sets them apart from other parts of society and defines them as the avant garde of a national modernization discourse.

This group of middle-class administrative officials shares more commonalities based on class, economic, linguistic and ideological criteria than its members maintain with their respective ethnic home communities. The cases presented in this book will show that this group identity leads to what is largely perceived as an ethnically biased practice of governance. Farmers, for instance, find easier access to national infrastructural resources because of their political and legal organization, which is closer to the principles of rule of the territorial nation state (See Mitchell, 2002; Scott, 1998; for discussions of legibility). At this point, the argument leaves behind models that perceive ethnicization of bureaucracy mainly as an over-representation of specific ethnic groups and the result of administration's recruitment practices.

Disadvantaged groups, such as local herders' communities, tend to frame their discontent in ethnic terms and perceive state administration and development agencies as ethnically biased. These groups are often excluded from infrastructural resources as the result of formally non-ethnic criteria, such as village size, forms of local political (civil) or legal organization. The preconditions, i.e. whether specific groups meet these criteria or not, are, however, created in a local discourse that is based on ethnicity and ethnic division of labour. Ethnic criteria thus determine access to administrative resources on two levels: the quasi-ethnicity of administration on the one hand and the production of ethnicity within the local agro-pastoral communities on the other. The practice of state and development organizations of formally disregarding ethnicity obscures its factual importance: some of the beneficiaries of this concealment are local landholding farmers who enjoy privileged access to modern resources, mostly to the disadvantage of migrants and transhumant herders.

In response to the formation of new quasi-ethnic elites and the ethnicization of the state bureaucracy, Burkina Faso – along with most of its neighbours – witnesses an increasing counter-movement of disadvantaged groups and elites that are excluded from direct access to national and development resources. In the wake of restructuring programmes, a rising number of herders' associations, unions and other civil organizations have appeared in the local and national arenas both offering assistance to the local population and engaging in the fight for political recognition of Fulbe (or 'Fulani') herders as a distinct ethnic and socio-economic group. On a national scale in a politically non-ethnic discourse, these organizations need to communicate their political and economic character, while simultaneously being largely defined by their ethnically homogeneous clientele and membership on a local level. In Chapter 5, I will discuss the implications of this new type of association and relate them to other forms of agropastoral political organizations in different national contexts. In its entity, the argument promotes a new approach to local economic and political systems and their transformation into the nation state and development-oriented governance regimes.

Much of this book deals with an ethnic group that occupies a prominent place in the anthropology of Sub-Saharan Africa: Fulbe herders (occasionally also: *Fulani* [Hausa] or *Peul* [French]). With over fourteen million people, Fulbe constitute one of the largest ethnic groups in the Sudanic belt, constituting significant parts of the population in almost twenty countries (Dafinger, 2004; Hagberg, 2004). For the most part, Fulbe livelihood is based on herding and pastoralism. Even in cases where certain Fulbe groups have been forced to give up herding (Burnham, 1999; de Bruijn and van Dijk, 2001) and joined the urban middle class or the intellectual elites, identity discourses still draw on notions of Fulbe-ness as connected to cattle-herding and a nomadic lifestyle.

The contribution of pastoralists to national economies is significant; in Burkina Faso cattle herders generate up to 20 per cent of national exports within the West African economic zone (Kagone and Reynolds, 2006) and account for 5 per cent of total exports to destinations outside Africa (INSD (Institut national de la statistique et de la démographie), 2010). Herders are, in other words, well integrated in the international political and economic maps of sub-Saharan Africa. At the same time, many Fulbe communities serve as paradigmatic examples of minority groups; mostly as a consequence of their spatial dispersion, they constitute only small fractions of the local populations (Dafinger and Pelican, 2006; Diallo, 2001: 4). Political Fulbe associations exemplify this paradox, as Chapter 5 will illustrate in more detail: many of these organizations are transnational in scope and powerful actors on the international scene – which sets them apart from most farming ethnic groups. At the same time, many fight losing battles for political recognition in the local and national arenas, where farmers seem to enjoy privileged positions in local politics.

The fact that different Fulbe communities are spread over a vast geographic area, almost two dozen nation states and different political systems, does not allow us to talk of a single monolithic Fulbe identity. Nonetheless, essential cultural aspects are at the core of a trans-Fulbe identity and are ideologically and politically reaffirmed: a common language, references to shared origin and history, a presumably shared mode of conduct, *pulaaku* and pastoralism as the dominant mode of livelihood, are repeatedly evoked in local and in international debates over 'Fulbeness'.

In this sense, Fulbe ethnicity has always had a tradition of vertical integration, embracing various strata within Fulbe groups, including nomadic and sedentary, politically powerful kingdoms and dependent sub-groups of local Fulbe communities. Under colonial rule, Fulbe ethnicity also extended laterally with homogenized Fulbe groups across different regions. Colonial administration did not discriminate between different Fulbe identities and created a homogenized and imagined Fulbe identity vis-à-vis the colonial state. If ethnicity is created at its boundaries, as Barth (1969a) suggested, then colonialism brought its own new boundary: it helped create a new meta-ethnicity, a trans-regional pan-Fulbeism, which continued to dominate the scholarly discourse of linguists, anthropologists, historians and politicians for a century. It is only during the past thirty years that social anthropology has come to acknowledge that assuming a general Fulbe identity would obstruct rather than advance analytical work and that we are looking at a plurality of different Fulbe identities in different contexts – Schlee (1997), along this line, speaks of Fulbe 'ethnicities'.

The recent politicization of Fulbe and the formation of a herders' organization has led to the renaissance of a pan-Fulbe identity. In striving for recognition and competition over national resources, Fulbe elites increasingly stress aspects of ethnic Fulbeness. This book (and especially Chapter 5) looks at the resurgence of the debate over a pan-

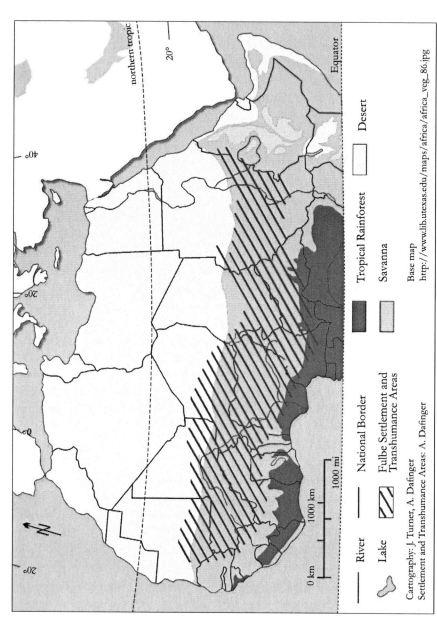

Map 1 Dispersion of Fulbe groups in sub-Saharan Africa (Dafinger, 2004)

Cartography: J. Turner, A. Dafinger
Settlement and Transhumance Areas: A. Dafinger

River — — National Border

Lake — Fulbe Settlement and Transhumance Areas

Tropical Rainforest □ Desert

Savanna

Base map
http://www.lib.utexas.edu/maps/africa/africa_veg_86.jpg

Fulbe identity and analyses these new, hybrid forms of political and ethnic organization as powerful brokers between a political non-ethnic and a local, ethnicized discourse.

Organization of the book

This book is organized into five chapters, starting with a description of the production of ethnic difference on a local level, successively moving on to ethnically framed conflicts and different forms of state intervention. Following on from this introduction, Chapter 2, *The logic of global relations*, introduces the area of research and locates it on the global map by discussing its regional features, natural resources and environmental schema and defining its position in the global political and economic system. Readers familiar with West Africa will find Boulgou a typical example of the social and ecological conditions of agropastoral savannah societies across the Sudanic belt in general. This chapter also reveals the specific political and historical conditions that allow later comparisons to other regions in West Africa, especially when the book discusses different forms of local political organization (in Chapter 5).

Leaning on the model of world system analysis (Hopkins and Wallerstein, 1982; Wallerstein, 2004a and b), the chapter also critically investigates how national and international agents assume control over local political, economic and social processes. The prevailing modernist ideology of building a formal economic sector is contrasted with the reality of subsistence-based production, by which more than 90 per cent of the rural population make a living.

Chapter 3, *Sharing the land: the ethnic division of labour*, focuses on the principles of group formation and local resource use arrangements, following questions of how user groups are delineated and how resources are being shared between these groups. The importance of land and landed relations is explored and the concept of the 'landed-landless continuum' introduced. This permits us to assess how the political and social order is established through differential access and entitlement to land, leading on to a critical assessment of the most recent land reform legislation in the wake of neo-liberal structural adjustment programmes.

The distinction between different degrees of landedness on the one hand and the landless on the other is also a marker of ethnic difference. Entitlements and obligations, which are inscribed in differing degrees of landedness, depend on ethnic classification: the ethnic division of labour, framed in positive terms and perceived as mutually beneficial, in fact reiterates and reaffirms the ethnic divide and persistently recreates the ethnic boundary.

Chapter 4, *Conflict*, describes how this ethnic boundary is perceived as conflict-laden and as a major source of disputes. As conflicts are not exclusive to the ethnic boundary, the chapter begins by describing the full range of possible conflicts in agropastoral Boulgou. Most conflicts are in fact based on tensions within kin groups and households. As entitlements are often legitimized through group membership, kin and other closely related individuals are most likely to have overlapping claims and to compete over similar or identical resources. The chapter's main point is to show how public discourse still focuses on ethnic differences as causes for conflict. The idea of cross-cutting ties will be re-examined in this section and the notion of 'concealment' developed.

Chapter 5, *Concealed economies*, investigates the social and political economy of the ethnic boundary and develops the book's main argument. The analysis shows how goods and services are moved across the ethnic divide and how various actors, local groups, elites and administration, all in their respective manners exploit this divide to secure resources and reify their respective privileged positions in local arenas. This is done by investigating two major agropastoral institutions: the practice of cattle entrustment and the institutionalized landlessness of Fulbe herders. Both are located on the ethnic border and allow the passing of certain goods and services by moving them onto a different sphere of exchange. Cattle and landed resources are converted into gifts, changing their property as commodities, which they possess within the groups.

In its second part, the chapter scrutinizes the role of the state and development organizations; it zooms in on the individual actors, highlighting the motives and practices of the members of the administrative middle class, and provides an alternative to models that take bureaucracy as an (over-)representation of specific ethnic groups. The cases reveal that members of the bureaucracy form a distinct social entity and tend to delineate themselves from local, ethnically defined groups. The administration's preference for certain ethnic groups is a result of the working of the bureaucratic machine and lies in the overlap of principles of ethnic and modernist ideologies rather than the administrators' own backgrounds.

2

The logic of global relations
Burkina Faso, Boulgou & the world

This chapter locates Burkina Faso on the global map and introduces the historical, ecological and political background of the research area – the southern province of Boulgou – and its connection with the wider region. International relations and the local national political landscape will be related to the country's position in the global political and economic network. Most of the modernization projects encountered are part of a wider international discourse: local intra- and inter-ethnic relations are largely framed by a development discourse that is determined by the country's historical and recent positioning in the global system. Using Wallerstein's (1974; 2004 a and b) 'world system' perspective, various threads in Burkina Faso's national and international relations can be tied together and understood as parts of an overarching process. The world system depends on peripheral states such as Burkina Faso largely for their reservoir of human labour as well as for the markets and resources they offer. Analysing the local as part of a global network helps make sense of the role of state agents, international donors and development projects and their interactions. Most organizations encountered on the ground are in some way implementing an agenda that is devised to maintain the new global world order.

Wallerstein's model, however, also received considerable criticism for disregarding the agency of states and other institutions as actors in the process. Evans, Rueschemeyer and Skocpol's 1985 attempt at 'bringing the state back' into this debate calls for a much more promi- nent consideration of states' autonomy in the capitalist core and the former colonial empires, and other institutions, mostly in emerging economies (e.g. Acemoglu and Robinson, 2012). Without disregarding the impact of strong states on developmental and post-developmental economy,[1] a look at many of the peripheries does not always make the state's role as easily discernible. The case of Burkina Faso has long been especially emblematic for the absent state, where international civil organisations preceded the state in implementing the rule of law and in providing modern social and political resources. From this view, the new bureaucratic elite that emerges as an important agent in Burkina Faso's civil society appears far from autonomous or independent of global dependencies.

A criticism that this book provides, draws on Africa's specific historical and cultural condition, an aspect which has often been overlooked in the dependency oriented literature. Many authors have stressed the fact that African agrarian systems of production have differed in fundamental ways from other parts of the world (see e.g., Berry, 1993; Cooper, 1981; Goody, 1976; Guyer, 1993; Shipton and Goheen, 1992; World Bank, 2011) underlining the importance of endogenous factors in shaping Africa's current position in the world economy. By taking account of the historical and cultural dimension of Burkinabe politics and economy and the autonomy of local economic and political agents, this book will contribute to a differentiated view.

In assessing the impact of a global economic system on local social relations, on national political strategies and on the economic avenues by which they by-pass the state, the world systems approach still provides essential analytical tools.

Burkina Faso

Burkina Faso mostly lies below the radar of international politics and global economic interests. Its GDP ranks at the middle of African states (540 USD per capita in 2009 (World Bank, 2011a); the 2010 UN Development Programme Report lists it as 177th of 182 states worldwide (UNDP, 2009). It attracts modest direct foreign investment (171 million USD in 2009 (World Bank, ibid.), and boasts no major industries.[2] Landlocked in central West Africa, the country is a far cry from being a strategic geopolitical asset and lies well off the 'axis' that determine the West's view of the global post-cold-war map. Burkina Faso, while aiming to catch up with its more powerful neighbours, is still at

---

[1] The emerging southern alliances, BRICs, IBSAs, MISTs or the N11s are paradigmatic cases for states that act as (semi-) autonomous agents, interdependent with capital interests, and making claims vis-à-vis the institutions of the established world order, addressing issues of global governance on an inter-state level, and underscoring the claims for the restructuring of the security council, internet governance, or a commitment to global climate control.

[2] A cotton and textile industry, alongside beverage industries (i.e., two local breweries that are foreign owned) and a bicycle and scooter plant, are the only notable exceptions.

the outer margins of the world's economic, political and strategic interests.

This changes slightly when one zooms in on the regional picture. Burkina Faso is a major supplier of labour within the ECOWAS zone: between 2.5 and 3 million Burkinabe live and work in the neighbouring coastal countries, notably Côte d'Ivoire. It is also in Côte d'Ivoire that Burkina Faso connects to a wider global system of economic relations by virtue of its 'human capital'. Wallerstein pointed at the essential role that 'semi-peripheral' states such as Côte d'Ivoire play in integrating outer periphery and core states. In many ways, semi-peripheral states act as proxies of the core in the peripheral region. Their economy is neither fully based on core production (such as high technology), nor exclusively based on the production of raw materials and labour either, and Côte d'Ivoire plays a significant role for the economic functioning of the region. It attracts international interest in consolidating its integration into a globalised network. Semiperipheral states, in Wallerstein's model, also tend to show specific political properties and act as a buffer between peripheral and core states to obfuscate the differential in relative wealth. This became apparent in 2002 – and to a lesser degree more recently again in 2010 – in the wake of the Ivorian crisis. To a large extent this was also the result of the global economic and financial crisis, and expressed itself as a regional affair of internal clashes between power groups, strongly marked by xenophobic undertones.[3] In 2002, most of the estimated three million Burkinabe in Côte d'Ivoire fled across the border into Burkina Faso: from the local angle, international politics and economic foreign relations are mostly and firstly experienced as outcomes of regional events.

Burkina Faso's population is to a large extent rural; over 80 per cent of its citizens live from subsistence-based agriculture and agropastoralism (World Bank, 2006: 81). Only 40 towns nationwide count more than ten thousand inhabitants, of which only five exceed the 50,000 mark, including the urban centres of Bobo-Dioulasso and Ouagadougou. The promise of modernity between the urban and the rural areas can hardly be wider: whereas all cities and major towns are part of the national power network, a mere 2 per cent of rural households have access to electricity (ibid.: 12); the differential in access to safe water, and educational resources is less dramatic but still profound.

The demographic development is one of the decisive factors in the

---

[3] People, born either in Abidjan or having lived there for decades were evicted from Côte d'Ivoire and accommodated by a huge 'repatriation' programme in Burkina Faso. The effects on the receiving communities and the refugees alike were enormous. See also Y. Diallo, 2005.

changes that local resource regimes are undergoing: with 90 inhabitants/km² (2010), land use in the agrarian sector has reached a limit that can no longer guarantee adequate access for large parts of the rural population. People repeatedly stress that arable land has become a major issue and source of conflict to a degree that it had not been before; many of the disputes and conflicts I will present in the following chapters are framed in terms of a growing population and resulting land scarcity. Most development organizations and national modernization programmes, too, have identified demographic growth as the main problem of the near future. Burkina Faso's population was 15.73 million according to an INSD (Institut national de la statistique et de la démographie) 2010b report, twice as many as twenty years ago and is expected to rise by a further ten million before 2025 (FAO, 2004). As the amount of land is limited and population and demand are growing, an increasing number of households have less and less arable land to distribute.

The same is true for access to safe water, which continues to be a major concern for large parts of the rural population. Surface water is only available for a few months during the rainy season and the wells, which are often manually dug, require favourable locations where ground water can be easily accessed. Farmers generally fare better than herders do in this respect; in some of the remote herding communities, water supplies are often so poor that people have to get it from wells hours away. Women leave the homesteads at sunrise to return before noon with the daily ration of drinking water for the household. Although state run programmes have significantly increased the number of safe modern wells since the mid-1990s (see Chapter 5); they often merely replace ones which already existed, while in smaller and remote communities the precarious situation remains unchanged.

Neo-Malthusian approaches that locate recent problems of scarcity mainly in demographic development, however, cannot sufficiently explain the causes of ethnically framed conflicts in their present form for mainly two reasons. Scarcity, for one, hardly seems to be a recent phenomenon; land conflicts had been a major cause for dispute before the present situation (Hallpike, 1973: 457–8). Population growth has certainly led – and continues to lead – to a decrease and shortage of free land that used to accommodate expanding farming communities. This should not deflect from the fact that arable land had always been a scarce resource on a local level: land outside the village communities is perceived as 'uncivilized', 'dangerous' and 'missing meaningful social relations' (Dafinger, 2004a: 168ff), while access to fields within the village is subject to a range of social, religious and political rules and conditions. The political and religious authorities of the land-holding clans base their power and control over the community on their right to assign and control fields. While several authors have argued that historically people – and not land – were the scarce resource, most acknowledge that control over people was and is exerted through differential access rights (Balima, 1996; Berry, 1989; 2002; Goody, 1976). The landed gentry, the patriclans, who derive their social authority from allocating land to members of the community, have a vested interest in restricting access to landed resources. Hence, land had already long been a limited resource in political and social terms. Likewise, neo-Malthusian approaches fail to take into account recent economically and politically induced forms of land scarcity. Significant areas of Burkina Faso's arable land are increasingly being used for cash cropping and agro-business and are under control of the cotton and sugar cane industries. Recent land reform programmes, such as the latest RAF, explicitly encourage the spread of agro-busi-nesses – to the disadvantage of small-scale farmers. Rather than providing a viable solution, this response to the scarcity question leads to a further shortage of arable land that would be available to small-scale agriculture.

Alongside land and water, modern resources, too, have become another major field of competition. These include infrastructural resources such as roads, schools and medical care. Other 'new' resources are responses to needs created in the course of the modernization process, such as access to schools and formal education and to the legal system and – notably – employment within these organizations. Some scholars have argued that competition over such positions in the administration often tends to their being allocated along lines of ethnic affiliation, leading to a reification of ethnic boundaries, and the politi-cization of ethnicity reifying and confirming ethnic boundaries (Wimmer, 2004). While this may be true in a number of cases, in this book I will propose a more differentiated view of the 'ethnicized bureaucracy' that does not depend on the demographical composi-tion of the administrative apparatus: Burkina Faso's notion of citizen-ship is distinctly non-ethnic (Burkina Faso (Le Peuple Souverain), 1997): access to national resources and questions of political partici-pation formally disregard ethnic affiliation. No quota regulates the composition of parliament or other official bodies; accordingly, census data do not include information on ethnic affiliation and no official documentation provides overviews of ethnic distinctions in the country. Still, the division along lines of ethnicity is recognized by most people in everyday matters and questions of group allegiance and identity play an important role in relations with the state and bureaucracy. Burkina Faso counts approximately sixty ethnic groups (Balima, 1996: 33). The two largest ones, Mossi (c. 40 per cent) and Fulbe (c.10 per cent), account for half of the country's population. Most other groups are considerably smaller. Linguistic closeness as well as historical connections, shared migration, geographical distribution and shared modes of livelihood (e.g., hunters, farmers or herders) move some ethnic groups closer together and separate others. In the central chapters of this work, I will return to the question of ethnicity and the ethnicization of bureaucracy.

Burkina Faso's peripheral economic and political position is in part a legacy of its colonial past. It was set up as a politically liminal territory and economic hinterland of the coastal trading posts and areas from the core territory. What was later to become Burkina Faso had been colonized from 1896 onwards as part of French West Africa, (Afrique Occidentale Française), acquiring a certain importance in the first two decades as a frontier territory against the advancing British colonizers from the then British Gold Coast. Subsequently, its status alternated between that of a formal colony and one joined to the neighbouring colonies, Mali and Côte d'Ivoire. It was eventually established as a distinct political unit in 1947, was part of the Franco-African Community from 1958 and gained formal independence in August 1960. A series of military coups (in 1966, 1980, 1982, 1983 and 1987) marked its first thirty years of independence. The last successful coup, which overturned the revolutionary government under Captain Thomas Sankara (who gained power in the 1983 putsch), was led by the current president, Blaise Compaoré.[4]

The period that had the highest ideological impact was undoubtedly the 'revolutionary years' between 1983 and 1987. Despite this short time span, the politics initiated by the revolutionary government made profound changes in the way the state was represented and how it was – and still is – perceived by its citizens. Under Sankara's regime, local chiefs lost much of their political influence. They were later only gradually and in most respects only informally reinstated. Colonial history also reverberates in today's relations with neighbouring countries. Burkina Faso is part of the Economic Community of West African States ECOWAS and the West African Economic and Monetary Union UEMOA, sharing the Franc CFA with six other francophone West African states. The freedom of movement that is assured within the ECOWAS zone is one of the prerequisites for the high number of work migrants in the coastal countries.

The colonial heritage is also obvious in the country's legal and

---

[4]   Still in power in 2012, Compaoré had since been reaffirmed through elections.

bureaucratic system, which leans on French legal and governmental principles. French is the official language in administration, in bureaucracy, amongst NGOs and in the educational system. Outside major cities, French is only used to communicate with the authorities and creates what Hagberg (2004: 45) referred to as 'la culture des fonctionnaires'. Functionaries are transferred to new locations every two to three years; they tend to form their own social communities, centred around a common language, shared professional interests and economic distinction. Mostly, administrative staff do not speak the local languages.[5] Likewise, functionaries are united by a shared modernization ideology that sets them apart from most of the rural population. Degrees of being 'civilisé' – educated and enlightened – are important markers of ethnic boundaries and stereotypical criteria in determining local perceptions of ethnic groups. As the later chapters illustrate, Fulbe are often labelled as less civilized and 'closer to nature' by their cultivating Bisa neighbours – a view which is often shared by development personnel. The same distinction holds true for the functionaries' relation to the local population, which is largely considered as backward by the educated public servants. Development projects, structural adjustment programs and attempts to industrialize agriculture build on a similar ideology of modernization and civilization.

Organizations, such as the World Bank, the International Monetary Fund and the European Commission, rank countries based on a series of criteria, the majority of which consider the state's formal economy, education and political governance as benchmarks of prosperity and the well-being of its people. 'Access to education' here always refers to officially recognized forms of school education and similarly, calculations of GNP disregard subsistence-based production. Hence, 'improving the standard of living' by definition implies integrating the largest possible part of a population into a formal, state-controlled and accountable form of production and education.

A description of Burkina Faso's economic system and its integration into a larger international economy faces the challenge to take account of a predominantly informal sector. The economy is to the largest extent subsistence-based; around 80 per cent of people living in Burkina Faso are engaged in rural production that never enters the formal market sphere. From the early 1990s onward, a large number of initiatives aimed at integrating subsistence farming into a formal sector through land reform programmes and related projects. Over a decade and a half of so-called structural adjustment programmes, which included the privatization of hospitals and utilities providers,

---

5   H. Asche, 1994; V. Kremling, 2004. This is different in the morephone parts of central Burkina Faso, where Mossi are more likely to be found in local bureaucracy.

Burkina Faso boasted an average annual economic growth of over 5 per cent, an achievement which no development report and assessment fails to highlight.[6] This growth rate is largely an expression and indicator of the successful and on-going effort of the transformation of the country's economic and public sector. One may despair at the cynicism of the argument that claims 5 per cent formal economic growth, when at the same time the informal agricultural sector, on which four out of five people depend, scored record underproductions of up to 45 per cent in the same period (see Table 1 on p. 34) These harvest shortfalls are at least in part owing to the lack of an agricultural labour force; a consequence of migratory work in the formalized capitalist markets in Burkina Faso and neighbouring Côte d'Ivoire (Berry, 1981; 1991; Weiß, 1986). Formal and informal economics cannot be separated or viewed independently of each other (Hart, 2011). The so-called 'growth of the formal sector' is only possible at the expense of the vast majority of the population that cultivate the 'periphery's periphery', to paraphrase Wallerstein (1976). Ethnic relations (Chapter 3) and ethnic conflict (Chapter 4) are a direct result of the progressive integration of the subsistent hinterlands into a global free market.

With a majority of its people living within a subsistence-based agriculture, Burkina Faso's economy has only a few resources to generate national income from exports; cotton production and cattle husbandry being the most important ones. Another large part of the country's revenue is generated either directly from labour abroad or indirectly through remittances.[7] Formally, Burkina Faso's most important commodity in terms of national GNP and export value is cotton. Most of the production is located in the western part of the country, usually carried out by independent small-scale farmers selling their annual production to wholesale dealers such as SOFITEX, the country's largest textile business. The export of cotton accounts for 60 to 70 per cent of worldwide national exports and Burkina ranks twelfth in the list of the world's cotton producers.[8] As a raw material, the price of cotton is volatile, which makes its production heavily dependent upon international markets and external money. Volatility in cotton prices especially affected small producers: between 1995 and 2002 when world market prices for cotton fluctuated up to 50 per cent (UNCTAD, 2009). As one of the first countries to grow

[6] For an overview of economic development in the ECOWAS zone see e.g. Bureau of African Affairs, 2007.
[7] Ibid.
[8] With an annual output of 292 kilotons in 2006, it even surpassed Mali as the leading West African cotton grower. Dagris, 2007.

genetically modified cotton on a grand scale, it will not only rely on international networks as an outlet but also increasingly on obtaining its cotton plants from abroad. As a palliative measure, the fluctuation in world market prices is partly compensated by external development funds.[9]

Cattle come second after cotton in the country's export statistics. They are raised locally and sold through local markets from whence they are driven across the borders to the larger meat markets in neighbouring Ghana and Côte d'Ivoire (almost all cattle are sold within the ECOWAS zone). Cattle sales are easy to tax and constitute an important source of revenue for the state. Attempts are under way to intensify cattle production and several pastoral zones have been delineated (See Chapters 2, 3), where cattle farming is controlled by state or development authorities. Cattle prices – and as a consequence cattle production – are, like cotton, dependent on the world market. Moreover, meat prices in West Africa have been highly affected by European export policies. European meat sold to West Africa accounted for 9 per cent of local consumption in 1980; a decade later this number had risen to 90 per cent (Moll and Heerink, 2007). This meat is usually sold at prices below that of local cattle (Diallo, 2004; Schlee, 2004). In light of the more recent meat scandals in Europe, where thousands of tons of rotten meat are being sold under the eyes of health inspectors, one starts to wonder what exactly is being dumped onto the African market. Given the enmeshment of the local and global, cattle rearing in rural Burkina is immediately affected by European agricultural politics and developments on the world market.

The third major factor in external economic relations is Burkina Faso's migrant labour force. Between 25 and 30 per cent of its population works and generates income abroad. The export of work force constitutes a major factor in the country's economic relations and especially affects the economy of individual households, underlining and adding to Burkina Faso's peripheral position and dependence on semi-peripheral sub-centres, such as Côte d'Ivoire.[10] The 2002 and subsequent Ivorian crises appear to have had at least as many rever-

[9] In 2002, 129 million US$ were granted as part of the poverty reduction programme by the IMF and IDA. In the same period the US government subsidised US cotton farmers, pushing the price for US cotton below that of West Africa.

[10] Figures on exports and remittances, as based on World Bank statistics, however need to be viewed with much caution. Numbers based on official money transfers are misleading because remittances are often not transferred through formal channels but sent in person, as banks and other transfer operators skim considerable amounts off this money (Boon, 2006). Moreover, the rupture of formal relations between Burkina Faso and Côte d'Ivoire affected the official transfer channels more than informal transfers. Data based on household surveys are built on small samples and cannot claim representativity (e.g.; Wodon, et al., 2006).

berations in Burkina Faso as in Côte d'Ivoire itself. Before the violent riots, remittances used to reach up to 190 million USD per annum, accounting for almost a tenth of Burkina Faso's GDP. By 2004, that share had dropped to fifty million USD, while overall transfers to sub-Saharan Africa have tripled in the same period (Mutume, 2005: 10). The flow of remittances never recovered and has remained below 50 million USD since (Ratha and Mohapatra, 2011).

Moreover, even in times of high foreign employment the net balance of this labour drain is difficult to assess. The negative count, by loss of workforce within, is unlikely to outweigh the benefit through remittances:[11] a disproportionate part of labour migrants are young men in their twenties, whose labour is most needed in agricultural production.

The largest officially recognized sources of international capital for Burkina Faso, however, are still international development pro-grammes. In 2009, development aid amounted to over 1 billion USD (up from c. 400 million USD a decade earlier) compared to c. 900 million USD export revenues in the same year: an amount almost six times that of foreign direct investments (c. 170 million USD) (World Bank, 2011). Unsurprisingly, the impact of development-related proj-ects on the national and local economy is substantial. The fact that state-led development schemes increasingly gave way to the privately funded NGO sector after the 1990s did not necessarily result in less political interventionism. Most small-scale development organizations still coupled material support with political agendas, notably promoting privatization and market-oriented production. The gover-nance of pastoral zones (see below and Chapters 3 and 4) is one such example, and most other projects related to the implementation of the land reform (privatization) programme follow similar trajectories. Financial funds are more often than not tied to the implementation of 'structural adjustment' plans, bylaws and the homogenization of national legislation with an international standard, largely defined by donor organizations.

Province du Boulgou

The 'Province du Boulgou' lies in the central south of Burkina Faso, sharing its southern borders with Ghana and Togo. It covers 6.852 km² (2,584 square miles), just under 3 per cent of the country's territory. With over 600,000 people (as of 2011), it is the fifth largest of 45

---

[11] For a study of the remittance economy in Boulgou: R. Weiß, 1986.

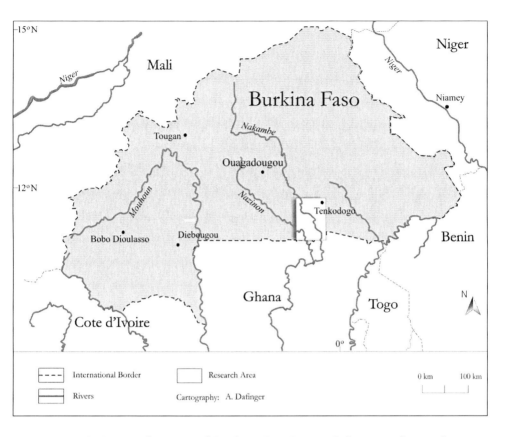

Map 2 Approx. location of Boulgou Province and the area of research
(Dafinger and Pelican: 2006)

provinces.[12] Its average of 90 people per square kilometre is close to
the upper end of what the extensively cultivated land can support.

Under formal criteria, Boulgou's position within Burkina Faso's
economy is marginal.[13] There is no industry, almost all economic
activity consists of subsistence farming and livestock raising: 98 per
cent of Boulgou's population lives off farming, herding and fishing.
The province's major export good is cattle: in 2008, 5100 head of
cattle (c. 1.25 per cent of nationwide cattle exports) were sold
abroad.[14] Exports mainly go to Boulgou's coastal neighbours, Ghana
and Togo (Kagone and Reynolds, 2006, Ch. 1; Pare and Yameogo,
2001: 72). Horticultural produce (notably onions and cabbages) is sold

[12] According to the Burkina Ministry for Economics and Finances. Figures vary depend on the
source. Population in 2006 was 543,570 (Pare and Yameogo, 2001). The estimate given (for 2012)
is based on the current population growth rate of 2.5%.
[13] i.e., referring to the criteria of a national, formal – and taxable – economic system.
[14] Ministère des ressources animales, 2008.

locally and in the capital. Other agricultural products, mainly cereals, rarely exceed the local demand. The following table gives a rough sketch of the local, subsistence-based economy; yields, according to this list, are not sufficient to supply to major national markets and hardly suffice to satisfy local demand, most of the time.

Table 1 Cereal production, demand and undersupply in Boulgou in tons
Source: DPA/Boulgou

	1994/95	1997/98	1998/99*
Net production	86 680	99 336	47 386
Estimated demand	98 377	104 283	85 032
Supply demand ratio	−11 657	−4 947	−37 646
(in per cent of demand)	−11.8%	−4.7%	−44.3%

(*absolute figures after 1998 are not compatible with previous statistics due to administrative reforms and resizing of provinces.)

At the same time, such statistics reflect the strategic interests of planning authorities. The administration and the development industry have a stake in documenting the inefficiency of subsistence agriculture and underscore the need for interventionism. Although the situation is precarious, such figures can still only be estimates as most staple foods do not go through the local markets. Yet the dependence of local production on climatic factors remains profound, as a look at the precipitation figures reveals (Figure 2, p. 36).

In addition to cereal production, milk is a major part of the diet and source of protein for the pastoral groups, while the expanding fishery sector around the Bagré dam perennially supplies the markets around the lake with fish. Completed in 1994, the dam serves as a major source of hydroelectric power,[15] mostly for the country's capital. Locally, Tenkodogo and Garango have been connected to the electricity network.[16] Besides this, the dam's overall benefit to the province is almost negligible: the perennial availability of water encouraged a small rice cultivation project, while the losses local farmers suffered when their bush fields were flooded (often without adequate warnings, and for which many were not compensated) had a much more immediate effect on the local population. The scarcity of arable land in many communities is partly owing to the dam and the flooding of fields. Herders as well were considerably affected by diminishing pasture: the areas around the river had been major destinations of transhumance routes.

[15] The power plant at Bagre produces 20 % of the national electricity.
[16] This mainly led to an increase in TV sets and boosted some entrepreneurial careers for operators of video centres.

Boulgou extends over an area of 60 x 90 km along both sides of the Nakambe, Burkina Faso's second largest river. Together with the Nazinon, which traverses Boulgou over a short stretch in the south-west, they are the only perennial rivers in the region. During the rainy season, the Mouhoun in the eastern half, along with numerous Nakambe tributaries, serve as the further supplier of water for horti-culture, cattle and humans.

Besides its rivers, Boulgou offers almost no discernible landmarks. The terrain stretches flat between 270 and 300 metres above sea level; a few isolated hills rise 30 to 50 metres above the plain. Boulgou's soils, like most others in Burkina Faso, consist mainly of the red earth (known to geologists as 'leached ferruginous soils') that gives the sub-Saharan savannah its typical appearance. Although they certainly add to the charm of the landscape, these soils are less desirable when it comes to agricultural use as they have poor water-retaining capacity. A large portion is also made up of raw mineral soils, which are not at all suitable for cultivation. Still, Boulgou is one of the few regions in Burkina Faso with 'vertisols', brown soils known for their excellent water retention. As they are mostly found along the riverbeds, they now especially attract rice cultivation.

Boulgou is part of the north Sudanic belt, characterized by low to moderate rainfall between 500mm and 1000mm annually and Savannah vegetation, widely dominated by shrubs and trees. Rainfall, however, varies widely between different parts of the region and between seasons. On average, the south receives 150 to 200 mm more rain than the northern parts and precipitation differs up to 100 per cent between the seasons.

The seasonal oscillation in the precipitation graph relates closely to the data on agricultural production and undersupply discussed above. Reasonable harvests that meet the population's demands for cereals are impossible to achieve when rainfalls drop below 1000 mm. Annual rainfalls have also been constantly declining over the past decades.

The low rainfalls hit herders just the same, as they depend on the availability of fodder plants. Harvest leftovers, an important source of animal nutrition, are likewise scarcer in bad years and streams or creeks, which fall dry after a short rainy season force the herders to move their cattle over large distances to access water. Rainfalls not only vary between the years, they also show considerable variation between different parts of the region. The graph below illustrates the stark differences. Although herders seem more flexible in dealing with these imponderables as they can move their cattle into the most nutritious pastures, they also need to adjust their transhumance routes each year, depending on the rains.

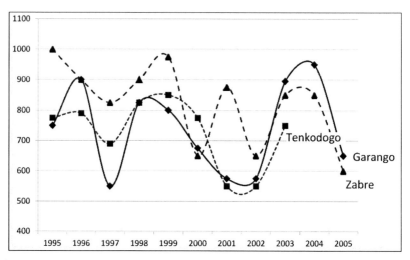

Figure 2 Precipitation (in mm) between 1995 and 2005, annual and regional variation

(Sources: Commission nationale de décentralisation, 2000; I. Drabo, 2002; MRA 2008. No later data obtainable)

Because of Boulgou's climatic and geological diversity, vegetation in the province is equally uneven. As a result of the poor quality of some of its soils, large areas of the region are agriculturally unused, keeping its original vegetation of shrubs and bushes. These stretches are unsuited for both agriculture and pastoral use, either because of their poor biomass or because thorny shrubs make them almost impenetrable. At present, some 120,000 hectares of land are under cultivation, c. 75 per cent of all potentially arable land. So, while there is a margin left for a mid-term agricultural expansion, the figures also indicate the pressure the region will face in the future. Even today, land is no longer fully abundant as some arable land is located too far from settlements, while other land might be considered off limits because of social or religious reasons. Regional imbalances make the situation still more pressing in the northern parts.

A look at the map (Map 3, p. 38) shows a slightly unevenly spread settlement pattern, with a majority of villages nestled around the Nakambe River. Almost 20 per cent of people live in one of the region's three towns, Tenkodogo, Garango and Zabre. Of these, only the first two show modest signs of urbanity. Both are to differing degrees administrative centres, host markets with shops that open daily and both are served by public transport: privately operated mini-buses connect both towns with the capital. They boast telephone networks, including cell phone infrastructure and are connected to the power network. Tenkodogo has many of the amenities of a true urban centre:

cinemas, several small hotels and the province's only hospital. It used to be an outpost of the colonial administration and is now the seat of the High Commissioner. Towards the end of the colonial era the colonial representative requested Ouagadougou if 'mail from the capital may be delivered to Tenkodogo by truck, at least so in the rainy season'. 'So far,' he lamented, 'letters are carried by people on their heads, often arriving soaked and illegible'.[17] Fifty years later, Tenkodogo is a major hub on the country's main axis with high levels of traffic from Niger and Togo passing through, ensuring frequent connections to the capital and its amenities.

Historically, Tenkodogo is considered the cradle of all the Mossi kingdoms, the predecessors of today's nation state. The king (*naba*) of Tenkodogo traces his ancestry to the very first Mossi ruler, and even the great empire at Ouagadougou is considered an offspring of Tenkodogo. It is for that reason that Tenkodogo enjoys at least symbolic recognition in the country's history. Within Boulgou, the reign of the *naba* extends over the eastern half of the province, comprising also roughly half of the population. Tenkodogo town counts just under 40,000 people; together with Garango (c. 30,000) and Zabre (c. 11,000) the three towns accommodate some 80,000 people.

The majority of the population lives in smaller villages of mostly up to 2,000 inhabitants. Villages are aligned along a horseshoe shaped band (see Map 3, p. 38), sparing the river zones, with a denser cluster in the northern parts. The areas along the Nakambe River had never been extensively settled nor used for bush fields until very recently. The major reasons for this were high risks of river blindness (*onchocerciasis*) transmitted by blackflies (*simulium damnosum*) and sleeping sickness (*trypanosomiasis*), through the tsetse fly (*glossina genus*), as well as other sicknesses prevalent along the rivers. Dynamics of settlement did not encourage the foundation of remote settlements either, so the stretch of inhabited land grew to form a somewhat continuous band, rather than forming isolated outposts.

The only exceptions to this rule are Niaogho and Beguedo, a few kilometres from the Nakambe at the northern fringes of the region (Map 3) and Yakkala as the southernmost outpost of the Lebri area, which is today on the verge of disappearance, having lost many of its fields to the rising waters of the Bagre dam. The lake also took a number of fields that were cultivated by farmers from more distant villages in addition to the house fields. Such bush fields have become more and more important in the light of an increasing population and

---

[17] *Rapport politique annuel Haute Volta : Cercle de Tenkodogo,* 1958. Centre des archives d'outre mer, Aix en Provence (CAOM)

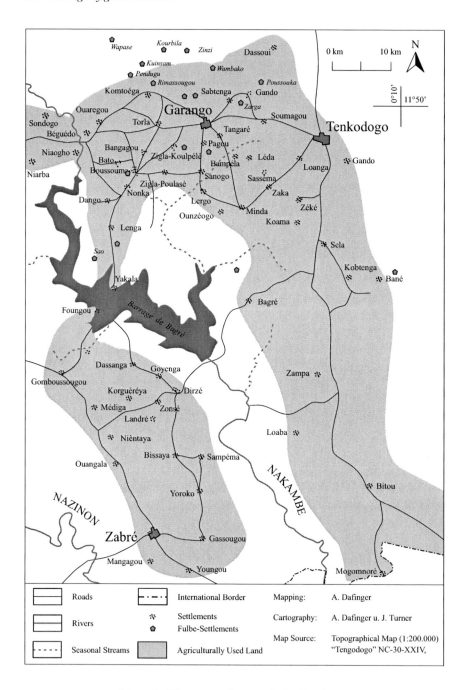

Map 3 The area of research in Boulgou

land scarcity; as a result, the loss of land to the lake had reverberations over a large area.

While Burkina Faso continues to experience considerable internal migration, this hardly affects Boulgou. Ecological conditions are – even by Burkinabe standards – not favourable enough to attract larger numbers of new settlers. The only recent noteworthy immigration followed the completion of the Bagre dam in the mid-1990s, causing a number of fishermen from the northern and western provinces to move into the area, and a smaller number of cattle herders resettling from the Sahel after the 1970s and 1980s droughts. Most people who leave the region do so temporarily: many young men take up work in Côte d'Ivoire and increasingly also in Europe, where many live and work for several years; only a few migrants decide to resettle permanently abroad or in other provinces within Burkina Faso.

In ethnic terms, Boulgou conveys a homogeneous image: three major groups live in the region: a majority of Bisa (sg; pl. Bisano; or sometimes Bissa or Bousance)[18], part of the Mande speaking groups and who for their largest part live off subsistence farming. Mossi (pl.; sg: Moaga), Burkina's largest ethnic group, account for c. 30 per cent, mostly in the eastern half of the region. With around 65,000 people, Fulbe (pl.; sg. Pullo; also Fulani [ha], or Peul [fr]) constitute about a tenth of the population.

Considering climatic, ecological and demographic aspects, Boulgou is doing neither better nor worse than most other parts of Burkina Faso. It attracts neither major investments nor unusually high numbers of development projects.[19] Although a number of state-run and non-governmental organizations are active in the area, the coverage with modern resources, such as schools, health centres, safe water and electricity is generally around or just below the country's average.

Officially, only about a third of Boulgou's children attend school.[20] In reality though, things are worse. A large number of children tend to drop out after only a couple of years, others seem not to gain anything from their time at school, simply because of insufficient language skills – all teaching is in French, which is not spoken by many of the children (see also the study by Kremling, 2004). In the light of rapid demographic growth, the future looks even dimmer: in order to maintain the present school enrolment rate, the number of schools needs to double over the next fifteen years. Access to education also depends on

---

[18] Thus, in proper terms, Bisa should be actually called Bisano (pl.); however, the general term Bisa (or, occasionally, Bissa) can generally be found.

[19] The major organizations that are active in Boulgou will be introduced below in this chapter.

[20] As of 2000, a mere 150 primary and 10 secondary schools allowed for a gross school enrolment rate of 36% – compared to 42% on the national level (Pare 2001; Thorsen 2007).

a variety of other factors, geographical proximity to schools being one. Some of the later chapters will deal more explicitly with aspects of gender, the economic diversification of households, as well as with the ethnic background as the most decisive factors in differential access to educational and other resources (see esp. Chapter 5).

If access to education is dire, the availability of health services is even more precarious. Besides the only hospital in Tenkodogo – which is supposed to accommodate patients from three more provinces – there are three medical centres, and around thirty local sick wards in the larger villages, run by nurses, serving more than half a million people. In statistical terms, there is only one doctor for every 36,000 people in the province.[21] Emergency medical aid is virtually non-existent for two thirds of the population. Access to health is not only determined by geographical distribution and the availability of medical centres, but also depends on social and financial standing, and Boulgou is no exception to this rule: in many cases, Western-style medicine will only be a last resort or an alternative to local healing practices.

Access to safe water remains another serious problem for large parts of the region. Starting in the mid-1990s, eight hundred new wells were built in a grand-scale project (the 'Projet Intégré Hydraulique Villageoise et Education pour la Santé', PIHVES). While this undoubtedly improved the situation for most people, it often did so only within an already existing infrastructure. It shortened the average distance between homesteads and wells and provided access to higher quality water; it did not necessarily provide wells in areas that had no previous safe water in the vicinity at all. A large number of people in remote settlements still live with no access to safe water – or only within hour-long walking distances. Access to water is the most immediate, most urgent and precarious need and competition over existing water sources and the struggle over new ones is one of the major triggers of social tensions. It is also the interface where local and state relations become most apparent in everyday life as the state and NGOs become major suppliers and brokers in water provision. Electrification of parts of the province is just starting to make its impact on everyday life, also because it went hand in hand with the rise of the mobile telephone network. Up to the mid-1990s, fewer than a hundred landlines existed in Tenkodogo and only a handful in Garango. Today, the number of households that have direct access to telecommunications is difficult to assess; it is a safe estimate that more than half of villages now have access to some form of telecommunication (Hahn, 2008). Research on the impact on changing communication patterns has only just begun.

[21] INSD, 2010.

Based on the estimates of the first colonial sources,[22] the number of people has grown almost five-fold over the past one hundred years. At the time of the first colonial census, just over 100,000 people lived in the area.[23] Previous research suggested that Bisa and Mossi groups had come jointly from the Gambaga area in today's northern Ghana, settling first in the region around Tenkodogo and only a little later in the area that is now known as the Lere (Keuthmann, 1998; Voßen, 1998: 99). In a second phase, Mossi immigrants from the northern kingdoms settled with these Bisa, founding a number of new villages (such as Busma and Niaogho, to which I will refer below). The arrival of the French drove many people south, towards the newly established borders between the French colony and the British Gold Coast.

From today's point of view, the Tenkodogo kingdom, linguistically dominated by Moore and the Barka dialect in Bisa, has the longest tradition of Mossi-Bisa cooperation. It also claims to have the longest history of settlement.[24] The north-west is dominated by clans whose origins lie in the northern Mossi-kingdoms and who came in a second wave of migration. The southern parts, the Lere and the northwest, Lebri, share the fact that villages are largely independent and part of distributed networks. This sets them apart from the Tenkodogo kingdom, which is hierarchically organized and focused on its capital as a political, cultural and economic centre. Lere and Lebri differ on other levels, mostly in their settlement history, dialectical variations and demographic development (the south used to be most sparsely populated and has seen a rapid increase over the past decades). In the following overview I will mostly focus on the dichotomy of the hierarchical system of Tenkodogo and the polycephalous network of patriclans in the northwest with which it borders.

The triangle that stretches 20 miles from Garango to Niaogho on the banks of the Nakambe in the north and 20 miles to Yakkala in the south is in many ways considered the Bisa heartland (see Map 3, p. 38), even if a majority of today's population does not even claim Bisa ancestry: most of the patriclans had migrated to the region only in the eighteenth century from the northern Mossi kingdoms. The newcomers soon took over the local language, married into Bisa clans and adopted the local political system, accepting most social and polit-

---

[22] *Rapport politique annuel Haute Volta*, 1919. Centre des archives d'outre-mer, Aix en Provence (CAOM) : 14MI 1691/2G19–8.

[23] It can be assumed, however, that more people lived in the area before the colonial conquest. Head tax and forced labour have led to a massive migration, mostly to the British Gold Coast. Tauxier assumes c. 120.000 people before 1897.

[24] Political rule is generally legitimised through autochthony or at least a first comer status. Local histories are often re-interpreted in this light and need not necessarily correspond to a factual order of arrival (Dafinger, 2004a; Dafinger and Ritz-Müller, 1996; I. Kopytoff, 1987; 1999).

ical institutions of their host society, blending them with institutions
they brought in from the north and that were previously unknown in
Bisa society. The institution of the *naba* (as the chief of a cluster of
villages) was also probably introduced to Bisa society by the Mossi
newcomers, leaning on the institution of the Mossi kings, or nabas
(Prost, 1950: 62).

Historically, Bisa country had been an important slave repository.
Bisa villages themselves played an important part in raiding neighbouring villages at that time. Submitting to the rule of the *Mogho Naba*
offered protection against slave raids from outside and, to a certain
degree, from Tenkodogo.[25] Most settlements, however, remained under
constant threat of attack by its neighbours. This advanced the emergence of local alliances of clans and occasionally of local chiefdoms,
such as Garango, Busma and Zabre, which united a number of villages
under joint leadership and in a military alliance, which included Fulbe
mercenaries, a fact that has its reverberations even today (see Chapter
3).

In the beginning of the colonial era, population density in the north
had already been high at an estimated 35/km² as opposed to only
10/km² in the southern regions.[26] In the first three decades of the
nineteenth century this difference slowly started to level out, as many
northerners migrated south across the Nakambe river in order to avoid
colonial taxing and the risk of being forcefully recruited as part of the
'travaux publique', the colonial 'work for the public good'. While the
population in the south continued to grow, the north only saw very
few new settlements after the colonial conquest; most of today's
villages already existed at that time.

As one of the consequences of the specific conditions of the north-
west (notably its particular settlement history, the hostile relations
between villages, and the villages' political autonomy), no major
migration took place within the region: patriclans remained concen-
trated in their original localities; even today only few villages consist
of more than one clan. Personal incentives to resettle between villages
were low: individuals who decided to join another community lost
their status as members of the local landowning clan. Low internal
mobility helped maintain the homogeneous composition of settlements up to the present date: In most villages, one or possibly two
patriclans account for 80 to 90 per cent of a local population. As a
result, patriclans in the north-west can almost always be associated

---

[25] Slave raids in most of West Africa used to be the domain of centralised polities, with slave raids
being a major economic field (Elwert, 1999; Goody, 1980), which is the case in Tenkodogo. The
smaller slave raids of the independent western villages, however, are exceptional in this case.
[26] For an overview of early settlement history see also Lahuec, 1979; 1983.

with a specific village: inter-village relations are largely synonymous with inter-clan relations (See also Dafinger, 2004a: 55–60). The only two major exceptions to this are the clan of blacksmiths, which is dispersed all over Bisaland, and the Fulbe pastoral communities, whose clans are equally not localized.

The kingdom of Tenkodogo in Boulgou's east, on the other hand, has seen profound changes to its local political and demographic landscape over the last century; its population has grown nearly six fold; it significantly expanded its territory in the colonial period and now stretches all the way from Tenkodogo to the Ghanaian and Togolese borders (Keuthmann, Reikat and Sturm, 1998). The *naba* is ethnic Mossi (*moaga*), while the majority of the population are Bisa; village chiefs are either Bisa or Mossi, depending on the village; all of them, however, need to be appointed by the *naba* in Tenkodogo. Especially in the first 20 years of the last century, the *nabas* of Tenkodogo have gradually extended their territory by incorporating conquered Bisa villages. Local chiefs were legitimized by the *Naba* and became representatives at the royal court.[27] The *naba* followed a strategy of *divide et impera*, encouraged resettlements within his territory and broke the dominance of the autochthonous patriclans. It was important for the *naba* to break the rule of the local clans; after all, at the time of colonial conquest the majority of villages were Bisa-speaking descendants of the firstcomer clan. Today, villages in the east have five or more different patriclans. As a result, individuals not only depend on their clan or lineage elders in many daily affairs, litigations and quarrels with neighbours, but are often also obliged to involve the village chief as a mediating and judicial authority. Many local disputes between members of different clans cannot be solved within the kin groups at all. As a result, relations between members of the locality are to a considerable degree defined through the super-ordinate power of the Tenkodogo *naba* and his sub-chiefs.

Fulbe, who constitute only about a tenth of Boulgou's population, are in many places an intricate part of local history. The specific character of the three sub-regions – Barka and Lebri in the north and the southern Lere – also reflects the presence and active interaction of the Fulbe population; the following chapters deal with the various ways in which Fulbe are attached to the political order of their farming neighbours.

A major difference that sets Fulbe settlements apart from the

---

[27] In Bisa communities, political authority used to be based on age – with the eldest of any clan at the top of the local hierarchy. One of the consequences was that hardly any elder enjoyed this office for too long, as most candidates had already reached an enviable age by their time.

farming villages is their non-territorial organization: members of each clan can be found in any part of the region (and in fact throughout all of Burkina Faso and West Africa, as illustrated above (Map 1, p. 20). Fulbe settlements tend to be rather heterogeneous, with up to five patriclans in one locality. Fulbe communities also maintain close relations between each other across the region.

The Fulbe's trans-spatial networks and non-territorial notion of community have major consequences for the resulting relations with the farming communities: on the one hand they are considered 'eternal strangers' (Guichard, 2000; Hagberg, 1998), always 'ready to move' and are by many farmers considered uncertain allies. On the other hand, Fulbe can draw on their far-distant relations in obtaining information and in trade. Fulbe traverse the local political boundaries and negotiate resource use with farmers irrespective of the regional political divide.

Historically, the migration of Fulbe into the area has seen two major phases, the first coinciding with the arrival of the Mossi migrants from the northern kingdoms in the eighteenth century and a second in the aftermath of the 1970s and 1980s Sahel droughts. Many Bisa settlements are closely connected to the presence of the Fulbe through their founding histories. Many settlements have only been set up with the help of allied Fulbe mercenaries and in some cases local histories claim that Bisa and Fulbe had actually arrived jointly from the northern provinces. As a general consequence, firstcomer-latecomer relations, a general topic in legitimizing power relations and political supremacy in most of sub-Saharan Africa (Dafinger, 2004a; Dafinger and Ritz-Müller, 1996; I. Kopytoff, 1999), mostly play no role in relations between farmers and those early Fulbe clans.

Besides these 'established' Fulbe settlements, a considerable number of Fulbe have migrated into the region from the drought-stricken Sahel over the past 25 years, now constituting a major part of the local Fulbe population. These newcomer villages are mostly located at the fringes of the settled areas and mostly outside the agriculturally used areas (Map 3, p. 38). Their relations with the farming communities differ greatly from the bonds between 'local' Fulbe-herders and the farmers, although both groups, the resident Fulbe, as descendants of the first migrants, and the newcomers consider themselves as the same ethnic group, sharing the same patronyms and ultimately the same ancestry and origin.[28] The resident Fulbe, however, generally enjoy more secure rights based on the shared history. Those first Fulbe were often mercenaries whose services were asked for by

---

[28] Most Fulbe in Boulgou claim to descend from Fulbe groups in today's Mali.

the small early Bisa farming communities to defend themselves against the slave raids.[29]

In pre-colonial times, only a small number of farming villages had immediate Fulbe neighbours. In the first half of the last century there were certainly fewer than ten Fulbe settlements in the northern Lebri region – compared to about thirty today, after many settlements had been founded by the recent wave of immigrants. Their choice to settle, however, was not arbitrary; most of those who came to settle knew the area from earlier transhumance and could draw on existing social contacts. While Bisa and Mossi villages over time have expanded in both number and size – many villages have up to 2000 (and occasionally more) members – Fulbe settlements tended to remain small; the increase in population here led to new settlements, not the growth of existing ones. As a result, Fulbe localities are significantly smaller in size than the farmers' and only few count more than 200 people. Most also tend to be of recent origin; of 21 Fulbe villages, only eight are more than 100 years old.

The prevailing explanation herders give for the small size of their communities is mostly ecological: limited pastures would not support larger numbers of Fulbe herders in any one place. Most who had left behind another village to settle here mentioned the shortage of pastures as their main motive to relocate. This is, however, only part of the story and in fact often not supported by empirical findings. In many cases, new Fulbe settlements were established in rather close proximity to the existing ones, in some cases even using the same resources, such as pasture and waterholes (see the example of Pous-soaka, in Chapter 5), so the actual reasons for fissions can only partially be accounted for by ecological conditions. Internal dynamics and collective action problems outweigh ecological considerations in many cases, as many of the later cases will highlight.

The historical and political partition of the province has not affected the mobility patterns of the Fulbe herders; transhumance and migration reach across the boundaries between the political systems.[30] The Fulbe profit from their trans-spatial networks by providing services for farmers; moving farmers' cattle into areas across the political and historical divides between the three regions, to which farmers themselves have no immediate access.

---

[29] With only one exception, all villages today claim a victim's history. Only Garango upholds its tradition as a former slave raiding community.

[30] Bisa, on the other hand, do not resettle from one zone to another. Even where mobility is high, as in the Tenkodogo kingdom, the divide between the political areas seems impermeable (Dafinger 2004a: 167ff)

Boulgou in the context of the Nation State

Formally, so-called 'traditional' political institutions have no role in the post-colonial state's structure and were effectively disempowered under the revolutionary regime in 1984, which instituted elected delegates as local representatives vis-a-vis the nation state. Still, many of the chiefs managed to retain a high degree of social, political and judicial authority. Notwithstanding their democratic legitimacy, the new delegates still had to operate within existing local webs of power. The village communities continued to be defined through either kinship or local political allegiances to the landowning chiefs and earth priests. Moreover, the historical boundaries of chiefdoms, historical distinctions and political relations were often the foundation of the national administration's spatial and social limits: in Boulgou, all of the province's thirteen departments build on existing local political units, correlating with the historical political partition of the region and often also with the internal differentiation along local chiefdoms. As the territories of *nabas* and village chiefs coincide with the limits of national administrative units, the local chiefs almost naturally compete with the representatives of the nation state. In the competition over new infrastructural resources, the established social and political units continue to rival along the same lines. In consequence, the state's political and judicial infrastructure coincides almost fully with the existing partition based on clan and other kinship allegiances and the official classification of villages – the 'villages administratifs' – is the formalization of local categories built on kinship (in the north-western regions) or the political rule of the Tenkodogo-*naba* (in the east). In practical matters, these departments, which are administered by prefects, are the most important units of state bureaucracy. The prefects are the first point of call for the local population in terms of administrative and judicial matters.

A major group of institutions alongside the state are development organizations. Most international organizations working in Burkina Faso enter joint ventures with national institutions and each of the projects in Boulgou is run as a joint international-national enterprise. The three largest, high-impact 'GoNGOs', governmental/non-governmental organizations, in Boulgou are the Projet du Développement Rural (PDR), Projet Hydraulique (PIHVES) and the Projet Nouhao, which manages the local pastoral zone, an area delineated exclusively for pastoral use.

PDR engages in a broad range of activities, which span from educational, instructional, administrative, to agricultural infrastructural programmes. PDR agents hold workshops in the villages to inform people about changes in the legal system (land reform), offer hygienic instructions and health advice. Their research department tracks transhumance routes, conducts geological and botanical surveys and advises policy makers in the design of infrastructural projects (see Chapter 5). PDR has been the subject and frame for a number of anthropological and developmental research projects (Juul and Lund, 2002; Oksen, 1996; 2001; e.g. Reenberg, 1997). It employs more than one hundred staff, making it the region's single largest employer and so has in itself become a major resource; positions in the organization on all levels are considered highly desirable – with salaries well above local standards.

Like PIHVES, the second largest development organization in Boulgou, PDR is largely financed through its partnership with European national development funds. PIHVES set out in the early 1990s to improve access to safe water by providing nearly 800 deep water wells within a period of ten years. Its explicitly participatory approach requires the involvement of local committees in the application and planning process. Chapter 5 will deal with the implications and consequences of this endeavour for the local social landscape.

The Programme de mise en valeur de la vallée de Nouhao (MVVN), is a joint Italian-Burkinabe project that was established in 2000 and which provides the technical infrastructure for the pastoral zone along the Nouhao River south of Tenkodogo (see the corresponding map in Chapter 3). Projet Nouhao will be extensively dealt with in the following chapter when the implications of the pastoral zone will be discussed. It is one of the first projects that is dedicated explicitly to the implementation of the new land legislation, the 'Réorganisation Agraire et Foncière' (RAF).

To sum up this overview, Boulgou's climatic background, its demographic development and its local political background are in many respects typical of many other regions in Burkina Faso and West Africa. Ecological conditions favour mixed agro-pastoral production throughout the Sahel and encourage the cohabitation of farmers and herders. The historical development of local relations from warfaring alliances to resource competitors is typical of many West African societies. The same is true of the increasing pressure on scarce land by its growing population: almost 90 per cent of Burkinabe live in the rural areas and in Boulgou this rate is even higher. Almost all of these people are engaged in non-market-oriented production, once again underscoring the importance of the subsistence-based agropastoral production as the backbone of local economies. A closer look also revealed that Boulgou's population is anything but a monolithic block. Differences in origin, political affiliation, different modes of production, all decide over differences in resource access and differentiate the local actors. Various local groups occupy, defend or contest their position in a system that is defined by criteria of length of residence, degrees of landedness, political visibility and social networks. This is the field in which state and development agents make their appearance.

The arrival of the state: transforming economic and social production

Supported by global donor institutions the state has a vested interest in transforming subsistence production and in integrating local agropastoral production into the formal economic sector. From a developmental point of view, subsistence agriculture offers little to no security in the face of unstable ecological conditions; it does not deliver adequate output to support a growing and increasingly urban population. From an administrative point of view, subsistence production is hard to assess, difficult to control and almost impossible to tax: subsistence production, in short, evades almost all classical fields of state control.[31]

Structural adjustment programs (SAPs) also aim at attracting foreign investment, especially by selling off the country's assets in natural and infrastructural resources (ECA, United Nations Economic Commission for Africa 1989). One problem that was soon identified as a major obstacle to modernization and development in sub-Saharan Africa was the lack of 'tenure security'. With no private ownership of the means of production and with the available labour force often dependent on kinship relations, sustainable development is deemed impossible, as no local or foreign business could be expected to invest in an incalculable climate (Gray, 2003; Stamm, 2004).

Attempts to transform subsistence economies affect both agricultural and pastoral production systems. Cattle are the second largest export product after cotton (INSD 2008) and the demand for beef in West African countries is soaring (INSD).[32] Moreover, pastoral lifestyle

---

[31] I refer to the 'arrival of the state' to indicate that in many parts of Africa, as opposed to many other parts of the world, decentralization programmes do not necessarily lead to a withdrawal of the state from local affairs. New, local and smaller institutions of governance (including NGOs) make the state and state rule more accessible and more relevant in local affairs than it often was before.

[32] (Kagone and Reynolds, 2006; INSD (Institut national de la statistique et de la démographie), 2010b). In the decade between 1990 and 2000, the number of cattle rose from just over 4 million to 7 million, with a slight increase to 8.1 million since 2008 (Ministère des ressources animales,

is often considered as incompatible with fundamental principles of state administration; transhumance patterns, such as the seasonal movement of cattle within the region, are deliberately misread as nomadism of people; as a result, sedentarization and integration into the political economy are two of the priorities on the agenda of the arriving state.

With 70 per cent of Burkina Faso's cattle held by Fulbe, the economic importance of livestock-keeping and its transformation has also become an issue of ethnicity.[33] Modernization programmes targeted at a restructuring of the pastoral sector need to specifically address Fulbe cultural variables and are, accordingly, mostly perceived under ethnic viewpoints by many Fulbe herders (see Chapter 3).

Although national land rights provided the legal framework for land transactions as early as the 1950s, virtually no land was privately owned in Burkina Faso before 1991. Instigated by the World Bank, most West African countries revised land legislation to accommodate local interests, aiming at a higher acceptance of the new laws by allowing village communities to formally 'acquire their land' (Cleaver and Schreiber, 1994; Falloux and Talbot, 1993). The new international urge for reforms was also backed by an increasing push for decentralization, insisting that privatization would facilitate local planning and empower local interest groups. The lack of formal security had been identified as a major obstacle to the modernization and betterment of rural sub-Saharan Africa or, in other cases, even as a causal factor in climatic change and environmental degradation (Bassett, Koli and Ouattara, 2003: 69. for a discussion). Moreover, such 'inefficient agricultural systems' are not seen as fit to sustain the rapidly growing urban centres in the long run. Proponents of privatization generally argue that traditional land rights encourage the borrowing – not renting – of land, leaving little incentive for users to invest in land that is not theirs. As an alternative, advocates of liberalized land regimes promote freehold rights in plotted land arguing that this would encourage farmers to invest in long-term land improvements, such as planting of trees and similar conservation measures: owners would eventually profit from these investments at a later stage. Similarly, land ownership would facilitate access to credit, which is widely perceived as a prerequisite for any agricultural investment. In addition, freehold titles would also guarantee the right to rent or sell plots: 'well defined ownership rights'

(contd) 2008.) and meat production increased from under 40 thousand tons to over 55 thousand. The number of cattle that were sold into the international market rose from 92,000 to almost 174,000 in 2000, passing the 400,000 mark in 2008), accounting for more than 20% of the country's total exports within the Ecowas zone. Meat is much more important for export than for national consumption, which only increased marginally.

[33] H. Kagone and S. G. Reynolds (2006, 6) estimate that 70% of all cattle in Burkina Faso are owned by ethnic Fulbe.

as a 1999 World Bank Note put it (Deininger and Feder, 1999: 1), 'make it easier to transfer land to more efficient users from those who are not as efficient'; a rather blunt euphemism for promoting agribusiness over small-scale farming.

A number of studies have engaged with this argument and refuted its economic assumptions: in a number of West African countries, land reforms and individual land rights led to neither an increase in investments nor an increase in agricultural output (e.g. Atwood, 1990; Gray, 2003; Kevane, 1997). One reason for this was that borrowing land actually proved to be a rather effective means of ensuring sustainable and efficient resource use, allowing maximum resource use of all arable land (de Zeeuw, 1997; Gray, 2003; Kintz, 1982; Saul, 1986).

Before 1984, pre-revolutionary land rights in Burkina Faso granted the state the right to appropriate lands for national projects, such as the AVV – a large-scale development plan of riverine lands – or on other grounds in the general 'national interest.'[34] Other land was considered the domain of local communities and clans, which controlled their terrain according to customary law and possessed the rights to allocate, use or borrow these terrains. Although this legislation permitted private land titles in principle, this was practically never made use of: following investigations by Ouedraogo (2001: 31–46) only 19 private titles had been issued in a period of almost thirty years.

In the attempt to curtail the power of local chiefs and feudal authorities, land laws were redesigned and all land was considered state-owned during the revolutionary years between 1983 and 1987.[35] Under these revised legal norms, the 'Loi pourtant la Réorganisation Agraire et Foncière' of 1984, land could henceforth no longer be sold or appropriated by private owners. The control of local authorities was restricted to allocating cultivated land within the communities. Claims to other potentially arable land, bush areas or grazing land were no longer possible.

There are two different ways of looking at this change in legislation. From one perspective, local elites were disempowered and everybody could now apply for patches of land: 'what was formerly considered a common land with restricted access' as French anthropologist Faure found, 'became a freely accessible resource', laying one of the foundations for waves of internal migration in the 1980s in Burkina Faso

---

[34] The Authorité des Aménagements des Vallées des Voltas (Volta Valley Authority) resettled thousands of settlers in riverine areas in twelve different areas, each of which was made up of six to seven new villages. The project included a programme to eradicate river blindness and providing technical and political infrastructure. The project was abandoned in 1989, many of the settlers moving to other regions (see D. E. McMillan, 1995 for an extensive debate).

[35] 'Loi portant réorganisation agraire et foncière', Loi n°014/96/ADP. Burkina Faso (1996).

(Faure, 1996: 200). From another angle, however, it does not take much to see that this land is not at all free. What had changed were simply the authorities allocating the land (now the state) and the criteria along which one could claim entitlements.

Meeting the demands of international donor organizations and development agencies the post-revolutionary government amended its legislation (in an attempt to 'rectify the revolution') and passed two further Réorganisations Agraire et Foncière in 1991 and 1994, providing for the systematic plotting of land and creating a threefold legal frame. Land in Burkina Faso now consisted of either state-owned terrain, including unused, uncultivated unclaimed lands, plotted individual or corporative terrain and so-called 'transitional' land, i.e. land that is controlled by the patriclans according to 'customary law' on a village or community basis.[36] This deliberate loophole (in fact an inconsistency) made it possible to implement the new legislation without having to face significant dissent on the local level. By constitution, Burkina Faso does not acknowledge any customary authorities, whereas the notion of 'customary law' presupposes the existence of such an independent local legal system. The pastoral zones draw on this legislation (of corporate terrain) and exemplify the political and economic trajectories of the land reform, as the following chapters will further illustrate. As a general consequence, the 'lotissement', the parcelling of land, became an integral part of urban construction schemes after 1994 in urban and semi-urban areas (Gensler, 2004). RAF's revision, though, was not mainly targeted at urban dwelling programmes but was mostly a direct response to the international development agenda, attempting to create tenure security, encouraging investment and – ideally – boosting agricultural output.

Government and state officials generally tend to welcome privatization as a means of establishing a reliable framework for agribusiness, such as large-scale extensive farming. As the mantra of neo-liberal readjustment agendas goes, those farmers who initially lose their land to the new corporations would eventually profit as they would get the chance to work as hired labourers.[37] As an initial step, the programme was to encourage local communities to pool their resources and run their own market-oriented cooperative. As of yet, however, only very few development organizations and local communities have taken advantage of the new legislation to reorganize their local legal relations and production systems. In Burkina Faso's west,

[36] New 'owners' are assigned permanent use rights, against paying a one-time tax of 5.000 FCFA. People, however, repeatedly raised concern that there is no guarantee that the state would not collect further taxes at later points.
[37] S. Diallo, 'Production Agricole: Les nouvelles …' *Sidwaya*, 16 August 2001.

where the privatization scheme has also begun to allocate agricultural land, almost two thirds of all new stakeholders are government officials and state employees, with another third working in other organizations or in business (Ouedraogo, 2001: 31–46). In total, less than 5 per cent of all newly allocated land is owned by development agencies, religious organizations or local communities, which seek to improve local conditions and more or less explicitly involve local actors in decision making. Investors from the first two groups generally get their income from other sources and invest the surplus in agricultural enterprises in their home regions often more for reasons of status than based on strategic economic considerations (ibid.).

The droughts West Africa experienced in the 1970s and early 1980s led to a profound change in Burkina Faso's social and economic landscape and prepared the ground for a number of reform programmes. Development and relief projects came to assist in the immediate aftermath of the disaster and to help secure sustainable productivity in the longer run. Herders in the Sahel had suffered severe losses of cattle,[38] and as a result, many of them decided to take their remaining cattle and settle in the more moderate climate of the Savannahs. Of those, many ended up in Boulgou, mostly settling in the areas north of Garango and east of Bane (Map 4, p. 73). These areas were neither inhabited nor cultivated so that most of the new settlers felt no need to seek permission from neighbouring farmers and attach themselves to local communities.

The newcomers were not complete strangers to the region, however, most of them had been there during their seasonal transhumance; this time, however, they had come with their families and intended to stay. In most cases this caused only little disturbance; the spatial distance between newcomers and established communities was big enough and land was generally available to avoid daily contact and to not let the cattle pose a threat to the cultivated fields.[39]

As an attempt to mitigate the impact of the drought and the subsequent migration, the administration launched several large-scale infrastructural adjustment programmes for the agricultural sector, the AVV – a river valley irrigation programme – being one. It established several pastoral zones, which were designed to accommodate the migrant herders from the Sahel, but also for herders who had been living alongside farmers in agropastoral cooperation in the Savannah areas for extensive periods. The main objectives of these zones were to reduce

---

[38] According to Kagone (2002), herders in the Sahel lost as much as 25% of their animals in the first drought and another 15% in the 1980s.

[39] Many other regions in the country were not as fortunate, like western Burkina Faso, which saw an increasing number of clashes over the sparse natural resources.

potential conflicts between farmers and herders, and encourage sedentarization of herders and control of herders' production methods in
order to 'rationalise the management of natural resources' (Kagone
and Reynolds, 2006: 8), especially in the light of the continuously
increasing demand for meat and other pastoral products in the country.
So the first pastoral zones predated structural adjustment programmes
and land reform and were linked to agricultural adjustment
programmes, such as the AVV. Resettlements in this period were often
carried out without the consent of those concerned – and often
enough met with their open resistance, as it was the case in Boulgou
where farmers were made to leave the area by the use of military force.

In the end, however, the economic success of the first pastoral zones
turned out to be as disappointing as the attempted boost in agricultural production through the privatization of land. While on a national
level the number of cattle has continuously risen and the production
of meat and dairy products has gone up by up to 50 per cent, this was
not the merit of the pastoral zones. Most of the increase was the result
of other infrastructural projects in mixed agro-pastoral areas, driven
by an increased demand for cattle in the neighbouring countries, as
well as a general recovery of stocks after the droughts (ibid.).

Since then, the RAF land reform has seen several amendments and
planning and management of pastoral zones has gradually been
changed to include better participation of both pastoralists and farmers
in the initial phase before actual resettlement takes place. Likewise, the
position of settlers has been strengthened vis-à-vis the managing
bureaucracy, granting, among others, more secure rights in the land
the re-settlers occupy (ibid.). Pastoral zones have become much more
part of a mid- to long-term trajectory to encourage agro-business
through either cooperatives or companies. In any case, the accounta-
bility and 'readability' of pastoral production is an essential dimension
and pastoral zones have adequate management techniques to monitor
and control the land's carrying capacity, pastoralists' production
methods and revenues. In the existing zones, the number of animals is
controlled, the size of the land for a household fixed at 10 ha, and the
amount of crop, such as millet or maize that is cultivated at the homesteads is set through by-laws, to which the herders are subject when
they settle and work in this zone. Likewise, the project administration
sets the maximum number of animals that may be sold and controls
relations of the herding community with the outside world,
prohibiting transhumance, the seasonal movement of cattle to
locations outside of the pastoral zone. Failure to comply with these
regulations is met with fines and eventually exclusion from the pastoral
zone and the project. A total of 2 million hectares of land had been

identified for future exclusive pastoral use, over 40 planned pastoral zones nationwide, including several areas in Boulgou. As a result of this restriction on cattle movement, no animals are exchanged between herders in the zone and those outside and the ties between those different groups are minimal.

Another objective of pastoral zone management is to disentangle farmer-herder relations and avert conflicts that arise through alleged resource competition. The FAO, the Food and Agricultural Organization, assesses reasons for farmer / herder conflicts almost exclusively as the result of spatial integration and cohabitation. Lack of fencing, poor supervision of herds, cultivating close to pasture areas, obstruction of traditional access routes to pasture and similar issues could, the FAO (2004) suggests, largely be resolved by the spatial segregation of farmers and herders. The report reveals the rhetoric of conflict management in modernization programmes and deliberately ignores those other fields of interaction, which are not directly related to spatial proximity, such as cattle entrustment or exchange of services. State and development agencies legitimize their intervention in reference to local conflicts by the implicit argument that the provision of material and political resources eradicates the cause for those conflicts. The resources, which the state and non-governmental organizations provide or protect, such as access to pasture, management of pastoral production and tenure security, legitimise their intervention and support their claims to political control of the local economy.

Locating Boulgou in the world system

Redrawing Boulgou's historical and political lines of economic and social transformation turns out to be part of a wider, global process: Burkina Faso is an integral – if peripheral – part of an international network of trade relations and of global financial restructuring. In the prevailing neo-liberal logic, the state's main raison d'etre is to provide a viable legal and political frame for capitalist development and free trade. In order to make its arrival in the local arena, however, the state needs to provide material and social resources. With only a tenth of its population employed in the formal sector, Burkina Faso needs to raise the necessary funds abroad, increasingly by selling its assets on the global market. Technical and other infrastructure, such as telecommunications and health, is imposed on semi-peripheral markets,[40] where

---

[40] Zain networks served 40 million subscribers in 14 African countries and controlled 50% of BF cell phone market. It was taxed at 10 billion $US when it changed owners (to the India-based Mittal conglomerate) in 2009.

it also sells major parts of its labour force. Development funds and increasing international investments are attracted by the price of implementing adjustment programmes, the privatization of land and the transformation of agro-pastoral production into a formal economy.

At the same time, there can be no romanticizing of local practice either. The history of warfaring Bisa, a predatory Mossi kingdom and mercenary Fulbe, the dominance of landed patriclans over new settlers and increasing demographic pressure give no cause for the glorification of local resource-use systems. Boulgou's scarcity of resources has always been the curse of its people and a legitimacy of its ruling gentry, excluding youth, women, newcomers and the landless from political participation.

The state and its proxies, the development machine, enter this local arena as competitors for political and social control; they have the same vested interest as the old elites in controlling and (re-) defining the local economy. Boulgou is not an economic or political *terra nulla*. That many (formal) economists like to see it that way and that the development machine ploughs through the region as if it was, is part of the legitimizing rhetoric of intervention – just as the local landed gentry had declared that the bush created a scarcity of 'civilized, inhabitable land' on which it based its political dominance. The actors who were introduced in this section – groups and subgroups of farmers, herders, landed, landless, newcomers, administration and development agencies – all attempt to impose their view of the land, which is tied to their claim to political legitimacy. Alongside gender and age, ethnicity and the degree of landedness are the major criteria in assigning economic and political authority on the local level.

3

IIIIIIIIII

Sharing the land
The ethnic division of labour

In Boulgou, as in most of rural sub-Saharan Africa, land is a major, if not the major, source of social control. The power to allocate land establishes a social hierarchy and a fabric of mutual dependencies. All parts of society refer to land in some way and are part of a complex field that spans those who hold land (the 'landed') to those who do not (the 'landless'): all groups and individuals in this field are related to each other in terms of their relative entitlement to the land. As opposed to the notion of ownership, which implies an abstract, exclusive right over an undivided whole, one is advised to look at property relations as 'bundles of rights and obligations' (e.g., Berry, 1993: 133): a flexible, permeable and temporary set of agreements, subject to continuous negotiations, opposed to the allegedly durable and often enough absolute notion of independent, i.e. allodial ownership. The complexity of land rights and property regimes in sub-Saharan Africa has been dealt with in great detail elsewhere (Bassett and Crummey, 1993; Juul and Lund, 2002; Lund, 2001; Moore, 1998; Sawadogo and Stamm, 2000; Shipton and Goheen, 1992 b; van den Bergh, 1996. For Burkina Faso especially: Brasselle, Gaspart, and Platteau, 2002; de Zeeuw, 1997; Hagberg, 1998; Sawadogo and Stamm, 2000).

Most authors underline the dynamic nature of landed relations: entitlements to land and access to landed resources are not fixed once and for all, but depend on a series of criteria that constantly need to be reified (membership in the landholding group; the capacity to actually exploit the land in an appropriate manner and so forth). Land, in most sub-Saharan contexts, is not only an economic asset but also a means of locating social relations, as I underlined elsewhere, (Dafinger, 2000; 2004). The dynamics and malleability of local land rights and the fact they are deeply rooted in social and political relations have been a continuous cause for concern for development and modernization agencies – which in turn have constantly been under attack by anthropologists underlining the actual complexity of African landholding (e.g. Berry, 1991; 2002; 2006; Brasselle, Gaspart and Platteau, 2002; Kevane, 1997; Wallerstein, 1984; 2004).

Organizations mainly criticized the practice of continuous re-negotiation of access rights as this fails to provide tenure security. People would feel reluctant to invest in the land, if they had no guarantee of profit from these investments in the future. Improvements that would ensure degradation control, irrigation and encourage general efforts to intensify agricultural production, however, had been identified as the silver bullet to economic development. Consequentially land borrowing is seen as a major obstacle to the improvement of the rural sector, as it offers no economic return for the actual landowner. The anthropological counterpoint stresses that entitlements to use land and its resources are not inscribed in the actual object (the land), but are rather immanent in the relations of the people (who relate to each other with respect to this land). Length of residence, the genealogical position within the landholding clan and aspects of social control are decisive factors and determine the respective rights of individuals and sub-groups to parcels of land.

The landed and the landless

In Boulgou, differential authority with regard to the land serves as a prime marker of social and political relations and dependencies. Being landed is a relative and contingent attribute that defines the relation between any two social groups or individuals. From the perspective of a landholding farmers' lineage, a member of a blacksmith clan will be considered landless, as the blacksmiths settle on and cultivate land, which is under the custody of the elders of the landholding clan. Religious authority over the land, too, is vested in the landed clan and is exerted by the earth priest. Nevertheless, in terms of belonging and autochthony, blacksmiths are still considered part of the landed gentry as they hold permanent rights in the fields they cultivate and the parcels of land on which they settle. In practice, then, most landed relations are gradient and drawing one clear line between groups in terms of landedness is almost impossible. The distinction between landed and landless is not one-dimensional but has several layers corresponding to the multiplicity of rights and relations to the land.

As a category of social relations, landedness has its inherent limits. Full material (economic and territorial) control over the land could

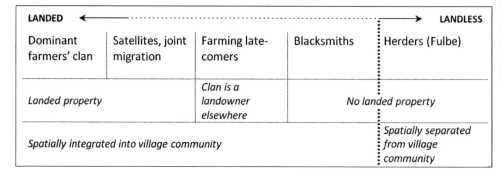

Figure 3 The landed–landless continuum I

only be achieved by excluding any others from the land. The more exclusive territorial claims are, however, the less will be the social control over the landless, in consequence: any landowning clan is only recognised in contrast to the other, 'less landed', that is those groups to whom landholders share out their land. Excluding others maximizes the potential economic and financial benefit but also deprives the landholders of their political or social authority and their privileged position in a wider social network. Land is traded against political and social power and authority; it is an economic as well as a political asset (Berry, 1987; 1989; Dafinger, 2004; Dafinger and Pelican, 2006; Downs and Reyna, 1988; P. M. Shipton and M. Goheen, 1992 a and b).

The same is true at the other end of the scale: the landless generally will still have their say in the definition of the land and, even if limited, over the allocation of resources. This model accounts for the social character of landownership and allows the alignment of all members of a local community within one socio-economic field that is defined by differential access to land and landed resources. Institutions such as land borrowing are an essential part of this fabric and of establishing social and political relations.

This system not only integrates all members of a wider local community, it also structures the local community hierarchically, from the members of the firstcomers' clan at the centre to the latecomers and semi-nomads on the periphery. All major offices, such as village chiefs and earth priests, are recruited from the descendants of the first-comer's group. Anyone who can claim membership in this founding clan is entitled to land in the community, as opposed to groups at the other end of the spectrum; newcomers need to seek permission to extend their cultivated areas – which nonetheless has hardly ever been refused.

The same principles hold true in Boulgou: land rights are the major means of expressing and reifying the region's social, religious and political order. Relations between different groups of settlers and the position of individuals within this hierarchy are expressed through their differential access to land. The allocation of, and control over, cultivated land is exercised by the clan and lineage elders and the earth priests, as religious authorities of the landed clans. The status of being a landholding group and claiming political supremacy is commonly legitimized through the acknowledged order of arrival (I. Kopytoff, 1987; 1999). The claim to a certain territory is ideally derived from direct ancestry of the first settlers in a particular place or else legitimized through myth, transferring rights in a locality's land to later arrivals.

The landowning clans are mainly defined through the prerogative of allocating land to members of the community. Land can be allocated to individuals or households for varying periods: members of the landowning and other resident clans, for example, receive land for the construction of compounds on a permanent basis. These parcels can be kept for generations and as long as the compound is inhabited. Other individuals, households or smaller groups of migrants from other villages who decide to settle in a locality are mostly granted the right to settle and cultivate for indefinite periods, although their rights may in principle be revoked, depending on whether the settlers are seen 'to fit' into the community (Zenner, 1996: 179).

The transfer of land rights is part of a rather formalized process. Most landowners had neither expected nor received any material compensation for letting land to new settlers apart from symbolic gifts, but the new settlers generally contribute to the annual *tarabale*: the sacrifice to the earth. The *tarabale* is carried out by the earth priest, who represents the landowning clan. This sacrifice claims to appease the earth and local spirits and thus endorses the spiritual and territorial authority of the earth priest and the landed clan. As a spiritual authority, the earth priest needs to sanction anything that affects the earth in any way: the opening of new fields, construction of new houses, births and deaths of people. Inappropriate social behaviour, adultery, treason or theft, are sanctioned by the earth through the earth priest, deferring moral and religious authority to the representatives of the landed clan. So while land is not considered a commodity that is freely exchangeable, it still cannot be seen as a gift either as it establishes well defined obligations through the relationship with the land; none of the returns and acknowledgments, such as sacrifices, symbolic parts of the harvest, labour in the chief's fields and political allegiance, are voluntary. Receiving land is the symbolic expression of the incorporation in the local community. In economic reasoning, land is exchanged for political control. As land is not sold or exchanged once and for all, the obligations established through borrowing are periodically renewed in the yearly and other sacrifices.

Similarly, the position of any individual or group on the landless-landed axis is not fixed persistently: over the course of time, rights become more permanent and some lineages may eventually install their own earth shrines after several generations. Within land–owning lineages, land is allocated to households according to their size, their specific needs and relative productivity. Most young men receive part of the patrimony at an age between sixteen and eighteen, when they stop living with their mothers and move into their own space *(kje)*, within the wider compound. Sons mostly claim their own personal fields at that point and fathers would only exceptionally refuse the request, if it happened when there was not enough available land within the patrimony. In any case, most of the young men's work at this point still goes into cultivating their father's and the parent's household's fields.

Possessing individual fields is a precondition for marriage and for setting up a household. Individual fields enable the young men to produce limited surplus and to establish a financial reserve and they are an essential foundation for the new household's economy. Although these fields are allocated to individuals, they primarily are meant to serve the household: as household heads, men keep the authority to control the labour and usage of the field and the right to distribute harvest among the members of the household. Further land for cultivation within the local community can be allocated to household heads depending on the availability of uncultivated land within the patrimony. The lineage eldest approves of any new fields or any new compounds to be built in the community, although in reality most decisions are based on a much broader consent. In my time with Lezigna, the *kiri* (eldest) of the Bangagne clan, I have witnessed a number of requests to construct houses, or transfer use rights between 'houses', often within the same lineage. Such decisions were in almost all cases negotiated within the kin group and, in the case of new buildings, had the approval of the *parza,* the household head.

Women have personal fields within the husband's patrimony in the locality, which they receive as part of the morning gift (or dower), the customary gift of the groom to his new wife. Other than the husbands' fields, which are part of the households, these fields add to the women's individual earnings, which they spend for their own and their children's needs. These property rights are tied to the marriage contract and in the case of divorce the field will revert to the husband's patrimony: women cannot bequeath their fields; their land rights are temporary and individual. The allodial rights in the fields rest with their husbands' patriclans. In the above landed-landless continuum women find themselves at the lower end of the spectrum, as a mere workforce on their husband's fields and exploited for both their reproductive and productive abilities. Their entitlements are not permanent, neither does their labour transform their entitlements into permanent rights.

The house fields in the immediate neighbourhood are the most important in terms of labour input and productivity. Here, the clans and lineages also hold the most explicit claims and exert the most rigid controls over their use. Here, nothing escapes the eyes of family members and neighbours, who generally keep track of the harvests and riches of their fellow farmers. To avoid prying eyes, most also keep fields outside the settlement. These more distant fields may also be of a more individual nature and incomes gained can be spent on more personal needs than from those of the collectively cultivated house fields. The increasing distance from the settlement also minimizes social control, which tends to be weaker in the bush fields.

Young men, moreover, can claim and cultivate fields in their mother's brother's patrimony. Such claims to land, like most other requests by the sister's son, are practically never refused. From an early age boys enjoy the freedom to leave their father's home and live with their mother's brother when they have quarrels within their own families. (In one case, an uncle had tried for months to convince his sister's son to return, but never actually sent him back against his will). Requests for fields, as well, will usually be granted to the sisters' sons, although this can be restricted by the limited availability of land within the localities. Land granted to sisters' sons, however, will always remain in the patrimony and cannot be bequeathed, sold or let in any way. The mother's brother also continues to be responsible for the land vis-à-vis the elders of his own clan. Nephews who decide to move with their entire household and family onto the mother's brother's land also form an important group within any community. They make sacrifice to the ancestor shrine of their own clan, as well as to the earth at their host's (mother's brother's) clan. Similar to houses in the interlocking socio-spatial relations of localities (see Figure 4, p. 63) these settlers are not considered strangers and are more readily integrated into the community on the grounds of existing affinal ties and establish a system of links, cross-cutting the territorial continuity of the kinship group (Dafinger, 1998; 2001; 2004).

Allocating land to members of other clans is common practice throughout sub-Saharan Africa, as it is in Bisa communities. One major reason for this is the highly valued status of strangers, *sanno*: new settlers are seen as bringing a number of advantages to any community: they add manpower when it comes to organizing work parties and bring in new potential marriage partners. In the past, they also added to the defensive force of a community. It is often part of the *tarabale*, the earth sacrifice, to pledge the earth 'to bring in more strangers to settle' and to ask for 'fertility of crops, of people of the earth and the strangers'; it is considered an expression and proof of the earth's fertility and reproductive capacity to accommodate strangers and increase the local population (Dafinger and Ritz-Müller, 1996). Only very recently and mostly in the densely populated northwest has land scarcity started to reverse this trend.

The number of newcomers and of other non-land-owning clans varies widely between the communities dependent on local ecological and political conditions. In the demographically homogeneous villages in north-western Boulgou, hardly ever more than 20 per cent of the population are non-landowners, whereas in the eastern regions of the Tenkodogo kingdom the landowning clans are a minority in the villages. In many of those cases, the other resident clans have strong rights in their territories and often have their own earth priests, which stand in a hierarchically dependent position to the *taraza* of the autochthonous kin group.

Assigning land for settling and cultivation offers several benefits to the landowning clan. In return for the land, newcomers are expected to accept the prerogatives of the landowners, contribute to the *tarabale* and accept the overall authority of the village elder, *kiri*. They become part of the political community and the right to use the land is tied to their loyalty to the local landholding and politically dominant clan. Most importantly, new settlers almost always entered some form of clientele relationship with the receiving community.

Integrating strangers into the local community, however, also poses a number of challenges. Social relations and economic obligations within the clans are mostly defined through genealogical proximity and distance; social authority is legitimized through the genealogical order, prescribing each individual's position in a stable and largely non-negotiable social fabric. As outsiders to the kin groups, the newcomers are a latent threat to this system, as they do not fall under the sanctioning authority of the lineages and their elders, nor are they woven into the solidarity network of the kin-relations. By defining newcomers through patronage, however, it is possible to affiliate them with a specific segment of the local kin group and assign them a position in the network: allotting land to new settlers is an important means of accomplishing this.

The elders of the landowning lineages are also often held responsible for the newcomers, both in terms of their well-being, as well as for their successful integration into the local community. In turn, the landowning group's status and political authority increases with the number of clients and the width of the social network: although the relative status of lineages within the local clans is largely defined through their genealogical relation, the actual impact and authority often also depends on several other factors. A wide clientele network and the capacity to mobilize a large number of followers is part of the social capital, which is used to achieve and manifest social authority.

As the landed–landless continuum suggested, land is exchanged for social and political capital that can be used in intra- and inter-village politics. Settlers from neighbouring communities are considered an equally important asset in inter-village relations as migrant settlers. In the villages in the western regions, most clans have at least one house on the territory of their neighbouring localities, creating a web of interlocked communities.

These houses fulfil the role of middlemen between the communities and create cross-cutting intra-ethnic ties, which overlap the territorial boundaries.

By cross-cutting social and territorial affiliations, these houses are

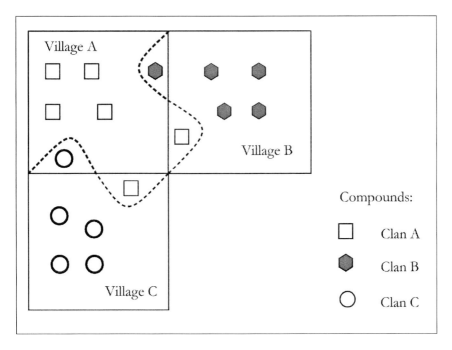

Figure 4 Interlocking of local and kinship groups (schematic)

also manifestations of two conflicting principles of group formation: that of territorial organization (expressed in the local community) and that of social organization (of the kinship group). Only in the landowning founders' lineage are both principles congruent; other groups are defined in relation to this centre: the social and physical distance to the founding lineage.

Giving land to new settlers and lending land to members of other clans thus is a matter of mapping the political and social rather than a primarily economic transaction. The permeability of boundaries creates an interface between neighbouring communities by overlaying two otherwise incongruous principles of group formation. Cross-cutting ties ensure a constant permeability of boundaries and flexibility of the legal and land use system. Formal economic models, which oppose the borrowing of land for renting, grossly underrate the symbolic meaning of land and the complexities embedded in patron-client relations. While their counterargument – that the times when land was abundant, while manpower was the scarce resource (Berry, 1976; 1993) are over for good (Cleaver and Schreiber, 1994: 44–66) – holds some truth, it still overemphasizes one means of production (land) while neglecting another (human labour).

The importance of land borrowing is one of the social institutions indicative of the significance of territorial organization within and between local communities. At the same time, it underscores some of the difficulties consolidating the territorial principle with other types of political and social relations and the challenges that arise from the incongruences of different modes of group formation. The model of a landed-landless continuum permits us to align a broad range of over-lapping social entitlements and obligations along a common scale that shows varying degrees of entitlements to land. Land rights serve as the measure and expression of social and political status. Being part of this system of land allocation is an essential prerequisite for integration into the local community.

THE LANDLESS

One group that stands at the outer margin of the landed-landless continuum are the cattle herders. Although many herders' settlements are considered part of some neighbouring farmers' village historically or in administrative terms, they are at the same time almost inevitably segregated from the farmers' settlements, both spatially and socially. An outward expression of this is that Fulbe, as a rule, do not participate in the ritual sacrifice to the earth – mostly on the grounds that they are Muslim and could not participate in what they perceive as 'pagan rituals'.[1] The spiritual authority of earth priests extends over the settled and cultivated areas and the arable land in a locality. Cultivated fields are unambiguously part of earth shrine territories, while other arable but uncultivated land at the fringes is less clearly defined. (The areas outside the settlements are generally considered bush land (*po*) and are often claimed by a particular community as potential agricultural land, but are not considered part of the earth priest's realm). The list of participants at these rituals is a good indicator of who is in and who is out of the local system of landed relations. Fulbe are rarely guests.

The Fulbe herders' concept of land is in crucial aspects different from the farmers' view. Herders' social networks are far less based on locality; kinship relations are to a great extent focused on the lineage,[2] which in most cases is synonymous with the residence group, and marriages between villages are much less formalized. Consequently, Fulbe settlements may migrate and resettle without breaking up kinship-based relations.

Studies in pastoral Fulbe communities have repeatedly underscored the different notion of territoriality – in fact non-territoriality – and that claims to landed resources are not so much regulated through territorial ownership but rather through controlling the access and restrictive allocation of specific resources (de Bruijn and van Dijk, 1995: 333; Hagberg, 1998: 58; Kintz, 1982; van den Brink, Bromley and Chavas, 1995).[3] The herders in Boulgou, where even resource control is exerted only to a limited degree, are no exception to this. Although many of the local Fulbe often complained about other transhumant herders, who come in from other parts of the country during the rainy seasons and use the bush-land pastures, most also stressed that they do not see themselves in a position to restrict or even deny access to these herders. Existing resources are either openly accessible (such as the banks of perennial rivers) or are considered the property of the landowning farming community. Moreover, the Fulbe share no higher authorities above the village level, which could possibly mitigate resource claims between the communities and facilitate collective resource management. Instead, local Fulbe delegate control over landed resources to the farmers' communities. Accordingly, the resident Fulbe find themselves having to stress landlessness to defend their resources against migrant Fulbe and simultaneously having to under-

---

[1] In a few cases members of the Fulbe community sent gifts, such as milk or chickens for the annual sacrifice as an expression of 'respect and friendship' for 'the custom' of their farming neighbours, as they put it. Still whenever I asked, no Fulbe ever acknowledged the earth priest as a religious authority (see also p. 90).

[2] Lineage endogamy is a strong preference and commonly practised.

[3] Ensminger (1991) makes similar points about pastoral societies more general.

line their landed entitlements to resources as part of the local community. Chapter 5 looks at how Fulbe communities deal with this intra-group competition over resources in more detail.

For the landed groups, giving or lending land is a means of expressing kinship and wider social relations, as well as a source of social prestige and political control. Here, groups and individuals in the local community define each other in terms of their relative land-edness. Fulbe communities stand outside of this framework and lack most of these social tools. From the point of view of the landowning clan, the Fulbe's contribution to the community's social and political economy is categorically different from that of farming settlers. They do not recognize the territorial and spiritual authority of the earth shrine and their political allegiance to the village chiefs and the local founding clans lacks religious or other moral dimensions and is there-fore often considered fragile. The weak ties to the land – in the percep-tion of many farmers, Fulbe continue to be considered nomads – maintain a permanent exit option, which makes many Fulbe commu-nities appear as less reliable allies in the eyes of many farmers.

Farmers also often point to the different modes of production that make it difficult to count on Fulbe in agricultural work parties. For a similar reason, intermarriage is restricted to a few marriages of Bisa (i.e. farming) women into Fulbe herders' families. In return, Fulbe women (*Reobe*) never marry into the farmers' villages.[4] As herders, Fulbe women are not accustomed to working in the fields. Under economic considerations, marrying a Fulbe woman is considered disadvanta-geous for a Bisa man. At the same time, an ideology of a distinct Fulbe identity, of appropriate conduct (*pulaako*) and rules of endogamy creates an environment on the part of the Fulbe communities that makes marriages into Bisa families practically unthinkable. The bonds that still exist between farmers and herders rest mostly on three pillars: the historically rooted ties – based on military alliances – individual bonds established through personal friendship and cattle entrustment and, eventually, links based on shared administrative interests of the local communities vis-à-vis state and development organizations.

As I set out in Chapter 1, most farming communities had invited Fulbe groups to join their neighbourhoods during the time of slave raids in the early phases of settlement. Fulbe were known for their martial skills and helped to defend the communities against raids by other villages. This historical dimension lives on in a number of cere-monies and social institutions, such as the inaugurations of local chiefs often assigning Fulbe representatives crucial roles in the process. This

---

[4]   In 15 years in the rural areas, I had never heard of a case where this happened.

also underscores the importance of 'longue durée' – which privileges Fulbe with longstanding relations over those who only recently migrated to Boulgou. On a second level, a web of personal, trust-based friendships knits together local Fulbe and Bisa and ensures continued resource access within the local communities. This is facilitated by an ethnic division of labour: herding and agriculture only partially overlap in their demands for resources. Most resources, such as waterholes, can be shared; other resources can be arranged along temporal divisions: land can be used for cultivation until harvest, while herders use the same land as pasture for their cattle between harvest and the new sowing season.

A third bond that connects farmers and herders is largely pragmatic and mainly a response to the requirements of national administration. Fulbe often depend on the farmers' mediation in accessing modern resources, such as wells or administrative representation, as the bureaucracy often recognizes herders' settlements only as part of neighbouring farmers' villages. Farmers, in turn, often profit from having nearby Fulbe communities attributed to their villages, as the additional strength in numbers is an asset in negotiations with development and state organizations over resource allocation.

These links, however, appear not to be very strong and overall the incentives to grant land to Fulbe communities have decreased. Existing relations can still draw on an established practice, personal ties and the fact that both groups occupy different economic niches – limiting resource competition and potential aggravation of conflicts. Those Fulbe, who only moved in rather recently, however, find that they are even less welcome in the vicinity of farming villages – their marginal location at the rims of the cultivated areas visualises this (see Map 3, p. 38).

On the other hand, giving land to the herders never bore much risk either. Other than the fields, which were granted to farming neighbours, land granted to Fulbe is part of an informal exchange, which involves only few or no mutual rights and obligations. Rights to pasture are often only seasonal or, in the case of settlements, can be (and are) easily withdrawn when farmers' villages need to expand their fields. So, while other farmers may gradually acquire permanent entitlements and move up along the landed-landless axis, land given to Fulbe can be reclaimed at any time. Between farmers and herders, the landed and landless distinction appears to be drawn much more clearly than the gradient transitions between resident and migrant farmers.

LANDED RESOURCES

While land is as much a source of political and social authority as it is an economic asset, other landed resources, such as water or trees tend to have much less symbolic importance attached and are seen much more in purely economic terms. Any waterhole or river is in principle considered an unlimited resource. In reality however, ponds, waterholes and streams are very ambiguous in terms of access rights – especially so outside the rainy season: considered open resources, on the one hand, they are, on the other, contained within a land, which often is part of an earth shrine's territory and often restricted to a narrowly defined user group (e.g., the land-owning lineage). Almost all ponds, lakes and riverbanks are used for horticulture by farmers during the rainy season and the few months thereafter. The produce, like onions, tomatoes or zucchini, need to be watered regularly and most farmers spend both early morning and the evening hours watering their plants. The fact that gardens are used to generate money outside the subsistence economy is a reason why disputes over damage by cattle generally offer much less room for negotiations than other conflicts (see Chapter 4).

SHARING RESOURCES

In general, like most resources in Boulgou, land is shared among different user groups and not perceived as exclusively owned by any individual or closed group. As opposed to a system of dividing resources by allocating them to exclusive groups, a system of sharing has a much higher capacity to integrate members of different groups within a common locality, based on shared access to the land.

In another study, comparing local land rights in Burkina Faso and Cameroon (Dafinger and Pelican, 2002; 2006), we have juxtaposed these two models and showed that the allocation of exclusive rights goes hand in hand with a diversification of economic activity within any of the groups and households. This eventually led to the segregation of these groups, following the decline of mutual dependencies. Farmers, in the case of the Cameroonian Grasslands, adopt cattle herding in addition to their farming activities to ensure meat supply, to produce manure for the fields and to keep cattle as a means of storing wealth. Fulbe herders, in their turn, engage in small-scale cultivation to stay economically self-sufficient. Exclusive land rights prohibit cattle movements between different areas and as a result, the economic and social exchange between the groups is at a minimum.

In Boulgou, on the other hand, the persistent economic division of labour creates a broad range of interfaces between the socio-economic groups. Here, too, resource use of the groups only partly overlaps.

In order to share, one also has to divide: even in Boulgou, land cannot be used by two people in the exact same location, at the same time and for the same purpose. While all members in a lineage have a general entitlement to the lineage land, the actual allocation of space depends on a number of additional criteria. Individuals and groups are assigned different parcels for cultivation depending on degrees of kinship and according to their relation to the landholding clan. As opposed to the division of many other resources, most of these boundaries are not perceived as fixed but are continuously negotiable. Changing criteria of membership, religious duties and political allegiance, as well as fuzzy standards of 'proper resource use' are major arguments in the (re-) allocation of land titles.

A second means of managing resource sharing is the temporal allocation of resources. Depending on the resource, access rights can rotate in daily, seasonal or longer cycles. In the case of waterholes and ponds, farmers work in their gardens in the mornings and late evenings, while herders may water their cattle during the day. Fields are used for cultivation from the onset of the rainy season in May until after harvest any time from October to December and land is then opened as pasture for the cattle. Land granted to herders for settlements is given for undefined periods, but this right is often challenged later, as Chapter 4 will illustrate.

Both spatial and temporal division of shared resources is facilitated by the differential needs of the respective user groups. Still, resource sharing is the cause of major scepticism within many development organizations and the state administration, largely because of the constant renegotiations of access rights; not only do patterns of group membership change; the temporal distribution of access rights contains a high potential for differential interpretation and tension. The division and exclusive allocation of resources, propagated by national and development organizations, would allow for clearly defined, formal economic relations. Access rights may be granted based on contractual agreements – whereas in a shared system these rights are necessarily fuzzy and largely framed in notions of friendship and mutual understanding. Often, the use rights granted to non-members are perceived as gifts. Principles of reciprocity demand that any such gift will be returned in the form of a counter gift (Sahlins, 1972: 149–84), but the value of goods and services that are exchanged is not formally established (see Gregory, 1982; Laidlaw, 2000). Gifts, as Mauss (1954 [1925]:

8) reminds us, are very much about creating relations between people (see also works by Carrier, 1991; Gregory, 1982; Polanyi, 1975). The sharing of resources serves at least two distinct, yet interwoven fields: it fulfils economic functions by maximizing resource exploitation and establishes relations beyond the kinship groups based on notions of friendship and thus contributes to the social order on the level of a transethnic meta-society.

Resource use and 'structural adjustment'

The following section will look at the general impact of development projects and programmes in the region and introduces some of the approaches used to integrate local economies into national and global markets. Local land management and the ethnic division of labour in economic, religious, social and political fields are the two main targets in this process. The development and modernization programmes, which attempt to change the economic and ecological practice, need to provide alternative solutions for the social field. As the Cameroonian case suggested, however, this is rarely ever achieved; many West African states are not in a position to sufficiently provide reliable social and judicial authority. At the same time, it just cannot be assumed that the model of resource sharing ever constituted a viable 'equilibrium' (Cleaver and Schreiber, 1994), which could balance out the social and ecological changes that most recent population growth and globalization impose on regions like Boulgou. Local land rights and perceptions of land and territoriality are a major interface in the interaction between national administration, development organizations and local communities. Especially among the farmers, the territorial notion of community is largely compatible with the administrative approach. The state itself acts as a landed institution, which builds its political rule on the division into territorial units (Alonso, 1994; Elwert, 1983; Gupta, 2001; Hansen and Stepputat, 2001).

The alleged fuzziness of local land rights, however, along with the continuous negotiability of local land rights and entitlements makes local landholding unacceptable from a bureaucratic stance (Bassett, 1993; Berry, 2002; Cleaver and Schreiber, 1994; Stamm, 2004). The ultimate authority of lineage elders over fields and the practice of land borrowing without formal agreements further fuel the scepticism of modernization projects. Driven by donor organizations, the World Bank and the IMF, the administration of (the then) Upper Volta undertook several attempts to formalize land holding and create a viable frame for external investment as early as the 1970s. None of these attempts, however, had lasting effects and practically none changed the practice of local landholding. Projects like the AVV resettlements scheme were of limited local and temporal scope. Things gradually started to change when neoliberal 'structural adjustment plans' moved to the top of the internal agenda from the early 1990s onwards. The last land reform has been part of a package of decentralization and restructuring remedies to attract foreign investment and eradicate poverty, alongside the selling off of the country's assets – a phenomenon common to large parts of the developing world .

The main difference from previous land titling schemes was that the current legislation now took into account existing land holding practices and assured a pre-emptive right of local communities to their 'traditional' land. This is based on the presumption that landholding is regulated by local legal systems that would exist parallel to the national legal framework: land within the communities remains under the control of the landholding clans. The reform of the land titling procedures pretended to only be concerned with the allocation of new lands outside the village communities and leave existing internal property relations on settlements and house fields unaltered.

The revised legislation is nonetheless of major impact on existing local resource use and on the way access rights are negotiated. This is especially visible in the case of the implementation of pastoral zones in Burkina Faso, which are based on the new legislation and which have led to a socio-economic – and de facto ethnic – segregation under the supervision of state controlled development programmes. The scheme disrupts the dynamics of conflict regulation and containment, without providing alternative institutions of conflict management. The politics of segregation eventually aggravated the tensions and led to increased use of violence (Dafinger, 2006).

The new titling scheme also enables urban professionals and public servants to acquire land in and around their native villages. So far, people who had left their local community to work in urban professions or to pursue careers in the bureaucracy, had few options of maintaining agricultural land in the home communities. Migrants can in principle maintain entitlements by virtue of being members of the landholding clan; local practice, however, also requires that field owners cultivate and improve the fields that they are allocated. Extended fallow or overly long periods of non-cultivation forfeit those rights and fields will eventually be reallocated to other resident members in the kin group. As a result, few public servants who have moved to the capital or one of the urban centres are able to maintain their entitlements. In addition, many are also reluctant to visit their home communities for fear of social pressure by their rural kin. With any visit, a functionary or officer faces a major dilemma: to either have to give in to the material demands of their rural relatives or hold on to the money and face enormous social pressure, including threats of witchcraft (Geschiere and Nyamnjoh, 1998: 85f).

The new scheme allows functionaries to secure lands in their home communities and in nearby towns, without the need to participate in local networks or having to obey reciprocal obligations. Most allotted parcels of land so far, are in fact building spaces in smaller towns such as Tenkodogo. These little towns were the first areas to be parcelled ('loti', in official French), in order to provide building space for a growing urban population (Gensler, 2004: 40–56). The initial euphoria that dominated the new housing market has also led to an over-investment in a number of cases. In one of Tenkodogo's neighbourhoods, a number of modern town houses have popped up over the past years; built by those who found employment elsewhere with development organizations, major enterprises, banks or in the state bureaucracy. Many of the new house owners have no intention of living in these houses and rather see them as an investment, hoping to create additional income by renting them out. The catch in these calculations is that the only people who can afford to rent a house would be other functionaries, largely pursuing the same strategies.

In a mid-term perspective, however, the main objective of the land reform program is the 'lotissement', parcelling and privatization of agricultural land. In line with World Bank policy, privatization of land is considered as an initial step in the transition to large scale agro-business, the development world's apparent silver bullet to increase the output of agricultural production (German Federal Ministry for Economic Cooperation and Development, 2005; United Nations (UNDP) and Government of Burkina Faso, 2006). In this vision, agribusiness will support a growing urban population and increasingly formalise the agricultural sector, allowing more efficient state control and facilitating taxation of revenues. Functionaries also increasingly start to invest in holdings and agro-business, which operate on privatized lands (Freidberg, 1996). Similar forms of 'land grabbing' have also been described for other parts of Africa (Bassett and Crummey, 1993; Berry, 2002: 652ff; Peters, 2007).

The pastoral zones, which Burkina Faso has set up in different parts of the country, are another outcome of the RAF and the land privatization programme. Although many of the programmes were designed as early as the 1980s, the full implementation was often only achieved

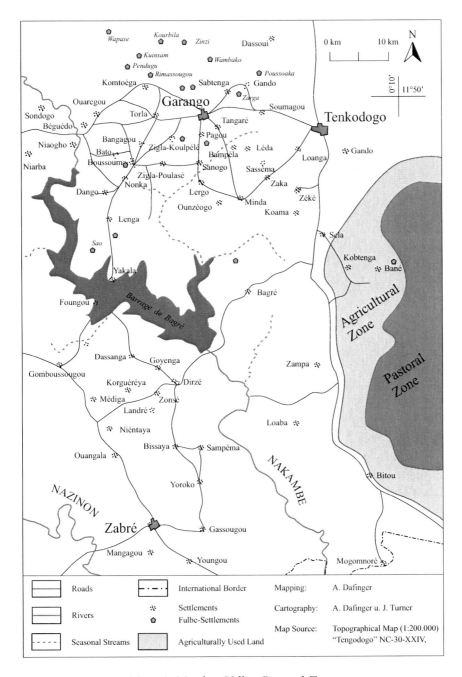

Map 4 Nouhao Valley Pastoral Zone

after the last phase of the land reforms from the 1990s onwards.[5]

One of these zones is located on the eastern fringes of Boulgou, in the Nouhao valley. Here, the resettlement of farmers happened as early as 1988. As an immediate response to an epidemic of river blindness (*onchocerciasis*) in the area, people were forced to resettle – quite against their will, however, and only after the intervention of national troops. In the late 1990s, Fulbe herders were eventually resettled into the zone, administered by a joint Burkinabe-Italian development scheme.

Today, farmers and herders both also acknowledge the negative consequences of the project: although the herders now enjoy easier access to pasture and the farmers appreciate that crop damage has diminished significantly, the history of forced resettlement still weighs heavy and the social costs of having lost relations across the ethnic border are considered high. A look at the above map shows the management region, which contains two areas of roughly the same size. The core of the area is the actual pastoral zone (c. 70,000 ha), which is enclosed by a cordon of agricultural land (c.100.000 ha), designated for cultivation. Infrastructural resources, such as roads, bridges, safe water wells, etc. are supplied by the project, partly in collaboration with other organizations like PIHVES (Chapter 5) and furnished in both the pastoral and agricultural zones.

A main point of anthropological criticism of most land reform and transformations of structural adjustment programmes was their narrow focus on formal economic dimensions of land tenure, largely ignoring the social importance of African land rights (Bassett and Crummey, 1993; e.g. Berry, 1975; 2006; Downs and Reyna, 1988). The importance of land also lies in its capacity to integrate social groups and as a means of coordinating the workforce of the local community. In the newly established pastoral zones, however, the sharing of land between groups and households is banned and parcelled land is reserved for either exclusive pastoral or agricultural use. Relations between Fulbe herders and Bisa farmers have broken up as a result of this spatial segregation. All this is explicitly intended to minimize frictions from overlapping resource use, to create optimized conditions for production and to boost agricultural output. Herders, in this model, no longer depend on the goodwill of landowning farmers to access pasture.

However, this new land is not as 'free to anyone' as Faure suggested in her assessment of the pastoral zones (Faure, 1996: 200), but comes at a price: in order to settle and work in the pastoral zone, herders

---

[5] L. E. Boudon, 1997. 'Rectifying the revolution' is the official terminology, with which the current president labels his turn from Sankara's socialist and anti-western revolutionary agenda toward a western oriented policy and the country's opening to foreign investment.

now have to abide by the bylaws set up by the project management. Failing to do so (that is, taking in additional cattle or cultivating other than prescribed crops) invokes fines and eventually leads to expulsion from the economic zone (as has happened on two occasions).[6]

Groups, ethnicities and metasociety

Taking what appears to be an emic category as a starting point for investigation (that is, taking Bisa and Fulbe as 'ethnic groups') is not without problems. Common-sense ethnicity is, as Roger Brubaker reminded us, 'a key part of what we want to explain, not what we want to explain things with. It belongs to our empirical data, not to our analytical toolkit' (Brubaker, 2004: 9). Nonetheless, turning to analytical models only leaves us with an occasionally over-debated, yet vaguely defined concept and the risk of over-generalizing the outcome of local historical, economic and political processes. Max Weber, first to scrutinize the concept, considered 'ethnicity … a weak analytical concept' (1968: 395), referring to a range of phenomena so broad that they have almost no explicative value. For Weber, ethnicity included any 'sense of common descent extending beyond kinship, political solidarity vis-à-vis other groups and common customs, language, religion, values, morality and etiquette' (1961: 301). In his view, ethnicity was simply out-dated as a concept and he showed himself convinced that it would eventually be replaced by other principles of group formation, such as class, nation, or religion.

> Ethnic membership does not constitute a group; it only facilitates *group formation of any kind,* particularly in the political sphere. On the other hand, it is primarily the political community, no matter how artificially organized that inspires the belief in common ethnicity. (Weber, Roth, and Wittich, 1978: 385, emphasis added)

Why then does ethnicity continue to play its dominant role eighty years later and obviously seems more important as a concept in social sciences than before? Publications on ethnicity have constantly risen since the 1960s (Cohen, 1978: 379; See Eriksen, 2002: 4f). When, almost five decades after Weber, Barth published his seminal contribution on ethnic boundaries (Barth, 1969a), it had already become clear that the malleability of the concept, so criticized by Weber, was

---

[6] In one case, the zonal management saw 'no alternative' but to evict a herder (i.e., the complete household and family), when the family ignored cultivation plans and had misused their allotted fields for the cultivation of maize (instead of the prescribed cereal-maize mix). The project feared this might set a bad example and, by evicting the family, decided to send out a message to the collective.

in fact one of its foremost strengths. Ethnicity permitted to draw lines around almost *any* group of almost any size, proved flexible in creating criteria of inclusion and exclusion; it made it easy to mobilize its followers on very emotional levels and obfuscated other (class, religious, linguistic) lines of solidarity and group cohesion. As an analytical tool, it offered an alternative to concepts of 'tribes' or 'race' (Cohen, 1978: 379), which were increasingly discarded because of their ethnocentric (Western) bias. For Wimmer, ethnicity mostly gained its relevance in relation to the nation state; questions of legitimacy of state power lead to claims for recognition and political awareness of ethnic affiliation (Wimmer, 1995: 464).

Although most anthropologists adopted what soon became a catchall term, only a few scholars actually attempted to offer viable definitions (Banks, 1996: 1–10). Barth distilled four criteria that were generally assigned to the 'ethnic group', in the mainstream of anthropological work at the time. Ethnic groups were largely considered to be a) biologically self-perpetuating populations, b) based on shared culture values and forms, c) constituting a field of communication and interaction and d) seen as identifying themselves and being identified 'by others as constituting a category different from other categories of the same type' (Barth, 1969b). This also stressed the fact that ethnicity is as much negotiated and generated in interaction with 'others', or 'them-groups'. It was increasingly the latter point that anthropologists picked up following Barth, focusing on the boundaries and aspects of cultural exchange. Ethnicity only made sense in relation to other groups (Lentz and Nugent, 1999).

R. Cohen saw the concept of ethnicity largely in opposition to the notion of the 'tribe', which disregarded the embeddedness of a specific group in a wider context (Cohen, 1978: 386). Similar to Barth in this respect, Cohen stresses that ethnicity is relevant at its borders and produced in interaction.

While Weber had erred in assuming that ethnicity would become obsolete as both an actors' model and an analytical concept, his view that ethnicity is constructed and a consequence rather than a prerequisite of political action (Jenkins, 1997: 10), constituted the backbone of instrumentalist (Bentley, 1987) or circumstantialist (Glazer, Moynihan, and Schelling, 1975) approaches to ethnicity. The reasons for the persistence and increasing importance of ethnicity (Banks, 1996; Jenkins, 1997; Ortner, 1984: 141f; Wimmer, 1995) are also owed to a political discourse that continued to use ethnicity as a tool in establishing and managing power relations (Hechter, 1974; 1976; Horowitz, 1991). The *divide et impera* of postcolonial states was often built on ethnic division (Dafinger and Pelican, 2006; Horowitz, 1991;

Wimmer, 1995). Often enough 'the boundary [between ethnic groups] is patrolled by the Europeans', as Banks observed (Banks, 1996: 27).

That ethnic groups are no longer taken for granted, as timeless, unchanging, quasi-natural units of human group formation (almost) seems to go without saying, in the wake of Weber's and Barth's observations on the political character of the ethnic group and on the importance of the ethnic boundary. Nonetheless, the persuasion persists in the discipline (see Esman, 2004), and even more so outside the academic realm (Allen, Hudson and Seaton, 1996; Allen and Seaton, 1999; Fardon, 1996), that there is more substance to the ethnic than being a mere contextually negotiated category, exploited by an interested elite and an often colonial invention (Lentz, 1998; Lentz and Nugent, 1999).

This primordialist stance defines ethnicity as built on 'the affective potency of primordial attachments' (see Bentley, 1987: 25; Dafinger and Pelican, 2006, for a debate) or, in Esman's words (2004: 31), 'historically rooted, deeply embedded in a people's culture, reinforced by collective myths and memories, (…) likely to persist over time':

> (1) ethnic groups are authentic and important social collectivities; (2) conflicts among them and between them and governments are critical realities that cannot be wished away; therefore (3) they must be critically examined and analyzed so that the dynamics of ethnic-based conflict can be better understood … (ibid.: 40)

Esman believes that ethnic groups, whether constructed or primordial, evolve into authentic collectivities (ibid.) over the course of time. He fails, however, to show us any such authentic collectivity. Although his examples of Nazi Germany or civil war Serbia underscore how ethnic sentiment was politically exploited, they are poor examples of corporate ethnic groups. The same is true for his claim that 'conflicts among them and between them and governments are critical realities'. Brubaker argued that

> ethnic conflict – or what might better be called ethnicized or ethnically framed conflict – need not and should not, be understood as conflict between ethnic groups, just as racial or racially framed conflict need not be understood as conflict between races, or nationally framed conflict as conflict between nations. (Brubaker, 2004: 9f)

Primordial argumentation does not necessarily reject the idea that ethnic identity had to be created at one point. As Kapferer suggested, ethnic identity once created, forms an often-unconscious part of specific culture and becomes part of an individual but collectively shared sentiment. For Kapferer (1988), mythology is a paramount example of these processes. In this, Kapferer follows the same line as Connerton (1989) who sees sentiments of ethnicity and nationalism rooted in collective commemorations.

Primordial sentiments of belonging, collective memories, cultural embeddedness and historical roots may well help to explain how ethnicity is built. It may also partly attempt to tell why and to which ends ethnicity is constructed. But primordialism fails to explain why in some cases we see manifestations of ethnic consciousness and outbreaks of ethnic violence (see Chapter 4) more than in others and why at times ethnicity prevails over other principles of group formation and not at others.

When, in the remainder of this book, I will partly draw on some of the primordialist-oriented works, I will also argue against the assumption that ethnic sentiments are subject to a historical inertia and largely beyond the individuals' agency. Ethnic (and nationalist) sentiments are deliberately exploited by the members of the political and social elites and can swiftly change their meaning and political relevance.

Weber and Barth's approaches to ethnicity are only among the most prominent examples that went beyond primordial sentiment – the 'foundations and materials' (Schlee, 2004: 148) of ethnic identity – and turned to interaction, to the boundaries and the political trajectories of ethnically defined groups. Ethnicity in this frame is a cultural, as opposed to an often biologically oriented primordialist view; because of its culturedness, ethnicity must also be considered variable and manipulable. Based on these assumptions, ethnicity becomes a powerful model in the toolbox of political and economic struggles.

A large part of Bisa are in fact descendants of Mossi migrants to the region who decided to adopt the cultural institutions and practices of their hosts and 'become Bisa'. These groups deliberately chose their ethnicity. But ethnicity also needs to *make sense* and help explain the pivotal cultural institutions and their connections; the ethnic categories, ascriptions and self-ascriptions that the following chapters deal with, revolve around particular modes of production, belief systems, linguistic practice and kinship relations, tying them together and creating meaningful connections.

The Mossi's early migration, and their assimilation into the Bisa societies support those models that locate origins of ethnicity before the colonial intervention. Nugent and Lentz, in particular, have made this point (Lentz, 1998; 2006; Lentz and Nugent, 1999; Nugent, 2008). Peel argued along the same lines in response to Abner Cohen's claim that ethnicity should be explained within its present functional context (Cohen, 1971; 2004). By re-drawing the ethnogenesis of what has come to be known as the Yoruba, Peel presents an image of a liquid and historically changing ethnicity (Peel, 1989). Yoruba identity today needs to be analysed in its current political and social context – but to the same extent can only be understood as the outcome of specific historical processes, and decisions by actors to assume and co-construct Yoruba-ness.

Another, likewise constructivist, position views ethnicity largely as a consequence of economic relations and as an extension of the economic and political world system. Labour markets in peripheral states are often organized around ethnic affiliation as Wolf and others had argued (Bonacich, 1972; 1973; Wolf, 1982). The congruence of ethnic consciousness and economic criteria advances ethnic mobilization, especially in contexts where other forms of political organization (unions, political parties) are not or 'not yet' at hand (Cohen, 1974). Ethnicity is seen as

> the outcome of intensive interaction between different culture groups and not the result of a tendency to separatism. It is the result of intensive struggle between groups over new strategic positions of power within the structure of the new state: places of employment, taxation, funds for development, education, political positions and so on.(ibid.: 96)

However, the view that ethnicity is mainly a means of securing collective resources furnished by the state, overemphasizes the role of the state as a supplier of resources and disregards that state and related organizations at the same time appear as competitors over political and social authority. Moreover, ethnicity is perceived as a strategy to compete over collective resources (Cohen, 1974) and a result of competition over scarce resources, rather than as preceding or even causing conflict. This model offers a viable approach to a range of ethnic conflicts, as both Cohen and Wimmer demonstrate, but still finds its limits in cases when scarcity is explicitly created in order to exert political control. Local elites, which propagate ethnic group formation to pursue political ends (as in the example of herders' associations – see Chapter 5) take a leading role in defining scarcity or perceived injustice. Control over people in Boulgou and the partial exclusion of Fulbe were built on the politically and religiously defined scarcity of land.

Likewise in a rational economic framework, Hechter views ethnic identity as a product of individual decisions: people do not usually choose their ethnic identity – although anthropology has provided us with a number of examples where this is the case (e.g. Bloch, 1995). Whatever is subject to individual control and contextually negotiated, however, Hechter's view is that ethnicity can always be over- or under-communicated i.e. be either considered a relevant distinctive criterion or not, depending on the context. In the case of agropastoral relations in Boulgou, ethnic difference within the socio-economic groups (Bisa-Mossi) tends to be much less articulated than is the case between two different production systems, farmers and herders. De Bruijn and van Dijk offer examples of pre-colonial pastoral elites, which used to actively maintain a shared (Fulbe) ethnicity as a means of exploiting nomadic pastoralists and controlling the income from their resources (de Bruijn and van Dijk, 2001).

While instrumentalist approaches offer adequate tools in showing how conflicts take on ethnic dimensions and in analysing how ethnicity is used to define the rules of inclusion and exclusion of political and economic interest groups, they turn out less helpful when it comes to the content of the ethnicized conflict. Often considered a product of 'unconscious and unspecified process of interest aggregation', or a fiction constructed by leaders and sold to their impressionable followers, a purely instrumentalist model will not tell us why the ethnic manages to impress its followers.

We need to take the primordialists back on board; only by looking into the 'quasi-natural character of ethnic sentiment', or the 'doxic world of the self-explanatory', can we address the question why individuals are willing to subordinate their economic and other interests under criteria of ethnic solidarity. A viable analysis needs to take account of both the content and the intention of ethnic rhetoric, as Schlee suggested:

> Take constructivism in its literal sense and speak of 'constructions' rather than 'inventions'. As in the building trade, which is the source of the metaphor, constructions are not arbitrary: (…) they make use of local materials. Sometimes old foundations are used, or old building materials are reused. Even very recent social constructs may be generated out of the same processes, thus achieving familiarity, plausibility and often a degree of pseudo-naturalness. (Schlee, 2004: 148)

Keyes (1981) has attempted to resolve the constructivist-primordial dichotomy by placing both aspects of ethnicity in dialectical relation to each other. Ethnic identities serve psychological functions, but they become socially significant

> only if access to the means of production, means of expropriation of the products of labour, or means of exchange between groups are determined by membership in groups defined in terms of nongenealogical descent. (ibid.: 3–30).

The later examples will highlight this nexus of ethnic identification and other (social, political, etc.) interests. Ethnicity is not only exploited by political elites (as Chapter 5 will explore), it is likewise a viable option for the so-called followers who have a choice in what to believe and who are free to embark on the ethnic discourse or follow other lines of identity formation. Hechter's notion of over- vs. under-communicating ethnic difference offers a key to describing this process.

To differing degrees both lines of thought, primordialist and instrumentalist, tend to overlook that ethnicity is not necessarily tied to specific groups (Brubaker, 2004). Politics in favour of one or more particular ethnic groups need not necessarily be carried out by members of these groups, but can simply be based on personal preference and strategies, or ideologies of modernization (some ethnic groups may be considered more advanced or 'civilized' in a local ideological context). The bureaucratic elite may act deliberately against the presumed interests of their own ethnic group, in order to show their intent to delineate themselves against rural backwardness, the prevalence of the kinship organization and to demonstrate an ideology of modernism.

Looking at Burkina Faso, it would be difficult – if not impossible – to define borders of societies, delineate social units or identify corporate groups. Communities are composed of several overlapping groups whose boundaries are often permeable and negotiable. Group affiliation is contextual and may be either stressed or played down, depending on the social field and the economic and political objectives. Ethnic affiliation is no exception: Boulgou's past and recent history gives no indication of corporate ethnic groups; even in terms of settlement history, we see small communities moving into the region, which in many cases had been pluri-ethnic from their origins. Ethnicity in Boulgou is not and apparently has not been a constitutive factor of corporate groups and corporate group action.

This does not mean, however, that ethnicity and ethnic affiliation would not be an important aspect of group identity in many contexts. When individuals act based on their perceived ethnicity, they tend to reproduce ethnic difference. Still, while the division of society along ethnic criteria is one of the most dominant social markers in Boulgou, it needs to be stressed that we are looking at a complex society that is structured along a plethora of differentiating criteria. While local rhetoric often stresses a quasi-natural or 'fundamental' distinction (Hirschfeld, 1995: 1434) based on ethnic common sense, which more or less closely interact, the following analysis will take ethnicity only as an – albeit important – part of the process and not use it as its starting point and so explicitly distance itself from primordialist approaches to ethnicity.

A major structuring element of socio-political relations is the alleged duration of residence, as indicated above. The length of residence not only defines entitlements to land, religious or political leadership, but also differentiates groups and individuals depending on their relative length of stay. As the previous chapter has shown, land-edness, full control over a given area and its people, depends on the credible claim of having descended from autochthonous population or first settlers. Settlers acquire increasing rights in land with the duration of residence; religious duties and authority are successively passed over to families, which at one point were newcomers.

Ethnicity, in this list of sources of political and social authority of groups, is only second to aspects of seniority and length of residence. Neither is it a major frame for collective action; historically locality prevailed over ethnicity in delimiting alliances in violent conflict, as the local Fulbe mercenaries suggested. The fact that 90 per cent of the people are of one (Bisa) and only a tenth of another (Fulbe) ethnic group, also means that – for the farmers – most interaction happens between members of their own ethnic group.

Still, most people tend to draw unambiguous lines between ethnic groups and ethnic affiliation is a major identity marker on a meta-societal level. Bisa farmers generally refer to other Bisa by clan or locality (e.g., 'someone from Sanogo', 'a Guem from Busma', etc.), whereas beyond their own group these markers are only secondary. For most farmers, Guieba would foremost be a *simbino*, a Fulbe and only as a secondary attribute would he be considered *simbino na Magourou*, a Pullo from near Magourou. *Nasano* ('whites') likewise comprise anyone non-African.[7] Whether stressed in a particular context or not, ethnic affiliation seems always consciously perceived and articulated. This is also the case between Bisa and Mossi, in the eastern part of the region, and most people readily enumerate stereo-typical traits about each of their ethnic neighbours. Differences between Bisa and Mossi, however, tend to be less pronounced, one reason being that both groups mostly engage in agricultural activity and also largely because of the fact that many Bisa clans actually claim to be of Mossi origin, acknowledging that a transition between the two is possible, as opposed to Bisa- (or Mossi-)Fulbe relations.

When talking about 'the Fulbe' in general, farmers frequently refer to the herders as a monolithic block, ascribing the same attributes to different local communities, irrespective of historical aspects, length of stay, integration into local farming networks, or differential trans-humance patterns. The examples in the following chapters, however,

---

[7] Appreciating the technical 'finesses' of a latest scooter model, a friend remarked that 'vous êtes forts, vous blancs', complimenting 'our' ('white') technical skills. On my objection that the scooter was after all a Korean product, he only commented '*a fo di:m* – that's the same thing'.

illustrate that the actual behaviour of farmers does discriminate between different Fulbe communities. Thus, while Fulbe are generally located at the lower end of the local landed scale, as landless, actual access rights depend on a variety of factors, such as length of stay, integration into the local community, friendship relations between local farmers and the herders.

So a number of Bisa-Fulbe (or farmer-herder) relations can be distinguished on an everyday, interactive level. Some of the agro-pastoral communities share a common history of settlement, mutually legitimize each other politically, engage in the exchange of services, live in a shared locality and have joint mediation institutions. Garango, with its prominent role of the local Fulbe community in the inaugu-ration ceremonies, exemplifies this type of almost 'symbiotic relation-ships' (Breusers, Nederlof, and van Rheenen, 1998). The local economy of these agropastoral communities is based on the principle of an ethnic division of labour and encourages generally amicable, although individual relations across the ethnic divide. Some of these communities do emphasize a joint historical and political dimension (as in Garango), in others this is less explicit (as in Zarga, Poussoaka), where Fulbe can claim no explicit right to membership in political representation in the locality.

Relations between recently founded settlements, such as satellites of 'old' Fulbe communities and the settlements of the post–1970 migrant Fulbe tend to fall into different categories. With no shared history or spatial overlaps, the new settlers do not integrate into the local community; they exchange no services and the relations with farming neighbours are generally marked by the absence of individual friend-ships. Satellites of established settlements, nonetheless, maintain close links with the established Fulbe communities in the agricultural areas and can tap into some of the landed resources that are available to the resident herders through kinship ties. The recent migrants from the Sahel are in an even worse position and cannot draw on such intra-ethnic bonds. They are generally left out of both farmers' and herders' networks. This drastically affects their chances to use resources, as later examples will show. Cross-cutting ties, in all the cases, are the single most important social asset.

Fulbe herders differentiate between longer established communi-ties and the newcomer herders, who arrived after the 1970s and 1980s droughts. Although occasional personal ties exist between the old and the new Fulbe settlements, only a little cooperation takes place on a practical level. Marriage between the newcomers and the residents is an exception rather than the rule, no exchange of cattle takes place (i.e. practice of mutual entrustment of animals by local herders as a

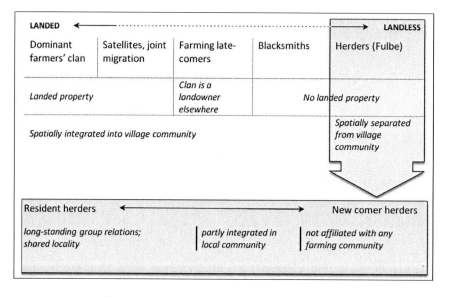

Figure 5 The landed-landless continuum II

means of spreading risk),[8] and transhumance patterns vary widely between the two sub-groups. Transhumance routes depend on the respective networks across the ethnic boundary; newcomers tend to be less connected and are hence more restricted in their choice of rainy season pasture. Zooming in on the lower end of the landed-landless spectrum reveals a more differentiated view of the 'landless' category.

The ethnic division of labour

As the above model shows, most criteria and distinctions that define groups and subgroups are gradient and do not imply categorical distinctions. The landed-landless continuum relates groups according to their relative landedness, assigning more authority to some and less to others. Likewise, kinship is not an absolute marker of group identity, but gradually and contextually incorporates units of varying size, extending well beyond the own clan; just as the economic diversification blurs the lines between cultivators and cattle keepers, herders also cultivate small patches of land and farmers mostly generally keep small ruminants. Almost all identity markers and group boundaries within the Bisa or Fulbe communities are negotiable and the transi-

---

[8] Cattle owners prefer to spread their animals over several herds. In case a herd contracts a disease, gets stolen (rarely), or confiscated (more often) only a fraction of the animals are affected.

tions between the sub-groups are to a large extent gradient.

As opposed to these permeable boundaries, the ethnic distinction appears the most categorical, even if some ethnic lines appear more relevant than others, as the distinction between Mossi and Bisa showed, which is much less problematic in everyday interactions than the divide between Bisa and Fulbe.

One indicator of the importance of the ethnic boundary between Bisa and Fulbe and its maintenance is the marriage restrictions between the two groups. Most Fulbe groups are endogamous and do not encourage marriages with neighbouring ethnic communities. Some Fulbe groups, including Fulbe in Boulgou, allow non-Fulbe women marrying into their families but consider marriages between Fulbe women and non-Fulbe (*habe*) as inappropriate.

Both among Fulbe and Bisa, intra-ethnic marriages are arranged by the couples' parents, a practice that still holds true today and applies to almost all first marriages – certainly in rural areas. These marriages are about establishing and maintaining links between the clans or, in the case of Fulbe marriages, often within the patrilineage. First marriages are almost as a rule never interethnic (I have observed just one case where a Bisa woman married an urban Fulbe as his first wife).

Most Bisa women who join Fulbe families do so as a second, third or fourth wife. The reasons the Fulbe give for this practice are pragmatic: as Fulbe women are not familiar with working in the fields Fulbe men prefer to marry farmers' daughters because they can work their millet fields. On the other hand, many Fulbe complained that Bisa ask for too high a bride price. These marriage restrictions are just one more outward sign of the practical relevance of the ethnic divide; the cases over the following sections provide examples of how this boundary (mostly between Bisa farmers and Fulbe herders) is generated in everyday action and through social institutions and will show *why* individuals work with and profit from this boundary.

Many relations across the ethnic divide are amicable and largely based on trust and friendship, other than a general, structural confidence in the intra-ethnic kinship web (see especially Seligman, 1997). Inter-ethnic ties are also often located on a different economic sphere of exchange. They are often hidden from the public eye and keep an aura of reticence.

Cross-cutting ties are an important asset in Boulgou's agropastoral economy. By exploiting these ties, its participants can shift resources, goods and services onto a different sphere of exchange and move them across the ethnic divide. In this way, the ethnic boundary also divides two principles of exchange: a sphere within the kin groups in which exchange is defined by formal entitlements and a field of inter-ethnic relations characterized by a much more fluid, informal and hidden gift exchange. The ethnic divide works as an opaque screen behind which goods, entitlements and social power are concealed from the public. As the book argues, this opacity of the ethnic boundary is one of its most important characteristics, and one which Fulbe and Bisa both consciously exploit. Concealment is crucial for keeping up the social and political order, both within and between the groups. Maintaining and regenerating the ethnic divide is as important as exploiting the differences. The following story (of spiritual parenthood) is an emblematic case of how the ethnic boundary serves to tie both Fulbe and Bisa together, by reifying stereotypical ascriptions.

Jambeedo's 'double descent'

One morning, during my time in Zarga (a Fulbe settlement of about two hundred people) I was excitedly told about a number of fellow *nazara*, 'whites', who had just arrived in Gando, the neighbouring Bisa village. Allegedly, they had come to help build a new school and apparently all stayed at the *naba's* house: the village chief's compound. I knew that the *naba* had a son who lived in Europe and so I assumed some connection here that would explain the presence of my fellow *nazara*. Indeed, when I went to Gando the following day, I met the *naba's* son who had just come home for a visit from Europe. He greeted me warmly, introduced me to his two European friends and started to tell me everything about his project. Francis, as he presented himself, was the *naba's* oldest son, and had studied and graduated as an architect, only the year before in Europe, where he still lived. His ambition was to improve the design of the standard school buildings and develop new adapted schools for Africa, eliminating many of the shortcomings of the traditional constructions. His prototype relied on local products, was relatively easy to construct and ecologically advanced and he discussed at length the importance of static cement-free bricks and ecological construction. Francis had raised substantial funds in Europe and convinced a few more architecture graduates to invest their time and assist with the construction works. So, here he was, drawing on the support of most villagers – albeit not all, as it would turn out – to supply the labour force and work on the site for several weeks.[9]

When the conversation eventually turned to my presence in neighbouring Zarga, Francis immediately got enthusiastic about the fact

[9] As throughout Burkina Faso, building a school is the task of the village community, whereas the personnel, the teachers, will then be sent and paid by the state.

that I lived with 'his father Bourema'. Bourema was a Pullo herder, a cousin of Kioponi and an immediate neighbour to my *wuro*. The fact that Francis claimed two different fathers (the *naba* and Bourema) was not unusual per se; in both a Fulbe and a Bisa context, all paternal uncles are considered and referred to as 'fathers'. However, Francis insisted that he had one Bisa and one Fulbe father – which to me up to that point seemed quite unthinkable. Claiming multiple fathers is impossible even across clans, leave alone between the two mostly endogamous ethnic groups. Taking into account that those few interethnic marriages always involved a Bisa woman marrying into a Fulbe man's family, then – if Francis was the son of a daughter of the present *naba's* father with Bourema (making the *naba* his mother's brother) – well, even then could he not address the *naba* as his father according to Fulbe classification, leave alone claim primogeniture and eventually succession to the *naba's* office as he did. I was confused.

When I brought up this subject with Bourema, the alleged 'father', he instantly expressed his feelings about the matter, lamenting about the fact that Francis had arrived a couple of days ago and still had not come to see and greet him. Bourema left no doubt about his special fatherhood and I was encouraged to hear the full story.

Preceding Francis' birth, I learned, the *naba's* first wife had had a number of stillbirths. When she was pregnant again, this time with Francis, the Naba Kéré, who was anxious to become a father at last, went to seek the advice of a *bagotodo*, a Bisa diviner, to investigate the cause of the stillbirths, find a remedy and ensure a safe birth. The *bagotodo* soon established that evil spirits, bad *kinkirga*, were determined to kill any *naba's* child at birth and hinder succession to the chieftaincy. *Kinkirga*, a Mossi concept that is also familiar to the Bisa in Boulgou, relates to the idea that all humans have an (evil) twin in the bush. The *kinkirga* needs to be placated throughout one's life (Bonnet, 1988: 57ff). In some cases, it tries to lure new-borns back into the counter world (Breusers, Nederlof and van Rheenen, 1998). The only way to ensure a safe birth and the continuation of the chiefly line, the *bagotodo* suggested, was to set up a ploy and trick the evil spirits. Around the time of her giving birth, the mother-to-be should be sent to a Fulbe home, where she should pretend she was giving birth to a *Simbino*, a Fulbe child, and that way fool the evil spirits (who were after all expecting the *naba's* son, not a Fulbe baby). After a successful birth and receiving a Fulfulde name, the new-born could then safely return home with its mother to her real husband. So Naba Kéré did as he was told; sent his wife to Bourema's compound, where she stayed for about one week, making the spirits believe she was giving birth to Bourema's child. The ploy worked, the spirits took no notice of (what they took to be) Bourema's infant, which accordingly received a Fulfulde name Jambeedo (*jam beedo*, literally 'the one who was made a cheater') before eventually following his mother home. This was the story behind the spiritual adoption and Bourema's mysterious fatherhood.

A Bisa woman giving birth in a Fulbe *wuro* is not a common occurrence and this was the only case I was able to document in Boulgou. The practice, however, is known and confirmed in several interviews among Fulbe and Bisa as *banfulbe*, 'Fulbe parentship.'

On the one hand, this is indicative of a more general view that Bisa farmers hold of Fulbe as having privileged relations with spirits and supernatural forces. The mere fact that they keep fires in their grass huts without setting them ablaze is a sign of some obscure power for many farmers, as was pointed out to me on several occasions. At the same time, Fulbe are moved closer to the realm of the wild, the uncivilized and the evil spirits of the bush, reaffirming the authority of the farmers over the civilized parts of the earth, the local genies and the biotic powers of nature.

Houis (1963) and Bonnet (1988), who had documented a similar practice between Fulbe and Mossi, stress the element of Fulbe inferiority. They locate the practice within Mossi cosmology, assigning a Fulbe father who, according to Houis and Bonnet, 'devaluates the child and places it outside the kin group and society', thus making it a less attractive target for the evil spirits, an argument to which Mark Breusers is reluctant to subscribe. For Breusers, who observed a similar practice in northern Burkina Faso, the spiritual parenthood establishes permanent relations between the child and the Fulbe family (Breusers, forthcoming). Within the farming community, friendship can eventually turn into kinship through the exchange of marriage partners; given that intermarriage between Fulbe and Mossi (or Fulbe and Bisa, for that matter) is restricted, spiritual parenthood is the closest way of establishing kinship between the ethnic groups. Much less than an expression of depreciation, the practice of spiritual parenthood appears as an attempt to render friendship permanent.

Houis and Bonnet's argument is supported by similar practices and beliefs throughout West African farming societies where farmers used to turn to Fulbe when new-borns were believed to be claimed by malevolent spirits. Baldus (1974: 361) provides an account of Baatombu farmers in northern Benin who abandoned children in the bush when they suspected them of bringing misfortune upon their family or, alternatively, left them with their Fulbe neighbours as slaves (ibid.). These children that were brought to the Fulbe, either grew up to live permanently with their hosts in a patron-client relationships or were sold onto the slave-markets or other families (ibid.; Hardung: 1997). That children were either left to starve in the bush or handed to the Fulbe, in order to exclude them from the kin group and the civilized village communities, seemingly corroborates Houis and Bonnet's interpretation as an expression of the child's devaluation, and the assumption that farmers associate Fulbe with the uncivilized realm of the bushlands.

In its social and political implication, however, the Baatombu account cannot help explain the permanent links and amicable relations established through the institution of the *banfulbe*. The Baatombu children had been part of a slave economy, they were expelled from their community for fear of malevolent spirits, and all ties to their families were severed. Neither Breusers' accounts of *banfulde*, nor the relation between Jambeedo and Bourema, however, contain reference to the Fulbe's slave raiding past,[10] and the bonds created by *banfulde* spiritual parenthood carry lifelong expectations. Children of double descent like Jambeedo-Francis are destined to take up a special role in their later lives, especially as mediators between the groups. They are at the same time the expression of a common identity built on history and locality and the basis of an inter-group identity. Francis-Jambeedo is, in a word, a personified cross-cutting tie.

The special mediating position corresponds perfectly to the role which Francis was meant to take on as a future *naba*, chief of greater Gando. *Naba* and *kiri* are considered chiefs of village communities and responsible for all members of the locality alike, irrespective of kin group or ethnic affiliation. Chiefs are the main mediators in conflicts between ethnic groups and are expected to take an unbiased position. In a climate of public animosity between the groups, chiefs usually uphold the ideal of a peaceful and mutually beneficial relationship between Bisa and Fulbe in their localities. Francis' father was no exception: respected by the farming and herding population alike, he expressed pride about his multi-ethnic community. Francis' role seemed clearly laid out as a future chief of all people.

Francis, as Bourema's complaint indicated, did not really live up to those expectations, at the end of the day. In one of the glossy brochures with which he continues to raise donations for his (highly laudable) on-going engagement in the village, he underscored the successful building of the school by reinforcing ethnic stereotypes. He pointed out that now 'alongside the resident parents *even nomads* send their kids to school although traditionally they did not want to be bothered with education.' The 'nomads' he refers to (and which I italicized) are the very same people he was born with, whose ancestors settled in

---

10 Although the village name alludes to a former slave settlement, Jambeedo's clan derive their position from their descent from Tenkodogo's royal lineage and their firstcomership in the region.

the very same spot 200 years ago, and who had lived in the very same houses for the past forty years, in which he had studied before he worked abroad.

In general, only a few spiritual or religious rituals and events span the ethnic division. As already illustrated, members of Fulbe communities do not take part in the local *tarabale*, the sacrifices to the earth. Farmers' ancestor cults, *zirobalen*, are confined to even smaller units (clans and lineages) within the (Bisa) ethnic community. Shared religious belief and practice – Islam – brings together Fulbe and Bisa only to a limited degree (mostly the common Friday prayers is the only regular event that occasionally brings the groups together). Mosques, however, are rare (only larger places such as Busma, Garango, Tenkodogo and Niaogho have mosques at all). The fact that Fulbe do not participate in the earth rituals is an expression of ethnic distinction and is perceived as a major reason why Fulbe herders cannot – in the perception of most farmers – develop a permanent relation to the land. Fulbe are also generally considered the 'better Muslims' by their Bisa brothers in faith, partly because Fulbe had adopted Islam long before many Bisa started to convert.

Nevertheless, the expertise of Fulbe in supernatural affairs is acknowledged on more than this one level. When farmers intend to build a new house, many seek the advice of their herding neighbours: Constructing a new house or a new compound is always a precarious undertaking. Even after all social and economic conditions have been met, lineage elders have given their approval and the earth priest has sanctioned the new location – a whole world of freewheeling spirits just seems to be awaiting the new dwellers. The closer the new compound is built to an existing cluster of homes, the less the risk, as most spirits avoid cultivated and settled places. The further a house is built from established homesteads, however, the higher the risk of being haunted by some malevolent variant.

Many farmers therefore call in Fulbe specialists to determine whether or not a specific location is safe for construction. The process is simple and actually requires no special knowledge at all, as one such specialist explained:

> …one makes three piles of small rocks. Then millet is put on top [of the piles and] a small calabash with milk [is] put in the middle.' Jinno are known to love both, millet and milk, so when the rock piles are still standing and milk and millet are untouched, the place is apparently free of any Jinno and it will be safe to build the homestead'. Many Fulbe herders use this procedure when they build their own homes; many however, prefer to rely on their animals: when the cattle sleep well for three days, the place is considered blessed …

This oracle is widespread, though not practised in every village. In fact, a closer look at the settlements reveals that the oracle was performed between those Fulbe and Bisa communities who stood in a longstanding relation.[11] In three villages that were inhabited for at least five generations all practised the oracle; out of the five 'newcomers' (two to three generations) only two were asked by their farming neighbours.

The practice reifies the stereotypical image of civilized farmers vs. uncivilized herders, that is part of ethnic ascriptions. Fulbe are considered as further from 'culture' – they marry their parallel cousins; 'a clear sign of lack of order', as one farmer had put it – and closer to nature, so they are apt to communicate with the wild, unlocalized spirits that can be detected by this oracle.

Many farmers and herders express the relation between Bisa and Fulbe in terms of mutual dependency. The idea of a 'symbiosis' of agricultural and pastoral lifestyle had, for a long time, also permeated anthropological studies (for a summary see Breusers et al., 1998; Oksen et al., 2000). Local narratives repeatedly underscore the ideology of a shared history and joint destiny. Local chiefs, *naba*, consider themselves the main mediators, responsible for the people in their territory and oral histories claim a strong nexus between Fulbe, Bisa and Mossi.

According to some versions, ancestors of all three migrated to the area together; in other versions Fulbe arrived together with Mossi groups, who were later to become Bisa (Dafinger, 1998; 2000; Dafinger and Reikat, 1996; Izard, 1970; Keuthmann et al, 1998; Lahuec, 1979). Either way, local histories claim no firstcomer arguments in ethnic relations; the landless status of Fulbe herders is legitimized through other institutions, such as religious specialization and ethnic division of labour. While over the generations, newcoming farmers acquire increasing rights in the land they were assigned, for the Fulbe communities the longue durée of residence helps them to a more privileged access to land, but does not infer permanence nor move them up on the landless–landed scale.

The example of the inauguration ceremonies of the chief at Garango (as it last took place in 1995 for the present *naba*, Naba Koom) and its annual commemorations, illustrates the importance of historical links between the groups on an ideological and political level.[12] Stressing a common history also reaffirms the ethnic divide,

---

[11] This observation draws on a small sample of eight villages.

[12] The Naba is ideally the eldest son of his predecessor. Various chiefly lineages, however, compete over the office and all put forward their claims. The 1995 Inauguration of Naba Koom followed a fierce two year fight between, at the end, two rivalling candidates. (Dafinger, 2004a; Keuthmann, et al., 1998).

inscribing the ethnic division of labour in the common past, as the story exemplifies. The inauguration ceremony restages the founding myth of the town and reiterates the role of Fulbe in the defence of the early settlement; it offers an example of the nexus between Bisa and Fulbe settlers. Garango's founding myth and its restaging are particularly interesting because they highlight the role the Fulbe played in establishing the settlement.

The story, in short, tells that the first Fulbe in Garango were warriors who helped the newly arrived Bisa settlers establish political rule in the region. During the (weeks long) initiation ceremonies, the new chief (or *naba*) spends a week in a Fulbe hut to pay tribute to the fact that Garango's political independence is owed to the Fulbe's loyalty. The Fulbe version of the story differs in so far as the Fulbe claim that they held political and military power at first and only later decided to hand the insignia of power to the Bisa chief.

The Garango chiefdom is the second largest political unit in Bisa country after the Tenkodogo kingdom, its fiercest adversary in the pre-colonial slave raids. It comprises several villages whose chiefs 'receive their chiefly *bonnet* ', the insignia of office, from the Garango–*naba* and vow allegiance to him. Defensive alliances of villages based on kin-relations, such as the exogamous clan-alliance of Guem and Bangagne at Busma, cannot comprise a larger number of villages and so the political solution of a common leadership seemed a viable solution. The political leadership, however, also came at a cost. Neighbouring groups and villages had to be appeased and at least partly integrated into the exercise of power. If a dominant group cannot lay legitimate claims to being firstcomers, as discussed before, their political primacy needs to be legitimized, to pay tribute to the firstcomers' special status and concede religious or other authority.

Although Garango's major clan can claim descent from the first settlers, their founding myth stretches far to include the wider network of the region. As the story goes, Barga, a Bisa hunter, came to Boulgou from the southern region of Lere. He decided to stay, brought his family and eventually founded what was to become Garango. Determined to extend his political power, Barga started to get involved in the rather lucrative slave raiding business and hired the help of some *konankobe:* Fulbe warriors. Following one story, five brothers, nomadic Fulbe mercenaries, arrived at Garango, offering their martial skills. When Barga, the chief of Bisa-Garango, invited them to stay and help defend the settlement, one of the brothers decided to settle and, furthermore, handed the *labbo,* a ceremonial spear, to Barga, asking him to 'accept the political rule'.

That this is reiterated in the inauguration ceremonies underlines the importance of Fulbe in the local history. Besides the Fulbe hut, in which Naba Koom spent his first week in office, the *labbo*, the spear that the first Fulbe handed to the Bisa chief, is displayed regularly in front of the *naba* as he processes through the town, paying his tribute to the various earth shrines. This regular re-enactment of the prominent role of the Fulbe-warriors as sources of political rule, publicly underlines the rights that Fulbe enjoy within the local community, and the Garango *naba* publicly reaffirms his obligations towards them. Although the Garango example is exceptional in its ceremonial dimension, other localities with a joint Fulbe-Bisa history also acknowledge the importance of Fulbe warriors in their founding histories. The history of joint migration and warfare establishes a general entitlement of herders in the local lands. Even though individual use rights still need to be regularly renegotiated, the resident herders find it easier to lay claims to land and pasture in their localities than those communities which lack these historical ties.

The friendly ties that reach across ethnic lines create room for economic manoeuvres and extend the limited possibilities that exist within each ethnic group. The numerous and permanent obligations of individuals within the kin groups and households all make it rather difficult to build up wealth. Under aspects of risk management, this redistribution within the groups works as an effective tool for coping with uncertainty. The goods and services that are exchanged between related households ensure that temporary labour shortages or field damage do not cause excessive hardship for individuals. But it is also true that this practice prevents the distribution of wealth over time to level out seasonal fluctuations. Accordingly, many farmers follow a split strategy of (public) synchronous and (concealed) diachronous distribution. This allows households to openly fulfil in-group obligations while at the same time accumulating surplus in a more hidden manner. As most agricultural products cannot be stored over longer periods, investing in cattle had become a major alternative to accumulate wealth, especially from the 1950s onward (Fafchamps, et al., 1998; van den Brink, et al., 1995). Besides spreading the risk of seasonal fluctuations, farmers prefer investing in cattle for a second reason. The possibility of entrusting them to Fulbe herders allows them to keep them away from their own compound and hidden from their own community. Although this practice is widely known and practised, individual farmers are very secretive about the fact that they keep cattle with their herding neighbours. Fulbe herders are much more open to talking about the cattle which they guard for the farmers – however they are anxious to conceal any specific information and maintain the farmers' anonymity.

In the negotiations over crop damage, which are often held in public, farmers always pressed for maximum compensation by the Fulbe herder. Herders, however, reclaimed part of this compensation payment from the farmers only a few days later in personal meetings – on the grounds that some of the cattle actually belonged to the same farmers. During the public negotiation, in the presence of their fellow cultivators, none of the farmers ever openly admitted to the fact that they had cattle entrusted to the herders.[13]

This helps in reassessing assumptions that cattle entrustment would be a largely inefficient means of risk management, such as Fafchamps' suggested. (Fafchamps, et al. 1998). Fafchamps argued that cattle sales never fully compensated for the agricultural underproduction and only partially levelled out seasonal income fluctuations. In his study, he found that the sale of entrusted cattle only compensated for around 30 per cent of the shortfalls of annual agricultural production. If cattle were kept exclusively as a buffer stock, Fafchamps believes, farmers would always sell just enough to be able to buy the amount of crops which agricultural work failed to deliver. This argument, at a closer look, contains two major flaws. Selling 'just enough' in theory requires knowledge about coming harvests; selling the maximum number of cattle in a given year would only make sense if the following years would again deliver sufficient yields and allow the regeneration of the buffer cattle. Under real life conditions, any farmer would try to keep enough stealth cattle to help through possible (and in fact likely) subsequent harvest failures. In addition, as harvest failures are likely to affect a large number of households, prices for cattle would drop if all farmers reacted in the same way and sold all their animals, while costs for crops would rise accordingly. Selling only part of the buffer is – in Fafchamps' own formal economic terms – the most rational answer.

A second major reason for not selling all the cattle lies in the social nature of animal entrustment. The need to hide wealth from demanding kin puts a limit on the amount of cattle that can be commoditized and liquidated on the market at one given time. Farmers who deny owning cattle need to keep a low profile when turning cattle into cash. There is a pronounced secretive aura surrounding entrusted cattle and relations between individual farmers and herders are generally framed in terms of friendship, stressing the importance of mutual trust in these relations.

Economic and social exchange *within* the own ethnic group usually involves middlemen: a third party vouches for both sides and acts as witness to the transaction. Transactions of wider significance between

---

[13] Breusers et al. (1998) give similar accounts for Mossi-Fulbe relations in Burkina Faso's north.

members of different communities usually take place in the market of some third clan or village (Dafinger, 2004a: 176). The entrustment of cattle, to the contrary, generally knows no intermediates and is dealt with rather informally. Relations between cattle owners and herders are mostly concealed from the public eye and cattle are often handed over in the absence of any witness. This obviously makes it very diffi-cult to deal with potential cases of embezzlement. Accordingly, these transactions require a considerable degree of trust especially on the side of the cattle-owning farmers. This stands in remarkable contrast to the public stereotype that depicts Fulbe in mostly negative terms. Farmers keep no official records of cattle they leave with a herder and herders assume no liability for animals that are stolen, hurt, or die whilst in the herder's custody. This is especially remarkable, given the considerable financial risk; the value of a cow may equal a small house-hold's annual harvest.[14]

Still, this entrustment of cattle merely follows a generally informal and often unspoken agreement. While farmers do not pay for the serv-ices which the herders deliver, they are nonetheless expected to return small counter gifts, such as salt or cloth for the herder's wife, in acknowledgement of the herding labour. That the respective owner also bears all immediate costs such as vaccinations, occasional fines and medication tends to be an unspoken part of the agreement and not discussed unless one of the parties fails to fulfil their duties.

The most important compensation, however, is the land which farmers grant to the Fulbe for settlement and pasture. These rights are also expressed in terms of mutual friendship and are considered 'gifts' (and acknowledged by symbolic counter gifts such as donations of milk to the farmer's family).

The fact that people locate cattle entrustment in a sphere of gift – rather than commodity – exchange, bears a number of important consequences. Gift exchange is mainly focused around establishing relations between people (Mauss, 1954 [1925]; Polanyi and Pearson, 1977).

The entrustment of cattle requires trust, but it also creates trustful relations (Gregory, 1982; Strathern, 1988). Guieba, in the case below, insisted that his friendship with Noël began the very day on which he started to tend his animals. Another service, which farmers may render, is to act as middlemen between the herders and the bureaucracy, with which they often appear to be on better terms than the herders.

Perceiving herding labour, access rights and other goods and serv-ices as gifts, permits herders and farmers to react flexibly to seasonal

---

[14] This is equivalent to 100.000 CFA (or 150 €), assuming all crops would be sold on the market.

fluctuations. No fixed value is assigned to any of the goods and services delivered and returns are flexible and depend on the economic
conditions of the giver. Even the smallest gifts, such as a symbolic
offering of a calabash of milk in recognition of rights to settle on the
landed clan's territory, are generally received with great joy, and repeatedly acknowledged with phrases such as that 'it may be a small gift, but
he is poor and cannot offer more'. The importance of the gift idiom
was stressed in many conversations. Tributes to political authorities are
often framed in the same rhetoric: 'after (Bisa) chiefs received some
milk as a present, they liked it and demanded regular gifts from there-
on'.[15]

Although the practice of entrusting cattle and other animals is most
common between farmers and herders, public servants, office clerks or
entrepreneurs also often invest surplus earnings in livestock, which
they entrust to herders rather than to their own families. Although
public employees are embedded in the formal monetized sector, they
are mostly also still integrated into webs of kinship obligations. Much
like the farmers, many of these city dwellers accumulate wealth by
acquiring animals in order to avoid revealing their new wealth to their
families. As they mostly make their earnings outside the agricultural
sector and mostly maintain different social and professional networks,
financial considerations to them are more important than to most
villagers in their farmer–herder relations. Aspects of social relations,
shared locality and mutual friendship appear less relevant.

The following account is an example that contains both rural and
urban elements of exchange as well as elements of formal economic
relations and friendship rhetoric. Noël, one of the two main protagonists, works as a butcher in Garango; as such he is a typical town-
dweller and runs his own business. Guieba, the second actor, lives in a
small Fulbe community just north of Garango and makes his living as
a herder and from small-scale subsistence cultivation. Noël and Guieba
had known each other for five years when I first met them – right in
the middle of a dispute over a number of allegedly embezzled animals.

As a butcher, Noël's interest in keeping animals is not only to invest
surplus and build provisions for low-income periods. By keeping his
own stock, he can also balance out fluctuations on the cattle market.
The relation between the two was established through a common
friend, Zeba, who knew that Noël was looking for a place to keep his

---

[15] Taxes and tributes as acknowledgments of political leadership are often expressed in the same
terms – when the French colonial administration introduced a tax system, this was seen as a 'gift'
of the population to the strangers, who then 'turned it into a habit', demanding it on a regular basis,
without apparently delivering an adequate return. Taxes and tributes are paid without immediate
and visible return.

animals. Noël entrusted to Guieba a smaller number of male cattle at first, subsequently adding more over the following years. During conversations, Guieba kept mentioning that many of these animals were bulls because the main incentive for herders to take care of other cattle is the milk they get from the cows as a compensation for their work. So, with a majority of bulls in his herd Guieba was rather unhappy in economic terms, while he continued stressing that he nonetheless raised all these animals with his 'own hands and labour'. While Noël's motives are clearly economic and less driven by ideals of a cross-cultural friendship, for Guieba – or so it seemed to me – the social prestige of having a *djatigi*, a friend in town, often seemed to weigh as important as potential material gains from this relationship. From a purely economic stance, the deal seemed not very lucrative to Guieba, which is one of the reasons he underscored the friendship character of their relations that expected no immediate return, but rather lays the foundation for a delayed reward and underscores their mutual trust. Guieba's rhetoric reveals a general pattern: herders, who take care of farmers' (or other non-Fulbe) animals, expect to establish relations of friendship upon which they can draw when the need arises. Intermittent requests (e.g., for salt) serve to assure the benevolence of the *djatigi* (the 'friend in town' and owner of the animals). Although he did not expect any payment as an immediate acknowledgement of the herding labour, Guieba underlines that it is part of a common practice and understanding ('accord commun', as Guieba put it in French) that the labour and the relationship should be honoured in some way or another.

The rapport between Guieba and Noël exemplifies an ethnic division of labour that certainly stretches the pragmatic dimension of friendship a long way. It appears less rooted in a common local identity and existing group affiliations and, unlike most previous cases, is not a farmer-herder relationship, as Noël runs a business in town. Guieba would not consider him his real *djatigi*, a broker for his urban affairs; nor would Noël want to take this part and assume the responsibilities that are associated with a patron-client relationship. Both nonetheless exploit the ethnic dichotomy that is based on the division of labour and which is at the heart of their relationship. Although Guieba's account closely follows the discourse of friendship and gift exchange, some of his actual expectations are quite explicit and very much focused on immediate payments. Noël, according to Guieba, had repeatedly refused requests to contribute up to 10.000 CFA (c. 15€ – a considerable amount) to his expenditures 'in the bush' during transhumance: a more or less open demand for payment for his herding services.

The pragmatism in this relationship is obvious and is only on the surface framed as the exchange of mutual favours. The special character of their relationship and the discrepancy between an outwardly trust-based friendship and the underlying pragmatic and economic intentions are also at the core of the conflict that eventually arose between the two (and on which I will elaborate in the next chapter). It also shows the flexibility of a social institution, which in this case is not restricted to relations between herders and farmers. As in the next case (describing the herding agreement between a police officer and the Fulbe of Zarga), cattle exchange allows Fulbe herders to enter urban and official networks. What sets these relations apart from 'traditional' farmer–herder relations is that the latter are generally marked by a genuine quest for friendship, stressing its emotional and social dimensions, a sense of shared locality and relations of longue durée that span several generations. The ties into modern networks are much more open about their pragmatic and economic character, in this respect.

Relations with Fulbe settlements are not only an important asset for neighbouring farmers and many urban entrepreneurs but also for public officials and the local police, to hide extra earnings from the public eye, as this next case illustrates. Partly as a legacy of the anti-corruption movements under Thomas Sankara and partly due to the fact that public servants in Burkina Faso are paid regularly, petty corruption used to be an almost negligible phenomenon. However, with the enthusiasm of the revolutionary years having worn off, the tendency to police checks, roadblocks and tougher vehicle inspections has increased, combined with an unofficial policy of 'on-the-spot-fines'. Scenes are becoming more frequent, in which chickens, goats or sheep are confiscated out of a small flock on their way to the weekly market, mostly on the grounds of some missing paperwork, if not simply pre-emptively offered as 'presents'.

Although such events had increasingly become part of daily life, I had never asked what actually happened to these confiscated animals until one morning at Kioponi's house in the Fulbe settlement of Zarga. I was watching the young boys take off with their herds for the day when my attention was caught by the local blue police pick-up, slowly coming up towards the house. When the car came to a halt just outside our *wuro*, I noticed about half a dozen goats on the bed of the truck. I also recognized one of the two police officers, who happened to be from the village where I had lived for more than a year in the 1990s and who I knew still maintained close links with kin there. My hosts greeted the officers; everybody appeared to be on good terms with each other, one chatted, laughed and then offloaded the flock. There was no haggling or negotiating and no indication that anything about the situation was unusual. Inoussa, as I shall call him here, the police officer, then walked up to me, we exchanged greetings and chatted for a while until they took off again.

After they had left I was told that Inoussa already used to keep a 'small number of goats and sheep' with the family in Zarga, 'for matters of convenience', as it would indeed be 'very difficult to keep ruminants in town', in Samba's, my host's, words. It appeared to be of no concern where those animals actually came from. The fact that he did not leave them with his own relatives only a few kilometres further on appeared entirely plausible, too. Although his own village was so close, my hosts also knew why Inoussa was rather reserved towards his own relatives: because of solidarity and other obligations, Inoussa would have lost quite a number of animals in the redistributive network. So Inoussa preferred to pay the Fulbe herders for taking care of his livestock.

Inoussa's example is a borderline case; on the one hand, he entered a clearly defined economic relationship as he paid the herders for their work and all expenses connected with keeping the animals. On the other hand, he relies on the concealment, which is part of most informal agreements. By leaving animals in the Fulbe compound, he is under no obligation to account for their origin or their prospective use (such as distribution). Samba, the herder, profits from this relation in two ways: as a paid service, this generates income and secondly he manages to build a friendly relationship with an official who carries out the checks on the road to the market.

What connects Inoussa's case with the other two in this chapter is that, like Noël the butcher and the majority of the farmers, Inoussa needs to invest money outside the reproductive cycle of his own household and kin group. In all the three cases, the owners violate in-group obligations of sharing and distribution of wealth and need to conceal this fact from the other members of their group. In Inoussa's case, we also assume that he has more reasons than one to hide the provenance of his animals.

By crossing the ethnic divide, the animals are concealed from the other members of the same group, such as kin, colleagues (the brothers in arms of a 'culture des fonctionnaires'), by moving them across the ethnic divide. Concealment and secrecy are the keys to this business and are assured through a number of institutions, mainly mutual trust and friendship. The bridge over the ethnic divide also leads onto a different sphere of exchange: goods and services passing between the ethnic groups are framed in terms of gifts: especially in the first two cases, the movement across the ethnic divide is a gift exchange. While within the respective groups, cattle are considered an important commodity: within the farming communities livestock is considered an investment; the herders, likewise, see the financial and economic importance of their animals despite the alleged 'cattle complex' (Evans-Pritchard, 1949; Herskovits, 1926). It is only when the cattle cross the line between farmers and herders that they do so in a spirit of gift exchange, marking the different nature of the relationship, and reducing the potential for conflict.

All examples depict Boulgou's agropastoral division of social, economic and legal authority as the backbone of its social, economic and political system. Differential access to land is a main expression of this division: land is not merely a means of agricultural and pastoral production, but also serves as a language expressing and defining social relations and economic exchange. To describe the emic notion of differential access to land and the resulting social and political hierarchy, I suggested the model of a landed–landless continuum. While some individuals and groups can be seen as moving along different points of this axis (notably Bisa farmers), others (the Fulbe herders) are located at the outer margin of this grid and have no possibility of acquiring permanent land rights. Most links that reach across the boundary established cross-cutting ties and bind people together, while others helped to generate ethnic difference.

The landed–landless axis also expresses a fundamental principle of social perception: the differential degree of social order and 'civilization'. In the local context, control over land, landedness is legitimized with reference to cultural and religious supremacy: firstcomership establishes privileged relations to the earth and its local spirits; the territorial organization of the landed clans expresses the high degree of social and political organization. Alleged 'nomadism' (in fact transhumance), non-territorial organization and – from many farmers' points of view – dubious marriage practices, move Fulbe herders to the bottom of the landed–landless line and simultaneously locate them at the lower end of the civilized/non-civilized scale. The same excluding principles that co-define the ethnic divide find their continuation in the distinction between the rural and the urban middle-classes in the later chapters.

The most important institution yet in terms of ethnic relations is the practice of cattle entrustment: it is only through the categorical ethnic divide that this institution gains its meaning. Trust-based and friendship ties also exist within the ethnic groups; there, however, they are likely to either collide or simply overlay existing formal relations that are established through the kinship system (Elwert, 1980). The categorical divide between Bisa and Fulbe, on the other hand, allows for informal and individual relations. This corresponds to the gift-economic character of services exchanges, such as herding labour in this instance.

A crucial part of the institution consists of its concealment. Within the ethnic groups – and even more so within the kin and household units – economic and social transactions are expected to be transparent and usually involve middlemen. The informal, malleable and individual character of inter-ethnic relations makes it possible to carry out transactions that are hidden from third parties. The following chapter will engage with the question of how this ethnic divide is further rendered opaque through the practice of permanent conflict and insecurity.

4

Conflict

The ethnic boundary is a precondition for the ethnic division of labour, which is at the heart of Boulgou's agro-pastoral economy. It generates cross-cutting ties, built on trust and friendship. This boundary is also a zone of confrontation and conflict and this chapter will turn to the analysis of the more conflictual side of the ethnic boundary. It will show how conflict helps to maintain the illusion of an impermeable divide and will identify the actors that profit from this concealment.

The anthropology of conflict

Anthropological conflict studies have predominantly dealt with conflict as occurrences of violent clashes and warfare. As I outlined in the introduction, this book aims at a broader perspective, taking violence as only one option. Much can be gained from a wider approach, from de-stigmatizing conflict and from looking at conflict and dispute as social institutions, as Richards and Helander (2005: 3) have done in their attempt to take the study of conflict further and in a different direction. In their work, they partly draw on the first generation of anthropological conflict studies with its focus on the social function of (both violent and non-violent) conflict. Earlier theorists had perceived conflict and violence as essentially positive social factors – including the view that 'dividing the inhabitants of a country into two different groups [will] lead to a conflict favourable to creativeness and progress' – as Gluckman cites from Eliot's 'definition of culture' (Gluckman, 1964; Goody, 1957; Sahlins, 1961).

Considering conflict inevitable, as Richards does, or simply as 'embedded' in a wider social field (see Elwert, below), does not imply thinking of it as a 'positive' social institution. By not stigmatizing violence as an option of everyday disputes, the analysis transcends the dichotomy between victim and perpetrator and views non-violence and the prohibition of violence as a strategy in asserting power (Mamdani, 2001; Schmidt, 1999). Third parties assuming a monopoly of violence (e.g., the state) or attempting to define the use of violence as outside the norm become themselves part of the (meta-) conflict. Violence needs to be thought of as a potential extension of any conflict in analytical terms. In this, Elwert's model of conflict as a field of embedded social action proves particularly helpful (Elwert, 2001: 2543). He located 'war, genocide, competition, feud, legal battle' along a continuum and proposed a two-dimensional model that looks first at degrees of violence and second at social embeddedness, which are present in any conflict (ibid.; Schmidt, 1999). These two factors allow conflicts to be related to each other and enable the prediction of possible developments in conflict situations.

Elwert's main line of argument (2001) is that when violence increases, groups which have no shared authorities and institutions of litigation are likely to enter non-formalized violent and destructive hostilities. Individuals who maintain established relations and share institutions are more likely to enter a formalized war, which can at least potentially be contained. To take account of different types of violent (war, genocide, destruction) and non-violent conflict (negotiations, legal cases, avoidance), Elwert identifies a second parameter: the degree of social embeddedness.

Social embeddedness as a parameter provides an analytical tool to compare and understand conflicts irrespective of type (normative-, actor-, meta-conflict: see below) or degree of violence. It takes into account changes and transformations of a specific conflict over time and between different social fields. An ethnic conflict may take violent forms between certain sections of ethnic groups, while remaining political between others, e.g., between intellectual elites.

	more violence:	**less violence:**
stronger embedding:	warring	procedure
weaker embedding:	destruction	avoidance

Figure 6 Elwert: differentiations of conflict (ibid.: 2544)

With this model, Elwert offers the frame for the interpretation of relations and conflicts between Boulgou's herders and farmers. Here, violent clashes are almost all confined to conflicts between those communities that have minimal or no relations at all and which belong to the least established in the region. Rare cases of arson and homicide only affect those herders who have settled recently; disputes between the established herders' and farmers' communities are mostly settled in a peaceful manner. In these relations, mutual consent enjoys a higher priority in personal assessments of disputes than material compensation of possible damages. Examples from Boulgou also show that the factors leading to aggravation and violent conflicts are already inherent in low-level and non-violent disputes. Taking violence as simply one possible parameter among others will help the understanding of both violent and non-violent tensions.

Every conflict builds on at least two conditions. It needs someone (that is at least two conflicting parties) disagreeing in their claims over something (material or immaterial goods, or norms). Again, theories of conflict are divided and focus on either of these conditions to explain the reasons and courses of conflicts. Earlier, functionalist approaches looked at the social dynamics of conflict processes, while a second generation zoomed in on the actual object of dispute. Most recent anthropological models of conflict have returned to the question of the 'who fights whom' – although within different conceptual frameworks.

The 1960s saw the introduction of a third model, which attempted to locate conflict in human nature, identifying innate aggression as a driving force of conflict and violence (LeVine, 1961; Rubinstein, 1994: 984 for debates). Proponents of the aggression model based their arguments on an alleged innate urge to defend one's territory (Ardrey, 1997; Eibl-Eibesfeldt, 1974; Lorenz, 1966).

One logical flaw of these models was that they presumed an innate (individual) urge to maintain a personal space and applied it to the defence of a collective territory or good, as I discussed previously (Dafinger, 2004a). A number of anthropologists set out to prove that non-territorial foragers were largely aggression-free (e.g., Guenther, 1981), without challenging the territory-aggression nexus. The assumption that people are driven by innate aggression is limited by favouring biological determinism over social and cultural factors and cannot inform about the legitimacy of claims, the function of alliances and the uses of specific forms of violence (Rubinstein, 1994; Sahlins, 1961). This leaves two main areas of study, the question of focus on actors and the focus on the contested objects.

Conflict models that focus on the contested object work more or less explicitly on a neo-Malthusian assumption – this is especially true for non-anthropological and non-academic approaches. The increase in ethnically framed conflicts is often explained in terms of population growth and environmental degradation (e.g. Cleaver and Schreiber, 1994). Their central argument is that resources are becoming scarcer while more and more people compete over them. This assumption is also at the heart of most development and interventionist projects; it is a major part of development agendas and infrastructural adjustment programmes, which pursue the intensification (and privatization) of agricultural production and the control of demographic development:

> [S]hifting or long-fallow cultivation and transhumant pastoralism have been appropriate under conditions of slow population growth, abundant land, limited capital and limited technical know-how. The ecological and economic systems were in equilibrium. The key to this equilibrium was mobility. (ibid.: 4)

Only through 'reversing this spiral' (ibid.), that is 'adjusting nomadism', subsistence economy and extensive land use and through population control, is it possible to reinstate the 'equilibrium'. Obviously, this model gets caught in the thinking of magic equilibriums which most likely never existed, and views conflicts as part of a downward spiral. Conflicts are seen as the result of scarcity and as a major obstacle to sustainable development. Conflicts create insecurity that prevents further investment in the agricultural sector, which in turn aggravates tensions and pushes further down the spiral (ibid.).

Conflict in this model is depicted as the root problem of failed development. This logic provides interventionist agendas with their legitimacy and serves as a standard device in the rhetorical toolbox of neo-colonial and neo-liberal economic adjustment programmes. Hallpike (1973) offered an early anthropological critique of this alleged nexus of conflict and resource scarcity, although, by doing so, he sticks to Malthusian assumptions. In Hallpike's argument, the pressure on resources

> …is a relatively recent phenomenon, where it exists at all, that is and should not be assumed to have operated long before the present. […] It is clear that migration […] has generally been the preferred response to situations of overcrowding. (ibid.: 469)

I tend to follow Hallpike's argument in the first part, but have my doubts about the second half. If migration was a standard response, then conflict would indeed be a recent phenomenon. However, we have no indication that this was the case. To the contrary, political power and social authority in agricultural and agro-pastoral systems was based on controlling and restricting access to land and landed resources (Goody, 1976: 31–40).

Given the general importance of land rights in sub-Saharan Africa and of land as a political power base, conflicts over land were part of local power dynamics and migration but one option (the 'zero' option of avoidance, in Elwert's model (2001: 2544)). Assumptions such as Cleaver's and Hallpike's tend to overlook the impact of seasonal and other fluctuations, which cause shortages and increase pressure on resources for limited but recurring periods. And not every seasonal shortfall could have led to outmigration (there is no evidence to suggest that) but, to the contrary, might rather be met with a strengthening of social and economic networks, which still are a key to coping with the risks of ecological fluctuations.

An implicit statement of both economic and ecological models is that competition and conflict are less likely to emerge where groups occupy different economic and ecological niches. This is also true for conflicts that focus on power and political control rather than material resources and in situations where certain groups are precluded from access to certain resources *a priori*. Wimmer's (1995) case of ethnicized bureaucracies falls into this category. Most importantly, formal economic and other approaches that concentrate on the object of conflict, such as the land scarcity, tend to underemphasize the political and symbolic meaning of such essential resources as land or landed property. As the previous chapter has shown, land is a means of social control, 'a focus for the definition and exercise of rights of access', in Berry's words (1989: 2) that needed to be kept scarce by definition. In short, looking at what people fight over is a crucial dimension in the analysis of any conflict (especially Klare's 2001 contribution). This material cause of disputes, however, cannot always be taken at face value. As the cases of agropastoral conflicts in this book illustrate, Berry's observation proves right: that scarcity, although framed in the rhetoric of ecological and demographic factors, is also created as a means of political and social control (Berry, ibid.:1, 44).

Knowing what contestants are fighting over, does not necessarily tell us why people choose to fight over a particular resource at a particular time, nor does it offer immediate insights into strategies of conflicting parties and the social implications of conflicts. The bone of contention may change over the duration of conflict, it may not be the same for each and every actor involved or may even become secondary and forgotten as the conflict wears on (Hagberg, 1998). From an anthropological perspective, the question of who fights whom has to be a primary concern. We need to look at the 'equally fundamental question that remains poorly understood, namely, who is fighting whom and why? How and why do people draw the distinction between friend and foe precisely where they do?' (Schlee, 2004: 135).

The question of how litigating groups are delineated has been raised before (Barth, 1969b; Brubaker, 2000, 2004; Brubaker and Laitin, 1998; Gluckman, 1964; Horowitz, 1985; LeVine, 1961) and the analysis of how conflict shapes and is in turn shaped by social relations was in fact at the core of first-generation conflict studies (Bohannan, 1989; Colson, 1971; Gluckman, 1964; Gluckman and Gulliver, 1978; Goody, 1957). These studies started from the assumption that conflicts are an integral part of social relations, in fact necessary to maintain social order as they provide a frame for the negotiation and renegotiation of entitlements and the reification and consolidation of group boundaries and political leadership.

Gluckman stressed the eufunctional, that is positive, character of conflicts and considered them integral and necessary parts of social processes. Cross-cutting ties, he argued, help to contain such conflicts and prevent violent outbreaks. Gluckman's model, however, rests on the quasi-Hobbesian assumption that people are by nature in a constant fight against each other and the resulting need for mitigating institutions. The case of cross-cutting spatial (village) and social (clan) boundaries in the Bisa farming communities above illustrated that the concept of cross-cutting ties may indeed provide pacified social and spatial fields.[1] Some of the following cases, however, also provide examples of how cross-cutting ties build alliances across the ethnic boundary. Cross-cutting ties here are much less a pacifying or conflict containing institution but rather aggravate existing and instigate new tensions within the respective groups.

Barth observed a similar pattern in his study of the Pukhtuns of Swat, where he described how the fiercest competition over land happens between close lineages of the same clan (Barth, 1981). As entitlements to land derive from membership in the descent group, close relatives are more likely to develop colliding claims. Barth describes how Pukhtun lineages build alliances across the segments of the descent group, with whom they are less likely to dispute land entitlements. Inter-clan alliances form local majorities vis-à-vis the excluded kin. For Schlee, the Pukhtun example shows the limits of Gluckman's model; cross-cutting ties 'do not produce any kind of "cohesion" at least at the level of the total society'. In the end, Gluckman's attempt to establish a general theory of conflict based on cross-cutting ties did not stand the test of time. We see cases in which cross-cutting ties are apparently of no effect and others where they even aggravate existing tensions and this book adds yet another variant: cross-cutting ties are used to ward off intra-group claims, while inter-group conflicts help

---

[1] People frequently referred to the era of slave raids in Boulgou in Hobbesian terminology, as the war of 'everyone against everyone', although – to add to my point – cross-cutting ties intensified the violence rather than containing it in any way.

maintain this boundary and the ideological rhetoric of the we-group.

Approaches that focus on alliance building or aspects of group formation and consolidation, moreover, risk missing the importance of the material causes of the conflict. As Wimmer has argued, relations within a group may have a higher potential for conflict, than links between different groups, which often do not compete over the same resources, notably in societies where the ethnic division coincides with a high division of labour between the groups (Wimmer, 1995).

An apparent problem with many of these models is that they leave little room to take account of individual agency and are mostly built on the assumption of self-regulating systems. Taking Roger Brubaker's objection to heart, that ethnic conflicts must not be mistaken for conflicts between ethnic groups – but rather understood as ethnically framed conflicts between individuals – we need to look at how and when individuals decide to enter a conflict, which costs they are willing to bear, along which lines they choose their allies, which type of conflict they pursue (the political, legal or ideological framework) and which allies they decide to align with.

To start the analysis by looking at ethnic conflicts bears the risk of making the second step before the first. In assuming that groups define themselves in ethnic terms and claim common interests against other groups based on ethnic criteria, we are confronted with the obvious problem that ethnicity may well be the consequence of a conflict rather than its cause. Ethnic groups may be defined through, or even be invented in the course of, a conflict (Allen et al., 1996; Appadurai, 1998; Tambiah, 1986; Whitehead, 2000). This requires us to have yet another critical look at models such as those of cross-cutting ties. We need to explore cross-cutting ties not only as opposed to conflict, but also as its by-product and consequence.

Another line that allows us to analytically differentiate conflicts – alongside degrees of violence and underlying motives (or objects) – is constituted by the ideological and legal framework in which the conflict is embedded. Georg Elwert proposed to distinguish two major types: normative conflicts and actor conflicts (Elwert, 2001: 2543). Disagreement over the type of conflict, its ideological and legal frame, can itself become a bone of contention leading to a third type of dispute, which Horowitz (1991) and Lemarchand (1996) referred to as the 'meta conflict'. Competing individuals or groups need to negotiate which type of conflict will be pursued. Whether a conflict will be violent or non-violent, ethnically-framed or class-based, the rules by which it should be conducted and ended are interpreted differently between the conflict parties.

In the context of the agropastoral conflicts discussed throughout this book, this distinction is especially useful; most of the conflicts, which start as actors' conflicts, will have at least one of their parties trying to substantiate their claims with reference to a more general norm. This inevitably invokes a larger group of people and often ends in questioning the specific norm as such (e.g., the rightfulness of a specific spatial or temporal border). Case studies illustrate how conflicting individuals and parties try to gain and maintain control over the scope and quality of the conflict. In practice, however, most conflicts show aspects of more than one type, calling for a multi-layered approach.

A majority of rural conflicts are disputes between individual actors or different user groups, who compete over resource access (to water, land, etc.), damage inflicted (to fields or animals), or alleged theft and embezzlement of animals. Few of these conflicts, however, take place in a field that would be void of rules and regulations: most conflicts are perceived as transgressions of existing norms – at least by one of the contesting parties.

Most commonly, problems arise over the interpretation and applicability of respective rules. One individual may claim rights to land based on 'longue durée', on the grounds that he and his family had this land under continuous cultivation for generations, while another contestant may claim the same patch of land, on the grounds that he is a descendant of the first settlers. Both are viable principles and both contestants can claim normative legitimacy for their cause. The conflict arises over principles of entitlements. In contrast, conflicts between claimants of different socio-economic groups may often be framed as infringements of existing norms, or by challenging the rightfulness of a specific boundary. In these cases, the applicability of a certain principle would not be contested; conflicts here often serve to renegotiate boundaries between user groups and their entitlements. The examples later in this chapter will provide models for both: showing how norms are constantly reified and how boundaries are redefined through acts of transgression.

With a focus on violent forms of conflict, anthropological studies have departed from these models that show conflicts as functional and essentially positive (T. S. Eliot, 1949; Gluckman, 1964). Conflict was increasingly viewed in terms of the malfunction and breakdown of the normal social order. Abnormality is also one of the contestants' claims in a normative conflict. Interventionism by state and development organizations is in part legitimized through the argument that local conflicts disrupt social order and 'normal' economic functioning. (Cleaver and Schreiber, 1994: 138).

In this book I take a different starting point, defining conflict in broader terms as an embedded part of social relations in general and considering violence as only one dimension, albeit an important one. The fact that the absence of conflict is formulated as a social ideal (as it is done by governmental or other mediating institutions) then enters the analysis as one specific actor's view. This permits treating claims to normality as part of conflict strategies: insisting that a person's or a group's claims conform to general norms, implicitly denies the right-eousness of a contender's claims.

Almost all conflicts dealt with here have pronounced normative aspects within which any one of the actors may try to move the dispute onto a normative plane, while the outcomes of conflicts feed back on the normative sphere by reifying and redefining existing spatial and temporal boundaries. Elwert understood normative conflict to be when 'a person or a group of persons clashes with a norm when violating other persons' or groups' rights' (Elwert, 2001: 2543), narrowing earlier philosophical legal approaches, such as Hill's, who defined normative conflicts in broader terms:

> … as a conflict of forces, forces which operate in different directions on a single point. One force, one norm, pushes in one direction, the other in another, perhaps opposite, direction. (Hill, 1987: 238)

Elwert's view is explicitly actor-oriented, assuming the rightfulness of one of the contestant's claims, while Hill's understanding merely assumes two contradicting norms. Both views correspond to different layers of normative conflict: actors indeed claim that their contestants are transgressing norms, while, on a different plane, each conflict also serves the redefinition of spatial and temporal boundaries.

Elwert also underlines another important aspect of normative conflicts, distinguishing between norms and moral values. A 'norma-tive conflict', he claims:

> …is a conflict in which a person's behaviour toward another person or to a thing, which is meaningful to a person, conflicts with a norm. In this context, norm is meant in the strict sense; it requires both monitoring and sanction. Prescriptive or prohibitive formulas without a sanction probability should be considered moral values, not norms. (Elwert, 2001: 2544)

The distinction between norms and moral values, however easily made on an analytical level, is much harder to maintain in the prac-tice of cross-cultural relations and culturally embedded 'doxic' ideals of conduct (Bourdieu, 1999). Norms may be monitored and sanc-tioned within any group but this may be much more difficult between two distinct groups, who do not necessarily share the same sanctioning authorities. The landed-landless continuum, as sketched above, provides a viable frame for setting, monitoring and sanctioning norms, while groups at the margins, such as transhumant herders, are not necessarily subject to the authority of the landholding institutions. This renders most political power and sanctions ineffectual. Elwert's distinction still remains useful as it directs our attention to the field of the monitoring and sanctioning institutions, which is created between farmers, resident and transhumant herders and with which I will engage in Chapter 5. It is through this field that state and governing institutions assume control over local relations by imposing themselves as normative institutions.

In doing so, national and international organizations also attempt to place conflicts in a specific ideological frame – often defined in terms of resource competition. They enter an arena that is already fiercely fought over on the local level: the control over the nature of the disputes and over the norms governing the process of the dispute. By attempting to define the type of conflict (e.g. as resource competition), contesting parties also define the criteria of inclusion and exclusion. The question of whether conflicts, for instance, are perceived as clashes between kin groups or as class-based struggles, has a direct impact upon the boundaries of alliances. The search for allies is a major part of any conflict strategy and one that has received surprisingly little attention. The politics of size (Schlee, 1999: 2002), the crucial act of delineating the group of followers, who are, after all, also competitors over the new resources, requires at least partial control over the decision on the type of conflict to be pursued.

As a state, Burkina Faso follows a pronounced non-ethnic policy. It is this claim on which the state bases part of its legitimacy. Official institutions attempt to redefine local conflicts, which are largely labelled in idioms of ethnic oppositions by its local actors, as competition over resource management and over control of the legal field. Fulbe herders, for instance, may be perceived as an ethnically distinct group in local discourse, emphasizing (or 'over-communicating', in Michael Hechter's terminology) their 'Fulbeness'. National institutions and international organizations address them as agro-pastoralists, stressing their professional specialization. Through this claim, the state enters the arena of local relations not only as a mediator but also as a contestant over the nature of conflict.

Approaches to conflict that focus on its material objectives (on 'what' is being fought about) often miss the role of the interventionist state and do not provide the tools to adequately assess its role and that of other mediating institutions in the process. To address differences over the type of conflict – including the question of whether ethnicity is considered a legitimate delineation – I intend to follow an actor-based approach. Decisions over the type of conflict do not necessarily have to be made by any of the conflicting parties. Just as different criteria of group formation (political, ethnic, or economic) may alternate or change over time or depending on context, so does the ideological and processual frame of conflict. Edmund Leach has analysed changing frames of self-ascription in Burma (Leach, 1954). Elwert focused on the element of 'switching' – the 'rapid change from one frame of reference to another' (2002: 35). Any conflict, we may assume, in fact happens simultaneously on several layers, drawing on multiple rules of identification and delineation. For analytical and practical reasons, conflicts can be dissected and analysed along these layers. In this way, the coexistence and interdependence of actors' conflicts, normative conflicts, violence and non-violence and the competition over the nature of the conflict can be accounted for.

'Ethnic conflicts' – conflicts considered to be predominantly organized along the ethnic ascriptions of the contestants – have risen significantly over the past two decades and have become a field of major concern in and beyond anthropology. This increase in ethnic conflicts is to a large extent due to a shift in classification both in academic and public perception: conflicts are mainly ethnic because they are labelled as such. In the 1950s and 1960s, most violent intra-state conflicts were framed as wars of independence; the 1960s and 1970s saw a significant increase in class-oriented revolutionary movements and anti-regime wars (Gantzel, 1997) and were reflected in the academic debates of dependence theory and neo-colonialism. Armed conflicts of the 1970s and 1980s were largely tagged as proxy wars and perceived as part of the super powers' scramble for domination over the peripheries. After the end of the cold war, a new label eventually moved into the centre of attention with 'ethno-nationalist' wars. The number of armed conflicts between ethnic groups has sharply increased from the late 1980s onward (Gantzel, 1997; Gurr, 1993; Turton, 1997: 2). By 1985, the majority of armed conflicts were eventually framed in either ethnic or nationalist rhetoric (Scherrer, 1994: 74; Wimmer, 1995: 465). Yet, the outbreak of ethnic violence is not related to the degree of cultural heterogeneity (Gurr, 1993). We may ask if are we indeed looking at a different type of conflict, or whether we are merely witnessing a shift in the way conflicts are framed through conduct and the structure of arbitration.

'Ethnic conflict' has in many ways become a catch-all phrase for a broad range of violent clashes and armed disputes and now serves as a general label for most sub-national-level violence and warfare in public representations (Allen and Seaton 1999: 3). It contains its own common-sense explanations; conflicts are seen as driven by the urge to find cultural roots in an increasingly globalized world or based on the antagonism of primordially distinct groups (Huntington, 1996). Ethnic violence is seen to occur when states fail to exercise sufficient control over ethnic units (Callahan, 2002; Kaplan, 1993). Neither is it considered an internal or intra-state affair alone. International organizations (such as the UN, EU or the Organization for Security and Co-operation in Europe) engage with conflicting groups and create a mediated forum for the contestants. On lower, non- or pre-violent levels, various NGOs and development organizations deal with 'ethnic tensions', often supplying substantial funds and playing important roles in the mediation and outcome of such conflicts.

Are we then looking at a new type of conflict or have conflicts simply been relabelled? Evidence suggests that we are looking at a combination of both: the framing of conflicts as 'ethnic' affects the way conflicts are led, impacts upon the strategies of contestants in terms of alliance building, invites certain actors (e.g. the state as mediating and controlling agency) and excludes others (economic and class-based, e.g. unions). We should remind ourselves at this point that although the number of ethnic conflicts has indeed increased since the cold war, it is primarily the publications on ethnic conflict that have risen exponentially, as the statistical chart in the introduction (Figure 1, p. 9) illustrates. An analysis of conflict must take into account the prevalence of ethnic explanations in public discourse; a field including but not restricted to media, politics, development policies and the social sciences.

This field also impacts upon the way conflicts are initiated and pursued, as it affects the options and strategies that specific groups or individuals can draw upon at different stages of conflicts (Grove, 2001: especially p. 361). Allen and Esman have shown the role the media play in shaping the political – and academic – field and its impact upon local conflicts (Allen et al., 1996; Allen and Seaton, 1999a, Esman and Telhami, 1995). The cases described in this book underscore this presupposition: the (non-violent) strategies of conflicting parties refer to different layers of group relations, including economic and ethnic dimensions, depending on the degree of entitlement, on considerations of group size and alliance building as well as access to international funds and support. As the history of herders' organizations in Chapter 5 illustrates, the paradigm changes in international rhetoric have an immediate impact on how minorities are organized (Dafinger and Pelican, 2006). In a study of Masai organizations in Tanzania, Hodgson showed that these organizations initially acted as representatives of an ethnically defined group and gradually redefined themselves as economic organizations and unions, responding to the fact that funding had shifted from independent, non-state organizations to more ecologically oriented and cooperative organizations that work more closely alongside or within state organizations (Hodgson, 2006). In a different paper we have shown that a similar process can be observed in West Africa, where herders' organizations are likewise attempting to bridge the gap between ethnic and economic interest groups (Dafinger and Pelican, 2006).

Anthropological attempts to explain what has been categorized as 'ethnic conflict' are split into two major factions, following primordialist or instrumentalist approaches, either building on the assumption that the reasons for conflict are intrinsic in the specific cultural settings (a result of the socialization of culture-specific norms and values) or are outcomes of general, global, political and economic processes. Most of the latter approaches locate ethnic conflicts exclusively in the modern nation state and the world system. After a brief discussion of both lines of thought, I will suggest an integrative model that attempts to take account of both, primordial sentiments and deliberate construction of ethnicity.

The public, mass-mediated Western perception of ethnic conflicts is to a great extent based on a primordial understanding of ethnicity and of ethnic groups as monolithic units (Ross, 2007: 19). It takes as a foregone conclusion that ethnicity and cultural differences are sufficient causes for ethnic conflict. These and other, similarly simplistic models of ethnic conflict are especially popular in the public view (Allen et al., 1996; Allen and Seaton, 1999) and among political elites (Schlee, 2006: 8–10; Wimmer, 1995: 472). They are propelled by analytical approaches of debateable provenance such as Huntington's 'clash of civilizations'(1996), or Kaplan's argument of 'ancient hatreds'(1993: 134), which are merely suppressed within the nation state, until 'the lid is removed and the cauldron boils over' (Bowen, 1996: 3). Not all of the contributions from within the primordialist line of thought, however, can be so easily dismissed. Bruce Kapferer, in his (1988) study of violent national riots in Sri Lanka, presents one of the more elaborate arguments in this tradition. Kapferer, who explained the outbreak of collective violence in Sri Lanka against a background of mythical traditions, stressed that historical factors and sentiments are withdrawn from open discourse. Conflicts and conflict resolution, he argues, can only be understood if analysed in the context of collective history. Kapferer, however, was strongly criticized by Spencer for overemphasizing historical and mythical content over political conditions. In Spencer's view the outbreaks of violence in Sri Lanka can only be understood as reactions to the political shifts and not in reference to mythology (Spencer, 1990), introducing a constructivist argument to the debate. Connerton (1989), in a similar vein to Kapferer, sees specific historical events inscribed in a collective memory, which is reified in anniversaries, spatial order, monuments and landmarks; Ross, in a more recent contribution, continues the argument, likewise following psycho-cultural approaches (1986; 2007: 2). Propagating a constructivist model, Cohen (1974) and Hechter (1976) see ethnicity take the place of other group delineators, namely unions and political parties, where the lack of civil society provides no alternative means of political organization. Sten Hagberg (2004: 199) showed how herders' unions in Burkina Faso also act as ethnic organizations in a local context, translating local, ethnically defined interests into the language of civil organizations within the nation state.

Brubaker (2004: 9ff.) similarly understands ethnic conflict not so much 'as conflict between ethnic groups, just as racial or racially framed conflict need not be understood as conflict between races, or nationally framed conflict as conflict between nations', as mentioned before. Instead, as Brubaker argues, conflict is ethnicized actors who are competing in other fields. Ethnic conflicts in these models are largely the result of competition over limited collective resources supplied by the state, an idea that had been raised before by a defender of a primordial approach (Geertz 1963: 120). Brubaker's point, however, is that partial groups manage to mobilize followers under an ethnic umbrella in their own aspirations for these new resources.

Approaches that are built on the congruence of ethnic and economic interest groups alone, reach their limit when not all members of the ethnic group find themselves in the same economic situation or when elites need to draw on different aspects of ethnicity to include those who do not share the specific economic background.

In this analysis, I integrate both models, primordial and constructivist, on the grounds that any constructivist approach still needs to take account of the persuasiveness of historically rooted ethnic sentiment. Ethnicity is used by social political interest groups and individual actors alike. It is a major criterion for aligning allies in conflicts and, as constructivists argue, often the largest common denominator, allowing small groups to mobilize a maximum of followers.

When does ethnicity become a political issue? For Wimmer, ethnic conflict depends on the fact that ethnic groups feel bound together by common destiny ('*Schicksalsgemeinschaft*'), invoking primordial understandings of ethnic identity and, in a second step, the politicizing of differences in order to produce violent conflict. He insists that ethnic relations and conflict reach an entirely new level within the nation state. Politicized ethnicity is the result of competition over collective resources supplied by the state: 'only when state power is defined as legitimized by the people, will they ask in the name of which ethnic group the state may act and which group gains access to its resources'.[2] A crucial step in this process lies in the ethnicization of bureaucracy, or the (over-)representations of members of one ethnic group in positions that decide over the allocation of collective goods (Wimmer 1995: 467–72). Wimmer makes an important point; he must, however, concede that no studies support the assumption that bureaucrats treat members of the own ethnic group in a privileged manner. He assumes that members of their own group enjoy a higher credibility and are more trustworthy and that shared language helps to access administrative resources. Here, Wimmer falls back on assumptions of primordial solidarity. His assumption, moreover, stands in contrast to his own observation that competition over resource access and positions within administration is fiercest within the group.[3] The issue of shared language, which he brings in as a possible explanation, can hardly account for the alleged preferential treatment of members of the group. Different ethnic groups may well share the same language, while members of the same ethnic groups often speak different languages, depending on political, economic and professional contexts. The prevalence of French by Burkina Faso's middle class over the vernacular of their rural kin is one example. The definition of the ethnicized bureaucracy, as based on the (over-) representation of members of a dominant group, limits the explanatory power of Wimmer's model to a rather narrow range. As the Burkina Faso case shows, ethnicization does not depend on recruitment of ethnic members, where the state pursues an explicitly non-ethnic policy. The constitution prohibits any ethnic discrimination and census data after 1984 contain no information related to ethnic affiliation (Constitution of Burkina Faso (Le Peuple Souverain), 1997, Articles 1, 19, 23). In this way it is practically impossible to judge whether members of any ethnic group are over or under-represented in the administration (see also Hagberg, 2004).

Mossi, who account for almost half of Burkina Faso's population, show a strong presence in official institutions and non-Mossi repeatedly stress that Mossi allegedly find it easier to deal with administration officials and have 'bras longues', long arms, that reach into the

---

[2]   In its German original:'... *erst wenn Volk und Staatsgewalt legitimatorisch aufeinander bezogen werden, stellt sich die Frage im Namen welcher Ethnie der Staat zu agieren hat, wer als rechtmässiger Besitzer in Erscheinung treten darf und Zugang zu seinen Ressourcen erhält*' (Wimmer, 1995, p. 464).

[3]   To uphold the argument, we would have to introduce a second, e.g. class based, distinction between elite (e.g., bureaucrats) and other members of the ethnic groups (e.g. peasants), who are not in conflict over the same resource. The shared ethnicity then becomes a cross-cutting tie that helps in preventing class conflicts.

administration, especially in towns such as Tenkodogo with a considerably mixed population (of Bisa and Mossi). There is no indication, however, that any of the groups actually is over-represented. In dealing with its citizens, differentiating lines are drawn less around single ethnic groups, but rather around clusters of related ethnic groups, creating 'meta-ethnicities'.[4] This, for one reason, lies in a perceived closeness of historically, linguistically or otherwise related groups: members of ethnic groups who share an alleged history and whose languages are closely related are likely to perceive of themselves as a larger unit vis-à-vis other major groups (although people strongly differentiate between them on other levels).[5] There is, for example, a major distinction between the mandephone (mostly Dyoula speaking) western part of Burkina Faso and the eastern half which is dominated by Gur-speaking groups (e.g. More). A second type of meta-ethnicity is based on more general criteria, such as a shared locality or socio-economic specialization, like farming, which unites Bisa and Mossi against the herding Fulbe groups. Another form of ethnicization refers to the 'bureaucratic tribe' or 'la culture des fonctionnaires' as a whole, which perceives farming ethnic groups as more compatible with and 'legible' to the state than pastoral, transhumant herders are. Questions of territorial organization and rural land rights are in principle compatible with national legislation and notions of territoriality, while the pastoral way of regulating access rights is perceived as largely incompatible with modern land laws (de Bruijn and van Dijk, 1995; van den Brink et al., 1995).

Administration is more likely to cooperate with established farmers' institutions, such as village chiefs and *nabas*, and acknowledges the prerogative of landholding village communities to register land under revised national land legislation. A general preference can be observed on behalf of the administration to cooperate with farmers and farmers' political organization, whereas pastoralists are considered to be outside the governable sphere and need first to be incorporated through sedentarization. The section on the national mapping policy (see below, p. 164ff) illustrates how depicting all herders as nomads literally keeps Fulbe villages off the official maps.

---

[4] I use the term meta-ethnicity to refer to levels of ethnic identity based on the perceived similarity of ethnic groups. In this it differs from the concept of the meta-society, which comprises different ethnic groups in one political or cultural field (Schlee, 1998). Examples of a meta-ethnicity might be Danish and English who (along with Germans, Dutch, etc.) form a perceived meta-identity based on similarity of language, dominant religion, or paleness, etc. as opposed to, for example Turkish people.

[5] Many speakers of Dagara or Kasim for example claim that they can follow conversations in More rather easily (all three languages belonging to the Gur-language family). Bisa on the other hand, is part of the Mande family, a different group of languages.

It is important to bear these considerations in mind before turning to the agropastoral conflicts in Boulgou. The deliberate production of ethnic difference will support the previous assumption that none of the conflicts are the result of primordial ethnic antagonism. Cases of intra-ethnic tensions, moreover, will underline that ethnicity is ascribed to certain types of conflicts, for political, economic or social reasons.

Differentiating different layers of conflict, as Elwert, Horowitz and others have suggested, will aid the analysis of the cases and help identify the actors who introduce ethnicity, who profit from an ethnicized discourse, and the agents who deliberately oppose ethnicity as a legitimate category and profit from a politically defined and mediatized perception of ethnic tensions.

Bureaucracy is a distinct focus of this study. The administrative elites are at the interface between local groups and the state or other international institutions; they are at the same time competitors over the state's infrastructural and local political resources. To explain the bureaucracy's role in these conflicts it is not sufficient to merely look at its ethnicization or view it as 'extended arms' of locally dominant groups. Bureaucracy – and the next chapter will support this view – provides the framework for a quasi-ethnic group of public servants with their own vested interests, seeking strategic alliances with ethnic groups without actually attempting to identify with them.

Intra- and inter-ethnic conflicts in Boulgou

The following discussion of conflicts in Boulgou continues the description of intra- and intergroup relations in the previous chapter. Although most conflicts are perceived as a disruption of normative social order by local actors, most conflicts are in fact low-level, everyday incidents that appear very much part of regular social relations. The fact that most actors defined conflicts as disruptive is in itself much more part of a standard narrative. The accounts will also show that low-level conflicts or negotiations over competing claims are located in the same social and communicative field as the economic and social interactions that have been described in the previous chapter. The boundaries between groups that are drawn by an ethnic division of labour are perpetuated through a public discourse of conflict.

The following sections will first look at the material causes of conflict before turning to the protagonists, investigating the stakes, which individual actors hold in the conflicts. Both in terms of resources and specific entitlements – the material causes of conflict –

disputes are most frequent between members of the same group, while inter-ethnic conflicts appear to be much more about political and social positioning of individual actors – and renegotiation of boundaries and their violations.

Crop damage caused by straying cattle is by far the greatest source of disputes in Boulgou. Damaged fields are a daily occurrence in almost any community especially during the rainy season. Despite its prevalence in public discourse and the attention it receives on an administrative and planning level, most cases are small-scale incidents and are generally settled between field owners and herders. Farmers often accept minor damages as an inevitable side effect of agro–pastoral coexistence. Major damage or recurring cases caused by the same herds, usually require negotiations and compensation by the herder or custodian of the herd.[6] Depending on the extent of the damage and whether cooperation between the conflicting parties is successful or not, these negotiations may be taken to the village chief or take place in the presence of a larger group of dignitaries and elders. Only a few cases ever reach the administrative level. Based on my observations, only about one tenth of all cases were taken to the prefects (the lowest judicial authority). However, whether amicably resolved between litigants, settled by chiefs or resolved by prefects – the outcome is always considered a compromise. As a general rule, farmers complain that the compensation is hardly more than a 'symbolic gesture', and herders continuously lament the amount they have paid. In the end, both parties, as part of a generally accepted rhetoric, just agree for the 'sake of friendship and peaceful cohabitation'.

Other major areas of conflicts and disputes stem from overlapping claims and disputed entitlements to specific, mostly landed resources: fields, gardens and pasture but also water issues such as access to river banks, ponds, streams and modern wells.

The major contested resource is water. Virtually every pond is surrounded by a patchwork of gardens, where nearby farmers cultivate onions, tomatoes, cabbage and zucchini, which are sold on the local markets. Generally, a few patches are left uncultivated to serve as paths for people and cattle but as waters recede in the months after the rains, the available area bordering the ponds becomes scarce and paths are often used for gardening – leaving no access for cattle. The conflicts over these ponds tend to be much fiercer than crop damage issues for several reasons. Other than subsistence-oriented millet cultivation, gardening mostly consists of cash crops and any damage is an immediate financial loss for the gardeners. At the same time, herders will

---

[6] The custodian is not necessarily the owner of all cattle and the herdsmen, who are often boys, are generally not held accountable.

more openly resist any attempts to increase garden areas and encroach on the cattle paths, given that access to water is crucial and a non-negotiable for their herd.

The second most important resource likely to be at the heart of conflicts is land. Entitlements to land are in most cases clearly defined, including rights to borrowed land. Any member of a landed lineage is entitled to a patch of land, provided she or he meets a number of other criteria. Depending on the position in the social network, rights to land can be accumulated. On marriage, a man receives land for his new household out of the patrimony; with children and subsequent marriages he will be able to claim more. These rights nonetheless depend on continuous cultivation and on 'taking good care' of the land. If, for some reason a household head decides to leave fields fallow for extended periods the land may be re-allocated to others who can make legitimate claims. Likewise, the size of the household is used as an argument in intra-lineage debates over land allocation.

As a result, young men are eager to found their own households. However, virtually no young man can get a wife before all his older brothers are married. This causes significant problems for many, especially when elder brothers spend years abroad as migrant workers in Côte d'Ivoire, having girlfriends and even children – without ever getting married. As a result, their younger siblings who stay behind cannot get married and have no chance of advancing in the social hierarchy and reaching economically independent status. This practice leads to a number of conflicts over access to land, which many un-married men in their twenties find themselves excluded from, as they are not permitted to lead their own households. The result is that a considerable number of conflicts over land are not the immediate result of scarcity but rather caused by social institutions and allocation patterns within the kin group.

Another frequent cause of trouble and fierce conflict – besides competition over land and crop damage – is the theft / embezzlement of entrusted animals. Quarrels over embezzlement, whether real or alleged, are frequent between individuals, both between the Bisa farmers and the Fulbe herders, as well as within the respective ethnic groups. Family members who let siblings watch over their small live-stock or who entrust them with other agricultural goods frequently complain about cases of animals getting 'lost' in their kin's custody. Such quarrels between family members, however, are mostly regulated within the family or lineage and social sanctioning is more immediate – and at the same time less talked about in the public sphere. Cases of theft / embezzlement across the ethnic divide, on the other hand, are much more of a public concern.

The fact that inter-ethnic conflicts receive more public attention stands in contrast to the historical background: as the example of Garango's history has highlighted, violence and warfare were more common within Bisa society than they were between the groups. In the following section, I will return to the historical dimension of intra-ethnic clashes and the importance of inter-ethnic defence-alliances and then look at recent forms of intra-group competition.

In Bisa villages, the pre-colonial era is frequently remembered as 'the time of great wars', referring to the slave raids that used to haunt the region. Raids often were targeted against neighbouring villages – both with the intent of capturing their men, selling them on the slave markets and of abducting their young women as marriage partners for their own group. A response to these permanent threats was that many villages entered defensive alliances – which effectively were non-aggression pacts. Villages mutually considered each other as brothers, prohibiting marriage and reducing the incentive for any potential raids between them. Over time, this resulted in a pattern of marriage avoidances within the exogamous alliances on one side and webs of preferential marriage relations between formerly hostile communities, on the other. Although today's relations between the villages are explicitly friendly and amicable, past hostilities are still part of oral history and are inscribed in the political and economic landscape (Dafinger, 2004a: 116–20). Many of today's political, social and economic networks have their origins in these historical configurations.

Garango still keeps a shrine dedicated to the slave raids where sacrifices were offered in preparation for any slave hunt; today, Garango's annual sacrifice at the shrine serves as a reminder of its 'proud past'. The local chief's inauguration ceremonies, too, allude to this past, underlining the importance of local Fulbe in these raids; Fulbe mercenaries helped both to defend against and attack other villages. Following local accounts, inter-village relations were marked by explicit violence and the boundaries of hostility were drawn around local communities. Even shared ethnicity played no mediating role.

Inter-village raids, warfare and political competition are part of a collective past that highlights the conflict potential between political systems and localities, irrespective of their ethnic affiliation and composition. In conversations, people perceive warfare in terms of alliance building rather than as an antagonistic relationship.

The historical background is not the only indicator of the conflict potential within the respective ethnic boundaries. In a more recent context, competition over resources and social status is a major cause for disputes among kin and members of the same ethnic groups, as the following accounts illustrate. The first highlights the internal competition over social status and the attempts to define the individuals' position in the formal genealogical and kinship hierarchy.

It is the story of one of the numerous young men who, after having returned from migrant labour, need to claim their position in the local community. In this, they compete with their fellow clansmen and with others of the same local (and ethnic) community.

If one arrives in Busma from the north, one of the first noticeable buildings is a small compound next to the main road. It catches the eye mostly because of its 'modern-style' architecture: it is constructed of bricks and cement, as opposed to the usual adobe and – equally noticeable – all of its houses have corrugated iron roofs. On a closer look yet, one will notice that there is no one to meet the visitor: the compound, new and modern, remains uninhabited.

The compound was built by a young local man, to whom I shall refer as Sanno, who had returned from a job as a migrant farm worker in Italy.[7] Sanno had decided to spend a substantial amount on constructing a compound that would set him apart from the rest of the community – the outward sign of his acquired wealth. His move, accordingly, was widely considered presumptuous; many people regarded his lifestyle as extravagant, as unsuitable for his age and generally as an attempt to jump the local social hierarchy. In short, by showing off his riches, Sanno managed to make more enemies than friends. Soon after the compound was completed and Sanno had moved in with his family, the house started being haunted by ghosts; at night, *gini* spirits started throwing rocks against the walls and on the metal roofs. This was, as I was told, the sign of discontent (of the spirits) that Sanno had built his compound in this location: he had failed to consult the appropriate diviners before starting to build his compound. I found it impossible to determine if anyone was ever fully convinced that it was actually spirits throwing the rocks – Sanno, at any rate, understood the message, left the place and built another, more modest compound in a location that was part of his lineage settlement cluster – subjecting himself to the social control of a dense spatial network.

So – what had the actual problem been? After all, what Sanno had done – investing his new wealth in a visible manner and thus publicly showing that he had achieved some modest wealth – is not unusual for returning migrants. Why then was someone – neighbour, brother, spirits – apparently unhappy about the location and appearance of the new compound?

---

[7] Southern Italy is a major destination for many temporary work migrants from the Bisa region. The extensive network of Bisa in Italy reaches back to the times before 1993, when Burkinabe could enter most European countries without a visa.

Social relations within the households, houses and kin groups are largely defined through the kin relations, based on descent or for women through the order of marriage (Dafinger, 2004a); this is true for farmers' and herders' communities, Bisa and Fulbe alike. Within these rather rigid networks, there are few options to advance one's status through means other than those provided within the kin group, mainly marriage and parenthood. For young Bisa men, however, any of these steps demand that all elder siblings have already successfully made these transitions; it is very difficult to jump the queue and move up faster in the social hierarchy than any other member of the group.

Working abroad and returning with some modest wealth offers one of the few alternative means to increase social standing, if within narrow margins and at a considerable cost. Most young men who return from abroad (mostly Côte d'Ivoire) tend to distribute and conspicuously spend their wealth to advance their social status. Local communities offer few options to invest this money within agricultural production – occasional public millet mills being the few exceptions.[8] The inalienation of land is one reason for that, the general feeling that money that is generated outside the household and outside the agricultural cycle is often considered not compatible with the 'proper' social order (Parry and Bloch, 1989). Just like 'bitter money' (Shipton, 1989) or 'money of shit' (Hutchinson, 1992: 304), the migrant's earnings cannot simply be used to jump the queue in social hierarchies. Money that is generated from non-household-related activities must be 'laundered' and passed on partly through proper redistributive channels and partly through consumption. So, showing off and conspicuous consumption when returning home is not only tolerated but even expected of returning migrants. The important thing is to respect the social network, distribute substantial parts of the earnings and consume other parts. Accumulating wealth, acquiring symbols of material wealth and trying to jump the queue by assuming prerogatives such as 'modern houses', is much less tolerated and socially sanctioned. The reaction to Sanno's inappropriate construction illustrates the narrow margins within which individuals can operate and indicates the high potential for conflict in the hierarchical systems of kin groups and the local communities.

Sanno's case is a normative conflict in Elwert's sense, including the 'monitoring and sanctioning' of behaviour, (Elwert, 2001; Elwert et al., 2001), although the sanctioning institutions are deliberately not

---

[8]   Power mills are found in the bigger markets and occasionally in smaller villages. For 100 CFA (0.15€) women can have a bucket of sorghum ground in a couple of minutes. These mills are often built and owned by people who live in the bigger towns and who have a younger relative run the mill for them.

named in the accounts of the incident. Obfuscating the real agents behind a rhetoric of spirits, ghosts and witchcraft is characteristic for conflicts with the kin groups (Geschiere, 1997; Geschiere and Fisiy, 1995). In intergroup tensions across the ethnic division, actors are more easily identified and publicly named.

An account of the village of Zarga offers a similar case of disapproval of individual behaviour that is considered socially inadequate. Here too, envy constitutes a driving force of quarrels within one of the groups – the community of Fulbe herders in this case. It also points to a feature of most Fulbe settlements: their tendency to remain small in number and split off rather than exceed a certain numerical size. Zarga is one of the oldest Fulbe villages in the region between Tenkodogo and Garango. It shares part of its pre-colonial history with neighbouring Gando with whose farmers most Fulbe from Zarga maintain close relations. It is the origin of many other Fulbe settlements in the area, which have been established by factions of the Zarga-lineage splitting off over the course of generations. The reasons for these splits were generally given in terms of availability of and access to, pasture. As all older settlements are in the vicinities of farming villages, the risk of crop damage rises with the number of herders. The expansion of cultivated lands and the decreasing availability of pasture in the vicinity places pressure on herders to resettle or migrate. Fulbe herders also frequently expressed their feelings that farmers, as landowners and political authorities, would mostly not allow a larger conglomeration of herders in their neighbourhood. Reasons, however, may also be sought beyond this rhetoric. The fact that even those Fulbe settlements that are located outside the cultivated zone (see Map 3, p. 38) never exceed 200 people, weakens the argument that the neighbouring farmers would be a driving motive in keeping the herder communities small. Neither have I ever witnessed any case in which a farming (Bisa) 'chef de village' had actually asked the local Fulbe residents to move or split. To the contrary, heads of villages repeatedly stressed that they had no objections to a larger settlement of Fulbe in their vicinities. The dominant rhetoric reiterated by the herders, however, still stressed the pressure of neighbouring farmers as a main cause for fissions and resettlements.

This narrative largely ignores potential endogenous factors in this process. Social tensions and intra-lineage conflicts (over entitlements and social authority) increase with the size of the local group; fissions often result from intra-group dynamics, but are expressed as a result of ethnic conflicts. When a part of the Zarga-lineage split off around 60 years ago they resettled on the fringes of the farming village of Poussoaka – at a distance of only a couple of kilometres from the previous location (see Chapter 5) – and accordingly continued to use and share the same pasture and waterholes as before. Economic and ecological reasons obviously were not the decisive factor. As is generally the case, relations between the settlements continued to be close throughout the time and over the generations and marriages between the groups remained frequent. The political alliances, however, shifted to the *kiri*, village chief of Poussoaka.

This opened new possibilities of amicable relations with the farmers of Poussoaka, including privileged use of their post-harvest fields. On the other hand, smaller settlements also have their drawbacks, not only in relation to the farming community, which will always be numerically significantly larger. The size of a local community is also one of the major criteria for local development projects in allocating their resources. Only communities of more than 200 people can formally request a modern water well under the PIHVES scheme.[9] With just under 200 inhabitants, the Fulbe community of Poussoaka had no chance of being reviewed for a well project. The community, however, had another asset; Abdoulaye, one of the village elders, worked for the mayor in Tenkodogo overseeing the local cattle market. Abdoulaye is fluent in French, the administrative language, and because of his position quite familiar with the administrative idiosyncrasies, the 'culture des fonctionnaires'. He obviously knows how to navigate the administrative space. Abdoulaye decided to put forward an application succeeded in convincing PIHVES officials that the well was to serve over 300 people, and so a well was eventually built and has become a defining landmark of the Poussoaka Fulbe settlement.

What is interesting, are the diverging narratives of how Abdoulaye managed to tweak the numbers. According to his own account and confirmed by the project, the well was to serve the neighbourhood, which included the Fulbe herders and the more than one hundred farmers, who lived in the immediate vicinity. As the project does not discriminate between wells for farmers, herders or mixed communities, this was not at all surprising. The Fulbe at Zarga, however, claim a different story. According to many of them, Abdoulaye included them in the count and made the Poussoaka community appear twice its actual size. The fact that farmers at Poussoaka now use the well is seen as an additional injustice. Although the fact that Poussoaka has received a well brings no disadvantages for the Fulbe community at Zarga, most inhabitants there still believe that they have been misused – simply by being counted as part of the Poussoaka group.

[9]   The PIHVES project, a Danish Burkinabe co-operation started to build a total of 800 modern wells in the province over the period of then years, beginning in the early 1990s (see below, Chapter 5).

When a similar well was built in Gando – at almost the same distance and in the heart of the Bisa village, none of the Fulbe in Zarga complained about this or referred to it as an injustice. The conflict arose because the beneficiaries of the new well were also Fulbe; and greed appeared to be a major factor behind these accusations. Despite their frequency such internal conflicts do not shape the public debate in the same way as tensions that happen along the ethnic boundary.

As a contrast to the rather covert character of tensions within the groups, the disputes between Fulbe and Bisa often form part of a public debate. The same institutions that tie individuals of both groups together – the entrustment of cattle and the sharing of major resources – are at the same time a prime cause for conflict: most arise from accusations of embezzlement or disputes over compensation for damaged fields and injured cattle. Cattle entrustment especially shows a high degree of ambivalence. It establishes friendship on the one hand but is also incessantly used as an example of the need for suspicion in dealing with members of the other group.

While cases of crop damage are often individually discussed in the community, accusations of embezzlement are of a more general nature, as most farmers are reluctant to reveal the fact that they own cattle on the other side of the ethnic boundary. These general allegations include complaining about the owner of the animals, who does not adequately fulfil his obligation to pay for medical treatment and damages in which his/her cattle were involved, whereas the owners tend to regard these demands mostly as excessive and inappropriate. Herders, in turn, are under a general suspicion of embezzlement. Farmers accuse them of illegitimately selling animals that have been confided to them (and then reporting them dead or stolen) or withholding the offspring of animals (which belong to the owner of the mother-cow). These disputes differ from quarrels over crop damage as they directly concern the personal relations between owner and caretaker. Whereas disputes over crop damage often have two sides: a public accusation and personal mediation, arguments over embezzlement are not necessarily discussed openly as it might compromise the owner: after all, a major reason for Bisa farmers to confide animals to Fulbe is to conceal their assets.

The weaker the ties between cattle owners and herders are, and the fewer relations both entertain on other levels, the weaker the foundation appears on which trust can build. Minor disruptions, mere allegations of embezzlement can tear apart the bonds of partners whose friendship stems from exchange alone. What Elwert referred to as weak degrees of embeddedness (see above, p. 103) manifests itself on the ground in the absence of mediating authorities, as mutual assurances of reliability and trust.

Guieba and Noël, whose rather pragmatic relationship has already been revealed in the previous chapter, illustrate the ambivalence of the practice of entrusting animals: trust and allegations of embezzlement often go hand in hand.

The general reciprocal nature of this exchange, however – following Sahlins' three tiered classification (Sahlins, 1972: 277–314) – should not be mistaken for general generosity: all sides involved generally stress the respective benefits of these transactions. The rhetoric of friendship and mutual trust cannot obfuscate the explicit self-interest and pragmatism that are inherent in these relations. Pragmatism, in fact, is one of the dimensions that allows for the malleability of these exchange relations and the extension of the ethnic division of labour beyond the farming and herding communities. The transformation and integration of gift exchange into bureaucracy and into the formalized economy, is gradient, as the case illustrated. As a butcher, Noël had an explicit economic interest in owning cattle in the vicinity of Garango and was quite able to calculate the costs and benefits of outsourcing cattle herding. This corresponds to a much vaguer expectation of general reciprocity on the side of Guieba and his family.

The expectation of return, however, seems significantly higher than in other cases, given the professional character of Noël's cattle business. From Noël's point of view, the relationship with Guieba is purely professional, it can be terminated at any time and serves no further social purpose. Noël uses the instrument of formal authority, such as police and the court system, to negotiate and draw the boundaries of the costs he is willing to pay. At the same time, he builds on the rules of informal economic networks by avoiding clear arrangements of payment.

Guieba's son, Diallo Ousman, was seen selling one of Noël's cows on the cattle market. Noël was informed by one of Guieba's neighbours, Muïdo, a herder himself. Noël immediately went to see Guieba and, upon realizing that the allegations were obviously true, he filed charges against Ousman, who was arrested by the police. When Noël tried to reclaim his other animals, he found even more animals were missing and decided to sue Guieba for an additional two missing goats. Guieba readily acknowledged the charges against his son and, in order to have his son released from prison ('a one month of unsupportable food', in the culprit's words) replaced the missing bull with another, which he had to buy out of his own pocket (the son had apparently already spent all the money). He was, however, reluctant to give in to the other charges directed against him and prepared a written statement for the prefect in Garango in order to make his case:

[Five years ago] I received the animals of Bambara Noël, butcher in Garango, that was because of his relative Zeba Seydou. The animals consisted of two bulls, two goats and two sheep. In the same year, he bought a goat off my wife, to make it a total of three goats. He continued to buy old cows for his butchery whose calves he took and confided them to me. That way he had a total of four calves, which I raised with my own means and capacity. I raised them with hay and bran, which I paid with my own money. Those animals are two females and two bulls. Later he sent yet another two bulls.

The goats, which my wife and my children took care of, rose to the number of 31, not including those which died and those he [Noël] took for himself. (…) on top of all that he sent two donkeys (…) of which the female gave birth one day to a male, which he [Noël] came to take, without even notifying me.

Despite all my suffering and tiresome work my wife and children's, too, he never thought of satisfying us; not one day. Today, as he saw that his animals have become beautiful and interesting, he comes here to pick them up without even saying thank you.

He was not forced to come here and entrust his animals to me. It is based on a general consensus that I worked with him, believing that, one day he would compensate me.

So after having given a full account of his responsibilities, labour and investments and having elegantly hidden the cause of disagreement (the missing goats), Guieba prepares the ground to make his point: his right to receive adequate compensation. Apart from the occasional bit of lamenting rhetoric, his account reveals a general pattern: herders taking care of cattle expect friendship, which they can draw upon when needed. Intermittent requests (often for goods, such as salt) serve to assure the benevolence of the *djatigi*, the owner of the animals. Although no salary is expected for the herding labour, Guieba underlines that it is part of a general practice and understanding that the labour and the relationship should be honoured.

After the case had been turned down by the Prefect's office, Guieba and Noël were again forced to settle the case between them. Although Guieba had repeatedly mentioned that their relation was established through their common friend, Zeba, they did not seek his services as an intermediary but soon decided to drop the mutual accusations. Noël, after having had his bull replaced, had lost a total of three goats in the affair. Given a total of over 40 animals, this apparently seemed an adequate opportunity cost – especially as he had in fact never compensated Guieba and his family for their labour.

Soon after all charges were dropped, Noël returned the animals, which he had removed at the height of the dispute, into Guieba's custody. The son, Ousman, however, remained unconciliatory, having been imprisoned for selling Noël's bull. Although he never denied the allegations, he claimed that he had no alternative but to sell the animal, after Noël, the owner, had repeatedly turned down requests to contribute (up to 10.000 CFA (*c.* 15 €)) to Ousman's expenditures in the bush. Ousman sold the animal in order to buy 'medication for himself, his family and the animals, as well as millet for himself and his four children'. Today, although the money which he had gained in the deal by far exceeded the amount he might have spent on such 'essentials' and despite the explicit disapproval of his father, Ousman still insists that Noël should apologize for having him imprisoned.

This story underlines that the transfers of goods and services across the ethnic border are framed in terms of gifts and mutual friendship. At the same time, it reveals the pragmatism of the actors in working in this gift economy. Both Guieba and Noël have clear expectations about what they are willing to give and what they expect to receive. Negotiations and quarrels over the extent and amount of gifts and appropriate counter gifts are an unavoidable part of the negotiation process. On the other hand, one may assume, this vagueness of exchange rates ensures flexibility when dealing with fluctuations in the ecological and larger economic framework. The story also illustrates the different types and degrees of reciprocity in the gift economy of cattle entrustment. One thing that emerged from the different narratives was that Noël had obviously been briefed by Guieba's neighbour, Muïdo, a fellow Fulbe herder. Both Guieba and Noël agreed that Muïdo was apparently motivated by greed. The fact that Guieba (and his son Ousman) seemed to create a substantial income from working with Noël was apparently reason enough to intrigue against the two. Muïdo and Guieba reportedly were not on the best of terms in the first place and Muïdo used Noël as a means to tackle a private – intra-ethnic and intra-clan – tension. The fact that Noël himself found that Muïdo's accounts at least partly exaggerated was one reason why he decided to resume his relations with Guieba.

As later cases will reveal in more detail, interethnic relations – cross-cutting ties – here are a means of pursuing intra-group conflict rather than an institution of conflict containment. Fulbe interlocutors repeatedly stressed that discrediting and talking badly about neighbours to *djatigis*, the 'friends' of the other ethnic group, was a real nuisance and a regrettable practice in many communities.

One more aspect that emerges from the account is Noël's strategy of using the police and prefecture as instruments and part of the negotiation process. Although Noël has no immediate profit from his formal complaints, his threats increased the costs for Guieba (and especially Ousman), warding off a number of their claims – e.g., compensating herding labour – and making them more likely to give in to his conditions. Noel and Guieba's case also exemplifies another important aspect of conflicts over embezzlement: as part of relations based on cattle entrustment and friendship relations, none of these conflicts are violent and are unlikely to escalate. The analysis will return to the social and economic implications of this practice at a later point (Chapter 5). Before that, however, I want to turn to a different type of conflict that is much less embedded in social ties: the relations between farmers and 'newcomer' herders. Conflicts between these groups rely much more on the intervention of state authorities and show a much higher potential for violence and aggravation.

Kourbila is a settlement in the vicinity of the farming village of Komtoega. Komtoega is a local sub-centre and 'chef lieu' of the canton of Komtoega and has its own prefect. Kourbila is an example of a Fulbe settlement that was established quite recently by Fulbe migrants from the northern Sahel regions of Burkina Faso. When the group of herders arrived in the late 1960s and built the first houses, the terrain around what is now Kourbila was uninhabited and uncultivated bush land. In conversation, the older villagers vividly recall how they had to put up with lions, hyenas and a generally unhealthy environment. These accounts are common narratives and do not always correspond to a lived reality. They are part of a narrative that stresses that the land had to be transformed from an uncultivated wild space into a civilized place. Despite these stories, that underline that the land was bush and hence without owner, the Fulbe settlers still went to see the chief of Komtoega on their arrival to receive permission to settle in the vicinity. Apparently not very keen on having Fulbe as allies, they were referred to the *naba* of Yaoghin, another neighbouring village, insisting that the lands were actually associated with this village. Yaoghin, however, did not want to act as hosts either, nor could the newcomers draw on existing relations with any other neighbouring farming clans. Eventually all attempts to establish a relationship with the local chiefs turned out to be futile. The local Bisa's interest in the new migrants was obviously very weak and in the end the Fulbe found themselves at the margins of all territorial units and polities (the case of Zarga offers a similar example, see Chapter 5).

Settling in bush land, with no farming village having laid claims on the newly found territory, the Fulbe now claimed full use rights and saw themselves under no obligation to any land-owning (farming) clan. All herding families at Kourbila maintain their own house fields for the cultivation of sorghum, making it a largely autonomous community.

Over the course of time, however, the farming area of Komtoega has steadily increased and in 2012 – 60 years after the herders' arrival, eventually reached their settlement. As a consequence, crop damage in nearby fields has steadily increased. In this respect, Kourbila shares much of its characteristics with most other new Fulbe settlements, notably its weak relations to the neighbouring farming communities. Differing from the older established herding communities, the newcomer herders are not entrusted with the farmers' animals, they do not participate in any of the religious ceremonies of the farming villages nearby, they maintain almost no personal relations with their farming neighbours and like most they are largely economically autonomous. Conflicts that arise between farmers and herders in these communities are rare, given the distance between fields and pasture in the past. When they occur, as they increasingly do, they are rarely solved through negotiations between the parties involved. With no clear or established litigation authorities, conflicts are more easily taken to the state authorities, especially by the farmers. The Fulbe herders, in contrast, are reluctant to involve officials for fear of corruption – a fact that is exploited by many farmers who make use of official chan-nels as a threat to obtain higher compensation. Sometimes, as Souleyman, a herder, complained,

> ….it is better to pay 20.000 CFA to compensate for a damage of no more than 5.000 FCFA than to see the prefect, where I might end up paying 60.000 CFA or more.

The year before, Souleyman's cattle had entered a farmer's garden, destroying some of his pumpkin plants. The owner demanded 60.0000 CFA to compensate for the damage, an outrageously high sum in Souleyman's eyes. The farmer refused any negotiations, however, threatening to take the case to the local prefect if Souleyman was not willing to pay him the full sum:

> I offered to pay him [the farmer] 30.000 CFA for the damage done. But he demanded 60.000 – although the garden had already been harvested – which I refused to pay. He went and called an *encadreur* instead. He [the *encadreur*] found the damage was 8.000 CFA. So he [the farmer] went to the prefect.

The prefect summoned Souleyman and, in a Kafkaesque turn, fined him 50.000 CFA on top of the 8.000 CFA compensation to the farmer. It is common practice to take cattle into custody, when they are caught 'red hoofed' destroying fields or gardens. They will be kept in a pound until a preliminary agreement has been reached. The herd owner is liable to pay the costs involved for keeping the animals in closure (500 CFA per day and head of cattle). According to Souleyman, the prefect charged him for 25 cattle, which should have been at the pound for two days, adding up to 50.000 CFA.

So in the end, Souleyman, the herder, ended up paying almost the amount he initially was reluctant to pay, while the farmer received a mere third of what Souleyman had initially offered – with most of the money going to the prefect's office. Souleyman added that he was not given a receipt and along with the comment that the prefect drives a BMW, alleged corruption on the part of the state official. Such accusations of corruption are almost commonplace – farmers often complain about the fact that herders simply buy their way out of prison, whereas herders mostly see that the majority of prefects have a non-Fulbe ethnic background and imply that they are biased towards the farmers' cause. The amounts given in Souleyman's story (30.000 CFA he allegedly offered the farmer) are also part of rhetoric rather than a realistic account. Beyond bias, rhetoric and extended truths, stories like that of Souleyman point to a number of relevant issues. First, while allegations of corruption are certainly not true in all cases, some state officials still see their appointment as a chance to generate extra non-taxable income. The prefect mentioned in Souleyman's story is indeed a recurring protagonist in many accounts similar to this one.

It remains noteworthy that evidently none of the parties involved – neither farmers nor herders – are perfectly happy to involve the state authorities and that either side would often be better off with a mutual agreement. The threat, however, to call upon official institutions is an important part of the negotiations – and occasionally exercised, as above.

The vast majority of all conflict cases in Boulgou are non-violent, low-level disputes. Violence in the form of arson, expulsions and killings is exceptional and often takes the form of personal episodes, focusing around the central actors, rather than outbreaks of collective violence and group conflict. They can reverberate for many years and are perceived as extraordinary events (see Spencer, 1997).

On one of my visits to Diallo Ibrahim, an elder of the Fulbe village of Rimasougou, I stumbled across a small gathering of young men, whom I mostly knew as household heads of the neighbouring compounds. They were visiting Ibrahim to discuss what appeared to be a serious matter. The reason they came together that morning was that the news had broken about a group of young farmers from neighbouring Komtoega who were about to be released from Tenkodogo prison. Some of those present appeared concerned while others were really upset. There were rumours that the convicts were to be greeted by representatives of a major political party.

Who were these men and why was everyone so concerned? The group, I was informed, had been convicted for setting fire to the compound of a Fulbe family several years earlier and their release raised the concern that the conflict might be revived. What seemed more troubling was the rumour that a member of parliament and a farmer from the village had sent two party members to welcome the convicts, to express the fact that he was happy about the parole and to counter allegations that he might have been too passive in preventing the arrest and conviction of the men. The MP had been blamed for not having used his influence to prevent the men from being accused and sent to prison and there were even accusations that he had been actively involved in their persecution and conviction. While all this reveals a very weak faith in the independence of police and jurisdiction, the gathering of the young herders at Ibrahim's also shows that Fulbe in the region do not feel adequately represented in the parliamentary system. They are represented through the neighbouring farming community through such ties as friendship or patronage to the local farming population. In cases when their immediate adversary is from the farming village, they see themselves in a precarious situation.

No serious incidents had happened in and beyond the village since the trial and, in fact, no serious clashes were known to have happened previously. The politician's reaction and the worries of the Fulbe herders, however, indicated that the conflict had only been temporarily contained and was still simmering: the men had allegedly issued threats from their prison cells to the herder they had menaced. The herder, however, had left the area with his family and settled elsewhere.

Stories like these play an important role in constituting and maintaining social order by demarcating violence as exceptional behaviour and underlining the value of existing orders and modes of conduct. They exemplify how farmer-herder relations are perceived over time. In conversation, stories of violent conflicts are juxtaposed to allegedly more peaceful relations in the past. This may not be objectively true, as most interlocutors would in the same conversations talk about the pre-colonial slave raids, stressing the peaceful relations of today. Such statements, however, are not necessarily contradictory; whereas pre-colonial violence was very much defined through inter-village wars, relations between different groups are perceived and remembered to have been more amicable. Thus, most complaints about the degrading inter-ethnic entente refer to the everyday relations between resident herders and their farming neighbours. The dividing line today runs along criteria of local integration, landed-landless relations and duration of settlement (see also Chapter 3).

Violent conflict, as expressed in the two stories above, occurs between groups that maintain no or only recent relations. In contrast, longstanding rapports between the two parties prevent the escalation of conflicts, even between individuals who are not related through friendship or other ties. This in part confirms Gluckman's assumption that cross-cutting ties help to contain conflict between the groups. In this case, as well as in many other conflicts, the original cause of the dispute was soon forgotten and hatred focused on secondary issues drawing on stereotypical sentiments about ethnic otherness (Hagberg, 1998) and allegations of nepotism and corruption –the infamous 'bras longues' of farmers. The fact that such an escalation and outbreak of collective violence did not occur in localities that had long-established relations, such as cattle entrustment or shared political institutions, indicates that it seems harder to mobilize followers for violent action among those who maintain friendship or economic relations across the ethnic divide.

Conflict and the ethnic boundary

After I discussed the production of ethnicity in the previous chapter, I have now focused on the conflicts that arise from this ethnic division and the ethnic boundary. Having looked at dominant approaches in anthropological conflict studies, I eventually proposed a multi-layered approach, taking into account the multiplicity of motives and types inherent in these tensions. Conflicts along the ethnic divide are much more likely to involve state authorities than intra-group disputes. This is in part due to the lack of mitigating authorities, which are, for instance, institutionalized in the elders of the kin groups. It is also a product of the secretive aspect of economic transactions, such as cattle entrustment, which leaves little room for mitigating institutions on either side of the ethnic divide. State authorities, such as the prefects, are seen as third parties standing outside local relations.

The analysis of the cases above revealed that conflicts increase the perceived impermeability of the ethnic boundary and prevent other members of the same ethnic group from accessing resources, which are being controlled by the other ethnic group. In the case of farmers who entrust their cattle to Fulbe herders, the opacity of the ethnic boundary helps in hiding assets from members of the same ethnic group; the institution of cross-cutting ties is one of the keys to understanding the social importance of ethnic conflicts (Gluckman, 1964; Gluckman and Gulliver, 1978). The ethnicization of relations and conflicts, however, also bears specific problems – in analytical terms as well as for the autonomy of the conflicting parties: conflicts provide legitimacy to interventionism by national and international institutions. The conflicting parties draw on these new agents as important resources in the conflict process: the threat of addressing the authorities is one part of farmers' strategies in negotiating compensation.

An important dimension of the conflict economy is its on-going, processual character: although individual conflicts may eventually be resolved, the general tension between farmers and herders persists. As Elwert (2002) pointed out, unresolved conflicts cause permanent legal insecurity. In this case, this insecurity is an important part of the conflict strategies. It discourages exchange across the ethnic divide and helps maintain its alleged impermeability, whereas individual actors who maintain friendship and trust relations create exclusive fields of trust and security. This turns cross-cutting ties into scarce resources themselves, which are consequently concealed from other members of the group. In the next chapter, I will return to and focus on the aspect of concealment and the opacity of the ethnic divide.

5

Concealed economies
The hidden dimension of conflict & cooperation

This chapter will turn to the economy of the ethnic boundary. While publicly exploited as a source of conflict, the ethnic divide simultaneously provides a space for social, political and economic activities outside local communities and kin groups. Ethnicity is also an important argument when dealing with bureaucracy and development organizations. The first part of the chapter engages with the hidden ethnic economy of rural agro-pastoral production systems, after which the focus is on ethnicity and national bureaucratic practice.

Previous examples have shown how the ethnic divide provides a screen behind which farmers hide their cattle and withhold them from the web of reciprocal obligations within the kin groups. The transfer of cattle and herding labour goes hand in hand with a shift in the modes of exchange: cattle are also moved from the sphere of commodity exchange into one dominated by the rhetoric of gift exchange.

Being landless, Fulbe herders often seem to accept inferior status and thus also accept dependence on farming communities to receive lands for settlement and pasture. At the same time, however, passing control over land and resources on to the farmers in turn allows the local herders to ward off claims by transhumant pastoralists without having to violate intra-ethnic (and intra-kin) obligations of sharing. In this respect, the Fulbe herders profit from the public over-emphasis of conflict and maintain the image of an impermeable and high-risk boundary: this helps to conceal cross-cutting ties that permit resident local herders to share local resources with the farmers, while the transhumant herders are excluded from this hidden network.

Spheres of exchange: intra-ethnic obligations, inter-ethnic friendship

Alongside cattle and herding labour, a number of other minor goods and services are exchanged across the ethnic boundary. Most of these are acknowledgments of mutual obligations and, like herding labour, are mutually regarded as gifts. The inter-ethnic gift exchange stands in contrast to the intra-ethnic principles of solidarity and the formalized exchange of services within the same socio-economic and ethnic groups.

For most of the institutions of governance, national administration and development organizations, this practice of gift exchange is perceived as problematic, as are most informal practices of borrowing land or gift exchange as they are in principle considered incompatible with rational economic planning. State and development organizations discourage local forms of economic and social exchange and promote privatization of land and resources and formal contracts over friendship-based services.

The relative informality of the inter-ethnic gift economy, however, is not as disordered as institutions of the formal economy tend to perceive it. In most cases, clear expectations exist of who has what to offer, even if, as in the entrustment of cattle, expectations of compensation are not formally regulated. In the words of Guieba (in the previous chapter) – one follows an 'accord commun', a general practice in which herders accept cattle from their *djatigi*, from friends and neighbours in the spirit of 'good neighbourliness'.[1] Tending entrusted cattle is seen as a service between friends, which both herders and farmers stressed repeatedly. Tending cattle serves as an expression of trust and friendship, and can also lead to friendship, as the story of Guieba and Noël has shown: they were friends 'from the moment they were introduced and [Noël] brought his animals [to Guieba].'

As the herding of farmers' cattle is seen as an expression of friendship, no payments or formal agreements are made. Most Fulbe households in Boulgou have their own herds, and entrusted animals are simply added to the existing herd. Immediately occurring costs, such as fees for vaccination, taxes, fines and compensation for damage to gardens or fields are (or at least ought to be) borne by the respective owners. While farmers pay no direct compensation for herding labour, there are a large number of services and payments a herder may claim

---

[1]   This practice is different from paid herdsmanship, which is also common within the ethnic group. Fulbe with larger numbers of cattle often split their herds and pay younger herders to tend the animals.

and receive over the course of time, including the right to settle, access rights and gifts consisting of agricultural products. Both the herdsmen's work and the rights or goods given or granted by the farmers are seen as voluntary gifts, exchanged in the spirit of friendship. Most entitlements (to pasture, to cultivate or to settle) cannot be transferred, although rights to settle are generally implicitly passed on to the next generation. Even when gifts take the form of money, this is generally not considered a payment for goods received, but is mostly given in response to a specific need, such as unexpected medical costs, food and similar expenditures. As the rhetoric in Guieba and Noël's case has revealed, most perceive the complexities of herding labour, access and use rights, as well as other services as a distinct sphere of exchange, reserved for gifts and favours. It stands in contrast to the explicitly regulated set of obligations and entitlements that determine the distributive process within the households and within the ethnic, clan and lineage communities. At the same time, Guieba and Noël's case has shown that the distinction between what is perceived as a gift and what is seen as a commodity is not obvious. In a digression into the anthropology of gifts and commodities, I will attempt to unravel the complexity of gift exchange and discuss its effects on the relations between the two groups.

The analytical distinction between gift and commodity has its roots in anthropology's (pre-Maussian) foundations. Gift economy has largely been defined in contrast to commodity exchange, often locating both on an evolutionary timeline, associating gift economies with early modes of foraging and agricultural production, which were then replaced by barter and market systems (Carrier, 1991: 246ff; Godelier, 1999; Mauss, 1954 [1925]; Polanyi, 1944). Gift economies may either designate societies where everything is available without immediate or direct compensation or those where several economic layers, such as barter, monetary exchange and gift-giving exist in parallel with each other.

Mauss established the study of gift economies as a major sub-field in anthropology (Mauss, ibid.) The exchange of gifts, he posited, consisted of three essential dimensions: the obligation to give, to receive, and to return. Mauss freed the gift from romanticized notions and unearthed the pronounced pragmatism inherent in these transactions. To quote Mauss, 'gifts'... are 'prestations which are in theory voluntary, disinterested and spontaneous, but are in fact obligatory and interested' (ibid.: 1). Mauss saw the major purpose of gift exchange in its capacity to establish and maintain social relations, thus setting the tone for generations of (economic) anthropologists. As opposed to the exchange of commodities, gift transactions are meant to create 'qualitative relations between persons, they take place in an existing web of personal relations', according to Chris Gregory (1982), whose summary of Mauss' model was to became the tenor of subsequent studies in anthropology. While in anthropology the gift continued to be seen as fundamentally different from the commodity, formal economists rebutted the concept as a whole, since any good or service given was aimed at a specific gain in other fields, such as prestige or political authority.

Mauss' theory, however, also met fierce criticism elsewhere: he neglected the economic dimension (Malinowski, 1926: 40) and he erred on the driving force behind the obligation to return a gift (Sahlins, 1972; Wilson, 1973) – which he saw enmeshed with the object in a mystical force ('*hau*'). Mauss' central assumption of the fundamental distinction between gift and commodity did not come under serious scrutiny until sixty years later, when a number of authors began to tear down the categorical divide (Godelier, 1999; Laidlaw, 2000; Parry and Bloch, 1989: 25–7; Strathern, 1988) challenging the idea of 'pure gifts' and 'pure commodities' (Gregory, 1982: 212). Anthropologists provided examples of intermediate and hybrid forms within practices of gift exchange in market societies. The theory of gift exchange gained new weight as a theoretical model, apt to explain major social processes in the anthropology of post-socialism and analysis of gift economy in Western capitalist societies (Hann and Hart, 2011; Seabright, 2000).

Breaking with the axiom of a division between the gift and the commodity constituted a major paradigm shift (Appadurai, 1986b; J. G. Carrier, 1991; 1994; Strathern, 1988). In Arjun Appadurai's words 'it means looking at the commodity potential of all things rather than searching fruitlessly for the magic distinction between commodities and other sorts of things' (Appadurai, 1986a: 13). The focus began to shift away from the object as a carrier of a specific quality, to the process of exchange and the social and economic context that turns an object into either a gift or a commodity. What, then, remains of Mauss' theory? He established three major obligations involved in gift exchange: to give, to receive and to return; and although the driving force may rather be found in principles of reciprocity (Sahlins, 1972) enforced by social sanctions (Laidlaw, 2000; Malinowski, 1967; Parry, 1986), the observation that gifts demand a return remains unchallenged. His distinction between gift and commodity was a firm base for economic anthropologists, although in anthropology the focus has shifted from the object to the process and social context that defines whether one deals with a gift or a commodity (Appadurai, 1986b; Gregory, 1982; 1997; Strathern, 1988). Gifts, as opposed to commodities, need to be given, and between individuals or groups that stand in socially defined relations, gifts are obligatory.[2] In most agropastoral societies in much of West Africa, new settlers must be given land (depending on availability and the friendly intentions of newcomers). Other than commodities, gifts cannot be refused without risking the break up of existing social relations. Mauss' focus on the moral obligation saw major modification, especially with respect to its economic importance (Appadurai, 1986b; Polanyi, 1944; Polanyi and Pearson, 1977; Sahlins, 1972). Gift exchange, however, remains largely defined in terms of social relations based on friendship and trust. This is a reason why gifts, such as temporary rights to pasture, can be refused on the grounds of lacking social relations or between individuals or groups who cannot provide permanence and continuity of existing social relations. Transhumant herders are not in a position to reciprocate access to land by a counter-gift like tending farmer's cattle. Whether trust precedes the gift (Breusers et al., 1998: 368–69) or whether the gift generates trust seems almost exchangeable. This is why Guieba, the herder, insisted that he and Noel were 'friends from the moment they exchanged the first cattle'.

Gift exchange often constitutes an exclusive sphere of its own, in which only a specific range of prestigious and in many cases inalienable goods and services are circulated (Bohannan, 1959; Dalton, 1961). The labour of cattle herding is part of such a confined sphere; it can only be returned with a limited number of goods and services and only takes place within a limited group of participants.

What makes a gift or a commodity, however, is less an inherent quality of the good or service itself or the process of giving or rendering that turns a transaction into a gift or a commodity. Both Appadurai and Kopytoff have made this observation a key argument in their models of the 'social life of things' (Appadurai, 1986b) or the 'cultural biography of things' (I. Kopytoff, 1986). While certain spheres of exchange exist, with differing degrees of exclusiveness, any object (or labour) can exist in more than one sphere of exchange – subsequently or at the same time: any object in a gift exchange has, in Appadurai's words, 'commodity potential' (ibid.:13).

The practice of cattle entrustment exemplifies the oscillation between spheres of gift and commodity exchange. Farmers acquire cattle at moments of surplus production; they use animals, among other reasons, to buffer ecological fluctuation and harvest shortfalls during less favourable years. Cattle are, in this respect, commodities. In principle, any other freely convertible object could fulfil the same

---

[2] Christmas is an impressive example of how a commodity-oriented economy is built on obligation to give.

function – including a bank account. However, cattle are not only a commodity – they constitute, among other things, symbolic and social capital – which helps understand why cattle are never fully reconverted into money or food in times of harvest failures, as Fafchamps suggested (Fafchamps et al., 1998). The non-commodity character of cattle is one of the prerequisites for permitting their movement across the ethnic boundary and entrusting them to Fulbe, outside the realm of formalized exchange. When cattle move into the custody of the herders they do so not primarily as a commodity but as an expression, or token of, mutual friendship. They are also part of a more generalized field of exchange, including herding labour, religious services or the provision of manure for fields.

The herding labour which pastoralists provide is framed as a gift notwithstanding the obligation on the part of the farmers to make a return in some way or another. Cattle in this context are not seen as a commodity and no exchange value is applied to either cattle or the herding labour. That also implies that cattle which are entrusted to Fulbe herders cannot be reclaimed at will, but that the herders acquire certain rights over the animals instead. Guieba's account gave a vivid example of this: the fact that Noël, the townsman, occasionally came to reclaim some of the cattle did not pose a problem. Picking up all of his animals at once, however, clearly violated the unspoken agreement, as Guieba the herder repeatedly mentioned and which he considered the general foundation of mutual relations and trust. For the herders, the animals are a source of social prestige in that having larger herds adds to social standing. Richer and elder Fulbe often even lend some of their cattle to younger kinsfolk who need to impress prospective parents-in-law with their apparently large herds. As a consequence, withdrawing too many or even all cattle affects a herder's means of economic and social production and is regarded as a serious breach of friendship. The implicit obligation that retrieving cattle needs to be gradually stretched out over time is part of the general understanding – the bundle of rights and obligations – enmeshed in the practice of entrustment. It was on these grounds that Ousman, the herder's son, found legitimacy in his act of embezzlement. He justified selling Noël's bull by referring to the labour, which he and his father had invested in the cattle, to refute the charges of cattle theft.

Both the implicit rights to retain cattle over longer periods and occasional practices of embezzlement are in fact essential parts of cattle entrustment between herders and farmers: moving cattle across the ethnic boundary involves costs in either direction and can generally not be done at will and without consequences for the social relations which have been established through the exchange. While under formal economic considerations such costs are considered losses and add to the incalculability of entrustment, the viscosity of transfers and re-transfers on the other hand also ensures loyalty, as it prevents sudden break ups of existing entrustment relations. The rhetoric of embezzlement – practically all farmers have stories to tell of having lost entrusted cattle – also helps to maintain the opacity of the institution: it allows farmers to talk about the practice in negative terms, an important aspect of how the ethnic divide is represented to the public.

Cattle and herding labour are not the only objects exchanged in this sphere. A number of entitlements such as the right to settle and access to pasture are equally framed in terms of voluntary gifts, based on trust and friendship between individuals or historical bonds between collectives. Like other mutual services, the exchange of cattle and herding labour requires acknowledgement but does not imply an immediate and fixed return. The difference from services and resources that are allocated within the kinship economy, is that internal allocations are distributed according to membership of the group: the labour of family members is part of the defined mutual rights and obligations that need to be given and reciprocally returned.

Inter-ethnic ties open new fields of informal relations. The question that imposes itself at this point is why these inter-ethnic ties are not generally formally defined and why most exchange is handled outside the monetized economy. What is the added benefit of moving goods and services onto a distinct sphere of gift exchange? To assume that the practice of cattle entrustment and gift exchange is a residue of past traditions of non-monetary exchange that has merely survived in the age of the market economy would, however tempting, be misleading. The movement of cattle across the ethnic divide is a recent phenomenon, a way of coping with a changing global economic framework. Farmers in Boulgou, as elsewhere in the West African savannah, had only started buying cattle in the 1950s, towards the end of the colonial era (Swinton, 1987; van den Brink, Bromley, and Chavas, 1995). Cattle entrustment therefore had its beginnings at a time when relations between the groups had already undergone profound changes. The absence of money in these transactions could not be taken as an indicator of the pre-colonial, non-monetary past either. Universal money[3] (in the form of cowry shells) was known and used in West Africa over the course of several hundred years before the colonial administration imposed the French franc on the region.[4]

Cattle entrustment also emerged in a context that had long been

---

[3]   Money which is used for payment, assessing and comparing value and storage of wealth.

[4]   C.A. Gregory, 1996: 197. Cowries, in fact, were used as a means of resisting the colonial administration and imposition of the *Franc* until the 1940s (Saul 2004).

accustomed to monetary alternatives of accumulation. Analyzing cattle entrustment, accordingly, cannot draw on 'custom' as an explanation and rather needs to look to the social and economic rationale behind the institution, keeping it separate both from the kinship economy and the capitalist market system alike.

As returns are not fixed in value or in time, gift exchange provides a viable response to seasonal and ecological fluctuations. If adequate returns are not possible in times of harvest shortfalls, small presents suffice to maintain the relation between the exchange partners. Gifts within friendships may also be demanded in times of need (illness, etc.) without the expectation of any return. State and development organizations, however, perceive this practice as highly problematic: as returns are not guaranteed in a calculable and predictable way, resources that are let, lent or given for undetermined periods are considered to be inefficiently used and not providing adequate security for investments. From an administrative point of view, the practice of cattle entrustment and gift exchange must indeed appear problematic: anything that is circulated within the gift economy is at the same time withheld from the formal economy.

It helps at this point, however, to recall that gift exchange is in fact not incalculable at all (Berry, 1993; 2002); exchange partners are aware of their social network and do have means to make their claims explicit, as Guieba and Noël's story illustrates. Martine Guichard recently made a similar observation in Cameroon, pointing to the high risk of exchange between kin. The closer the degree of kinship the higher the risk of never receiving an adequate return at all (Guichard, 2007), as opposed to friendship relations which depend on appropriate counter gifts in the long run. While kinship is a lasting good, friends might be lost.

Moving goods and services across the ethnic boundary as gifts can also involve considerable cost. Embezzlement is a frequent occurrence and the fact that it is constantly talked about, underlines the fact that farmers are aware of the risk when they entrust cattle to herders. As the examples have shown, friendship relations and gift exchange, too, run a permanent risk of delayed or insufficient returns. Still, the risks within the ethnic groups are considered much higher than in inter-ethnic exchange (Guichard, 2007; Schmidt et al., 2007).

Differing again from intra-group relations, individual friendship ties that provide the framework for exchange between the ethnic groups, generally do not extend to other members of the group, such as immediate kin or other members of the same household. This difference may in part be due to the often-secretive character of friendship relations and in part to the fact that friendship is a personal affair and does not require the backing of the kin group, as opposed to economic transactions within the ethnic group (Fortes, 1971). Again, Gluckman's assumption that cross-cutting ties help to minimize conflict shows its limitations. In the case of Boulgou, the cross-cutting ties actually help prevent *intra*-group conflict by moving contested objects across the ethnic boundary but they do not help to contain conflict *between* the ethnic groups – owing partly to the particularistic, i.e. individual character of friendship over kinship.

Outsourcing social control: the herders' dilemma

While the practice of cattle entrustment has its apparent advantages for the Bisa farmers, its benefits for the herders are less obvious. In the case of the farmers, the ethnic divide provides the opacity behind which they can hide their wealth. The practice of cattle entrustment rests in the myth of an impermeable divide and a wall of permanent conflict. For the herders the motivation seems less apparent. The milk the herders get as an immediate compensation and the prestige of bigger herds hardly seems worth the additional effort and the constant hassle over crop damage – even less so as cows only give milk during the rainy season. The effect of boasting of a big herd is also limited in a face-to-face community, where many herders have a good idea of how many cattle any individual actually owns. The benefit of tending farmers' cattle seems to lie in individual friendship relations, which are established through the exchange. These friendship relations cross the ethnic divide and allow herders access to essential resources. Personal ties and the practice of resource sharing allow adequate access to resources for the herders on the other side of the ethnic boundary.

Still, these institutions only partly explain the rigidity and negative connotations that are associated with the ethnic boundary. Economically speaking, there is no extra gain in passing through the opaque screen of ethnic difference when laying overt claims to the resources might turn out to be less cost-intensive. Why then do herders engage in maintaining the ethnic divide?

The practice of accessing resources through cross-cutting ties, of refraining from overt claims to land and of accepting inferior status as landless, obviously bears a number of disadvantages for the Fulbe that reach beyond immediate resource access. As a result, Fulbe communities find themselves in an inferior position with regard to the modern infrastructure supplied by the state and development organizations, and Fulbe children are grossly under-represented in the educational system. At least in part, this is due to the herders' under-representation on the political landscape.

On a different scale, Fulbe are one of the largest groups in the Sudanic belt, as mentioned in the introduction. However, because of their spatial dispersion, they are usually minorities in the local context. In Burkina Faso, they constitute just under 10 per cent of the population. Apart from some of the northern Sahel provinces, Fulbe are a minority vis-à-vis local ethnic groups. In Boulgou, most Fulbe communities deliberately maintain this status by keeping local communities small and would rather break up than increase their numerical weight in a locality.

Why do Fulbe communities apparently accept their landless status, why do most herders seem reluctant to fight for recognition and entitlements, or exert (political, social) pressure on the landed in their communities? The extremely low schooling rate among Fulfulde-speaking youth[5] is not only the consequence of inadequate infrastructure and a biased bureaucracy (Chapter 5); it is also the expression of the reluctance of many Fulbe parents to send their children to school and a tendency to keep a low profile on the local political stage.

Zarga, the settlement near Gando, exemplifies how Fulbe communities perpetuate their low profile in local farming polities. Gando was founded at around the time of the French colonial conquest of the region, about a century ago. The Fulbe settlers had allegedly arrived at around the same point as the neighbouring Bisa farmers and were granted approval to settle by Gando's *naba,* the Bisa village head. The small Fulbe community settled halfway between the new village and Soumagou in the south and close to the small stream that marks the boundary between Gando and neighbouring Poussoaka.

Zarga's location at the fringes of Gando is characteristic of the ambiguity of many Bisa-Fulbe relations. On the one hand, spatial segregation expresses the marginal position of Fulbe in the local community and is indicative of their inferior status on the landed–landless axis. At the same time, Zarga also occupies a strategic location. Halfway between Zarga and Soumagou and on the way to Tenkodogo, most people pass through the Fulbe settlement on their way to and from Gando several times a week and the Fulbe of Zarga have a very good overview of what goes on with their neighbours. It corresponds to the many personal relations that the Fulbe of Zarga and the Bisa of Gando sustain.

Moreover, Zarga is also at the crossroads of Poussoaka and Soumagou,

---

[5]   An estimated tenth of the figure for farming boys; Fulbe daughters practically never make it to school. This is based on my own observations in a number of Fulbe villages and schools and interviews with teachers.

maintaining relations with both localities. A closer look at the map shows that some of the house fields, which most Fulbe keep to cultivate millet, are on the grounds of Soumagou. Some households maintain small fields to complement herding on both sides of the village boundary, 'borrowing' land from farmers in both Gando and Soumagou. Should, at any point, the relations between the Fulbe and their landlords turn bad, the herders will always have the option to activate their links with the farmers from the other village. The waterhole, too, which Zarga used before a new well was dug in the settlement, was located at the stream that marks the border between Gando and Poussoaka. The herders in Zarga diversify rather than intensify their social and economic relations and maintain a permanent exit option – as opposed to claiming permanence in landholding within their local community or 'raising their voice' (Dafinger and Pelican, 2002; Hirschman, 1970).

The community at Zarga has maintained its small size over the generations and never seemed to consist of more than six *wuros*, compounds, at a time; the community always preferred to split up rather than grow in size. As a result, Zarga is the nucleus of a number of other settlements in the bush-lands north of Gando and Poussoaka. One of the reasons for maintaining a small community is the farmers' alleged reluctance to accept more cattle around their fields. This, however, seemed much more part of a rhetorical topos than a realistic account: neither did the *naba* of Gando confirm this view, nor had there been major evidence that Fulbe herders were asked to leave Gando. When two generations ago, a part of the Zarga community split off, the migrants decided to settle in nearby Poussoaka, a mere two and a half kilometres from their old settlement, at about the same distance from the heart of Gando as Zarga. As I described (on page 124f., above) the overall presence of Fulbe in Gando's vicinity neither decreased nor increased with that move, nor was the risk of crop damage through cattle in any way minimized. The move had two main consequences: by breaking away from the community and moving over to Poussoaka, the Fulbe minimized problems of competition within their local group and chose a path of 'conflict avoidance', in Elwert's words (Elwert, 2001: 2544) or the 'exit option' in Hirschman's model (Hirschman, 1970). At the same time, they minimized the weight of the Fulbe within the local agropastoral community by keeping their numbers small. Why, to return to the initial question, do most Fulbe communities maintain and perpetuate their minority status in this way? In referring to the 'collective action theory' of Hechter (1988) and Lichbach (1995) I will investigate how diverging individual and collective claims and interests are negotiated in the absence of an

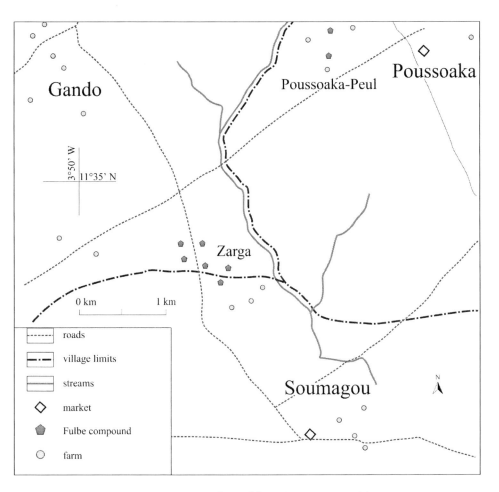

Map 5 Zarga and neighbouring communities

exertive super-ordinate authority. In Chapter 5, I will contrast this with cases of centralized control. The assumption is that an unresolved collective action problem on one side of the ethnic divide (the herders' dilemma) solves the problem of coordinating collective action on the level of the overarching (meta-) society, restraining Fulbe claims to landedness.

On the one hand, maintaining small communities, high mobility and spatial dispersion is a means of avoiding pressure on shared resources and disputes with farmers, as well as preventing retaliatory actions by landholders. Spatial dispersion also helps establish extensive trans-spatial herders' networks, which offer an effective means of risk management, in case local conditions turn bad: disruptions of local political and social relations between farmers and herders had often forced Fulbe households to move. In ecological crises, small communities may quickly react and migrate to other regions, as was the case in the 1970s and 1980s with droughts in the Sahel belt. The Fulbe communities that arrived in Boulgou and other parts of the southern Savannahs of Burkina Faso were small units, of a small number of households. Therefore, for a number of reasons, a politics of smallness has always been in the interest of both the collective and the individual. Members of resident herding communities have a clear economic interest in restricting in-migration and in keeping local groups small. However, limitations on group size have an apparent downside and collide with other interests of the herders, as they also restrict options of mobilizing sufficient local allies. Smallness in relation to the Bisa majority prevents Fulbe communities from making their voice heard in local negotiations over resource claims and rights to land, and reduces their weight in political decisions.

Herders, in other words, are trapped in a fundamental dilemma. Their immediate individual interest lies in securing best access to pasture and waterholes and in maximizing the head of cattle. In trying to achieve this, however, they face two contradictory problems: as a group, herders need to deal with the farming communities, which control all crucial resources. As individuals, they are confronted by their fellow herders who claim access to the very same resources. The strategies in each of the cases are mutually exclusive.

To claim resources vis-à-vis the Bisa farmers, Fulbe herders need to 'raise their voice', to use Hirschman's terminology (ibid.), organize in strong local groups and explicitly formulate their entitlements to the land and its resources. Organizing as a larger group, however, increases the number of internal competitors over these resources. The herders' collective interest of raising their voice and laying claims on landed resources collides with the individuals' interest of trying to exclude competitors.

Following Hobbes, any collective finds itself in a dilemma (Hobbes, 1968 [1651]: 'everybody wants everyone else to voluntarily renounce the use of force. At the same time everyone also wants to unilaterally retain the force option' (Lichbach, 1998: 413). In Hechter's broader understanding: 'that the social order is a common good constantly at risk of subversion by the action of free riders' (Hechter, 1988: 27). This dilemma applies to both the internal organization of the herders and the overarching agropastoral community. Within the herding community, any individual Fulbe herder wants to increase the number of cattle and maximize resource access, while having an interest in seeing to it that as few others as possible will do the same. Between the groups, both farmers and herders aim at maximizing resource use while at the same time trying to prevent the other group from doing so; negotiations are being made even more difficult by the absence of local superordinate authorities or shared political institutions.

One answer to this problem has been suggested within collective action theory: Mark Lichbach, in a work on political resistance, argued that dissidents or critics in a society face a particular type of problem: in order to successfully express dissent in a society, dissidents need to cooperate and form a dissidents' group (Lichbach, 1995: esp 410). In this Lichbach detects a solution to the Hobbesian dilemma: 'the paradox that social order in a state results from disorder in dissidents' groups', 'when the rebel's dilemma is not solved, Hobbes' dilemma will not arise' (ibid.: xii). Turning to Bisa-Fulbe relations, Lichbach's model offers clues as to how the overall social order – resource allocation under the farmer-dominated principle of landedness – is achieved. By limiting the herders' capacity to lay claims to landed resources, they are prevented from claiming landed status and challenging the preponderance of farmers in control over resource allocation. The herders' individual interest of maximizing resource access vis-à-vis their fellow herders collides with their own collective interest in establishing a numerically and politically potent part of their local community.

A change to the overall order, which locates Fulbe herders at the spatial and legal margins of society, could only be brought about by a collective and concerted action of the Fulbe herders: as individuals, herders have little chance of altering the spatial and temporal boundaries. By encroaching on farmers' territory or waterholes, conflicts over resources soon provoke concerted action by the farmers and the herders risk having their cattle killed or hurt, or being precluded from future resource access. Disputes and negotiations over crop damage, which was caused by negligence generally have no lasting impact on social relations. People, nonetheless, tend to be very sensitive towards transgressions of borders that were aimed at challenging the legitimacy of others' claims.

Following Lichbach's model, the Fulbe politics of keeping a low profile in the local political arena and maintaining small communities can be seen as a consequence of lack of internal organization. However, we are left with another problem, to which Lichbach's model offers no immediate solution: the question how resources are allocated and social order is maintained within the dissident group, despite clashes and the internal dilemma. How, in other words, do individual herders manage to solve the problem of restraining their fellow herders from accessing the same resources – while everybody attempts maximization for themselves? Fulbe communities, to recapitulate, have little possibility of denying other herders access to these pastures or preventing them from settling in close proximity: the established communities and the newcomers do not share super-ordinate authorities or other formal institutions that might regulate resource allocation and rights to settle. As ultimate rights over land and individual resources rest with the farmers, legal arguments cannot be brought up against the newcomers. Moreover, groups are generally too large to permit other means of coordinating individual and collective interests, as this might be the case in face-to-face relations.

As useful as the collective action approach proves to be in assessing agropastoral resource allocation, it is of only limited help in determining how strategies and claims are coordinated within the herding community: approaches to collective action problems are principally divided into endogenous and coercive models (Hechter, 1987; Hechter et al.,1982; Lichbach, 1995). None of these, however, seems to fit the case described. Between farmers, resource access is managed coercively through kinship and normative landed relations; between different groups of established, newcomer and transhumant herders, however, these options are not easily available. In the described case, the most practicable solution is found in a triangular relation between two herding groups and the farmers. In the absence of endogenous solutions and super-ordinate authorities, the farmers act as a sanctioning institution. If transhumant or migrant individuals or groups wish to stay in a community for any period, they first need to approach household heads in the resident Fulbe community who will act as intermediaries and help negotiate with the local farming village. This institution of go-betweens is central to almost all economic, social and political relations, within and between ethnic groups in large parts of West Africa (Dafinger, 2001; 2004). Marriages are negotiated through third parties; market exchange is often defined through triangular relations (Dafinger and Pelican, 2006). Petitions and complaints to the local chiefs are often negotiated through a third person.[6] The local herders need to vouch for their fellow herders and ask on their behalf for temporary access to the village land. Herders from established communities often enjoy privileged access to resources; transhumant herders from outside are only allowed to let their cattle on to harvested fields or water holes after the farmers and resident herders. Beeler

---

[6] In the early months of my fieldwork, unaware of the omnipresence and importance of the institution of go-betweens, I brought a pack of smoking tobacco as a gift to an elder, who I had first met a few days before. To my astonishment, he passed on the tobacco to one of his younger brothers and thanked – not me – but my assistant. So I realised that even gifts should not be given directly but are *supposed* to go through a middleman and in public. In contrast to this practice, 'hidden friendships' (Guichard, 2007), such as the exchange across the ethnic divide, are often immediate, which is taken as a further expression of the trust that underlies these relations.

describes a similar practice in neighbouring Mali, where resident Fulbe were granted access to harvested fields up to ten days before transhumant herders were permitted to let their cattle in (Beeler, 2006).

The perennial disputes between the ethnic groups and the staging of conflicts are important parts of this process. Conflicts and the rhetoric of ethnic stereotypes not only serve the negotiation of boundaries and resource access between Bisa and Fulbe, but – in line with Lichbach's model – also help regulate potential conflict within the respective ethnic group. The perennial character of conflicts – even if an individual dispute is settled, the general tension between the groups is largely maintained – contributes to the 'insecurity of on-going conflict' (Georg Elwert's term). Perceived in positive terms, permanent tensions and the resulting insecurity of boundaries also serve as a strategy in coping with ecological variables, as resource sharing can constantly be renegotiated. Moreover, it provides an effective means of controlling intra-group relations. The following example of the different transhumance patterns of resident and newcomer Fulbe illustrates both the ecological and political dimensions of conflict maintenance.

Map 6 (p. 153) visualizes the bipartition of Fulbe settlements: while a number of villages are located within the agriculturally used areas (shaded), a considerable number are also outside the cultivated lands. In Chapter 2, I suggested that this corresponds mainly to the order of arrival: almost all the newcomers, most of whom have come in the wake of the 1970s and 1980s droughts, are located outside the farmed areas. These remote communities enjoy the fact that they are not surrounded by agricultural land and as a consequence hardly ever have disputes with neighbouring farmers. As a result, these herders today own much bigger herds (of up to eighty animals) than the Fulbe who had been resident in the area for generations, where herds of cattle hardly consist of more than 20 to 25 heads. Unaffected by daily conflicts with farmers on the one hand, the newcomers are also excluded from most infrastructural benefits associated with farming villages – including access to modern resources supplied by the development programmes.

Newcomers' settlements share virtually no personal or friendship ties with the farming villages in the wider vicinity. No religious and other services (such as the house oracles or construction works, I described in Chapter 3) are exchanged between farmers and the newcomer herders: they lack most cross-cutting links that shape the relations between farmers and established Fulbe communities. Consequently, none of the newcomer Fulbe guard any of the farmers' cattle. With no farming neighbours, their cattle have no access to harvested fields either.

To add to this, the newcomers are also cut off from the social and economic network of the established herding communities. Although relations between the different groups of settlements – which after all share the same language, the same religious and economic backgrounds – are generally amicable, few links bind the two together. Almost all basic structural elements that connect the resident communities within, are absent between the newcomers and old settlers. Individuals of the two groups almost never intermarry and many other social and economic ties, which are usual among the resident herders, are similarly absent between the groups.

This analysis of seasonal cattle movements illustrates the point. The period of the first annual rains is very important to the herders; after the long months of dry season, they often run out of fodder and the first grass that sprouts after the rains is considered especially nutritious. But rainfall is variable and unpredictable within the region and making the right choice for transhumant movements is crucial for any herder. To balance risks and potentials, herders often exchange animals between their herds. The fusion of herds and the shared use of pasture also establishes and expresses close links between the communities. This exchange, however, is almost exclusively confined within the group of the long established resident Fulbe communities.

Herders in different localities exchange cattle during transhumance to ensure at least some of their herds have access to the best pastures. They also do this to minimize the risks connected with transhumance.[7] There is a greater danger of contracting disease, as cattle from different regions move into the same areas. By spreading cattle over different herds and different regions, herders make sure not all cattle will be affected in the event of an epidemic. Distributing cattle balances the differential quality of pastures: ultimately, some cattle will fare better than others, but all herders will be able to profit at least partially. The exchange of animals between herders is an expression of mutual trust.

Both kinship and friendship relations are crucial assets in decisions over transhumance routes and pastures. Moving one's herds to distant pasture is also often only possible through the mediation of local Fulbe middlemen who will vouch for their transhumant fellow herders in the farming Bisa villages. It is important to consider that resident Fulbe have no means, and no intention, of expressing their discontent about more temporary herders. The decision over whether or not to admit additional Fulbe in a given area is left entirely to the farming landowners. Whether transhumants receive such rights, however,

---

[7] Transhumance generally starts with the first rainfalls around May and lasts until farmers finish harvesting in October.

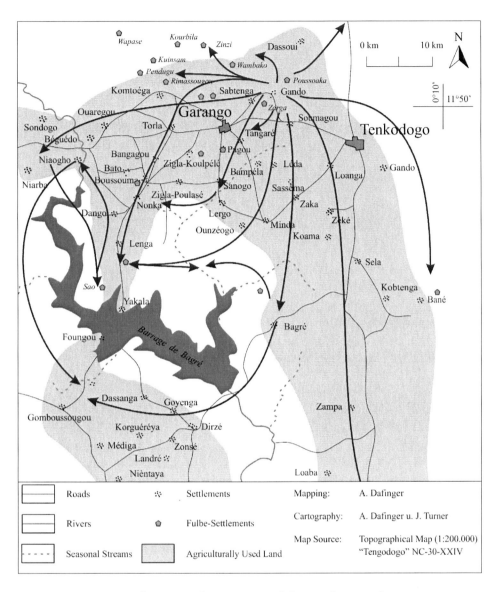

Map 6 Transhumance from Zarga and Poussoaka over four years.

The map shows that most seasonal movements of cattle happen within the cultivated zone and herders from the two villages generally seek permission to graze their cattle in the neighbourhood of villages. (Data based on information given by the herders in Zarga and Poussoaka about their transhumance tracks over three years, complemented by data collected by PDR, taken during transhumance)

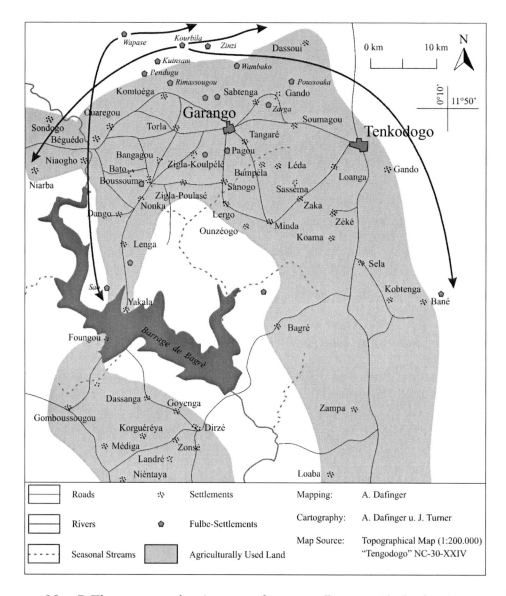

Map 7 The same map, showing routes from two villages outside the farming area.

Kourbila and Wapase were founded only around 40 years ago. The new settlers practise less transhumance, have much fewer options for pasture and almost all of their destinations lie outside the farming area. The newcomers have few ties to the resident Fulbe communities who might negotiate resource access for them vis-à-vis the farmers. (Data based on information data collected by PDR, herders interviewed during transhumance) depends on how much the local Fulbe middlemen are prepared to exploit their cross–cutting ties for their temporary herders.

Making the choice on whether to share pastures with visiting trans-humants is difficult. On one hand, each additional herder is a competitor for existing resources and potentially contributes to the aggravation of existing tensions between herders and local farmers, as the result of crop damage. On the other hand, the same herders may be able to offer pasture the following year in return, if rainfall requires the movement of cattle to other areas.

Map 6 shows the seasonal movement of cattle from two Fulbe villages, Zarga and Poussoaka, over the course of four years. Almost all rainy season pastures are in areas that are considered to be farming territory and arable land. Although not all of these areas are actually under cultivation, they are still part of farming communities and are under the authority of earth priests. Transhumant Fulbe, in most cases, need to seek permission of the landed clans before installing them-selves in the area. The relations between the Zarga- and Poussoaka-Fulbe and those of the receiving herding communities are generally amicable; the high frequency of movement is also an indicator of that.

In the case of the newcomer herders, on the other hand, this looks fundamentally different (Map 7). In interviews, Fulbe herders insisted that resident and newcomer Fulbe are equal in terms of entitlements to pasture and stressed the normative view that Fulbe would welcome any stranger and negotiate on their behalf with the local farmers. The difference in actual movement and resource use patterns, however, suggests otherwise (see Map 7). The transhumance routes from Kour-bila and Wapase, two Fulbe newcomer communities in the bush lands north of Komtoega, reveal that very few seasonal movements took place from these villages at all (over the same three-year time span). Herders tended to keep the cattle in close proximity to the home-steads all year round and the few transhumant pastures were all located outside the farming areas, also avoiding settlements of resident Fulbe. This pattern reveals that links with the farming communities are seen as an asset in intra-ethnic negotiations over resource access, despite but also because of the rhetoric of distrust and ethnic conflict.

The analysis of transhumance eventually enables me to answer the initial question of why Fulbe communities show a tendency to keep a low profile in local politics and largely refrain from making overt claims. Assuming inferior roles (as landless) and maintaining small communi-ties increases the impermeability of the ethnic divide, which is associ-ated with the distinction between landholders and landless. The (potential and real) conflicts associated with the ethnic divide allow resident Fulbe to ward off claims made by competing migrant and transhumant herders. Smallness, too, reduces the number of competitors over one of the most important resources: the cross-cutting ties, individual herder-farmer relations, which allow individual herders to eventually access resources. As in the farmers' case, the concealment of these cross-cutting ties is an essential part of the practice.

Exploiting the ethnic divide

The two cases covered in this chapter help to illustrate the economy of the ethnic boundary from two different angles. The practice of cattle entrustment helps farmers to withdraw cattle from the commodity sphere and conceal them from their own kin. The Fulbe herders concede control of access to farmers and unburden themselves of the task of barring access to fellow Fulbe herders. Analysis of these practices allowed the reassessment of the main tenets of established anthropological conflict theories. In both instances, cross-cutting ties (between Fulbe and Bisa) help avoid conflict within the ethnic group, rather than (as Gluckman's initial model suggested) merely contain inter-group tensions. In the first case, this is achieved by moving commodities behind an ethnic shield and thus withdrawing them as potential objects of dispute from the intra-group sphere. In the second case, cross-cutting ties likewise prevent clashes within the same user-group by shifting responsibility across the ethnic divide. Local Fulbe communities outsource control over resource access to the land-holding farmers and secure their share in the local resources in return for accepting their subaltern position in the landed-landless field. The same actors – local herders and local farmers – over-communicate ethnic difference and conflict in public discourse, while emphasizing locality and friendship (above ethnicity) in the non-public sphere.

At this point, it seems useful to turn back to Georg Elwert's model of the on-going dispute (Elwert, 2001; Elwert et al., 2001). Conflicts, as processes, are embedded in a wider field of social action and any conflict settlement contains, following Elwert, a normative dimension, redefining boundaries and creating security for all future action for all actors. At the same time, on-going conflicts are also a source of insecurity, restricting the actors' range of options. The disputes between farmers and herders in Boulgou allow us to re-assess Elwert's model in a new light. Conflicts, in this case, may indeed be seen as perennial and potentially endless. Even if an individual case is settled, and reaffirms norms and boundaries for the immediate actors (as Elwert predicted), general relationships between Bisa and Fulbe remain conflicted and maintain an atmosphere of insecurity. As we have seen, this insecurity is exploited by specific actors and groups as a means of exerting social control. Wealthier farming household heads build on these tensions to maintain control over household production to the disadvantage of other members of the kin group by moving resources over the ethnic boundary. Resident Fulbe, in their turn, have a vested interest in keeping up ethnic tensions in order to ward off non-local herders, as the previous section on differential transhumance patterns of resident and newcomer Fulbe has illustrated.

The motivation of farmers and herders in building the ethnic divide and in maintaining cross-cutting relations comes from two different directions: farmers attempt to conceal their intra-ethnic ties in order to maintain the invisibility of the entrusted cattle. In the case of the herders, cross-cutting ties are likewise concealed before the 'strangers', the newcomer herders, whom residents seek to exclude from the shared resources. At the same time, however, these contacts are social and economic assets which are traded against access rights. In both cases, the ethnic divide serves as an opaque screen that helps to ward off intra-group competitors.

An ethnicized administration?

In the local arena the ethnic boundary emerges as both a historically rooted categorical divide, as well as a strategic narrative in social and economic relations. The rhetoric of ethnic division, however, is also a reality in the offices of the national administration, which paradoxically both officially disregards ethnicity and engages in de facto ethnic stereotyping in its bureaucratic practice. In the remainder of this chapter, I will look at the practice of ethnicization of administration and show that occasional occurrences of ethnic violence can indeed be related to an increasing ethnic component in administration. There will be no ground, however, to assume that ethnicization is a consequence of the over-representation of one ethnic group in the bureaucratic machine, as suggested by other authors. Instead, we witness the formation of a new quasi-ethnic group: an emerging middle class of bureaucrats and administrators.

IMPORTANT VISITORS

Garango, like many other communities in Burkina Faso, maintains a 'jumelage', a partnership with other towns in Europe. These partnerships, or 'twin relations', are an important economic factor and a major form of development cooperation, often providing relatively non-bureaucratic and small-scale assistance. On the Burkinabe side, these links are of major importance and constitute a significant resource, several hundred of them exist between small towns in Burkina and abroad, mostly Europe. Competition over these resources is equally as fierce as over any other government or development funds. Garango has two European partner towns; one of them is a small and quaint German town, Ladenburg, in the foothills of the Black Forest.

The relations between the communities are managed by committees on either side, both working 'in the spirit of understanding, mutual respect and friendship between the peoples' (as a 1983 brochure reads) and in practice taking on the more mundane role of semi-official development cooperation. Funds are raised in Germany and projects which apply for funding under the partnership programme are evaluated and managed by the local committees. The committees also arrange the annual visits of the representatives of the project and members of the city council. Despite the interest of many of the Ladenburgers, information on Garango and Burkina Faso as a whole is difficult to obtain for their German counterparts. Local politics and social conditions reach the German partners (if at all) mostly filtered through the channels of official representatives of the Garango township. Details of internal politics hardly ever reach the German side.

So the annual visits are a major source of information and a chance for many of the active members to gain individual insights on the progress of some of the projects that are supported by the partnership and of those sites where a new school or a new dam ought to be built. Obviously, the 'comité de jumelage' in Garango and its members are powerful brokers between local communities in the Garango region and their German counterparts.

A few years ago, shortly after Christmas, I took part in an official opening of a school building in Koumbouré, a small village a 30-minute drive south of Garango. The school had already been in operation, but the official opening was going to take place in the presence of the guests from Ladenburg, which had made a major contribution to the building. The Koumbouré school building had been neatly decorated and as always on such occasions, the windows and doors were newly painted and a canopy had been set up to provide shade for the delegation. Some twenty people were on the visitors list, half from Germany, and half from Garango. Such a big group posed quite a logistical challenge in itself. At least five cars were needed to bring in the visitors. At this time not one car was registered in Garango.[8]

---

[8] In the first 20 years of its existence, the Ladenburg cooperation contributed to the building of 14 schools, assisted the electrification of the local infirmary and contributed substantially to the dam

Next to the canopy, a choir of school children waited to welcome the guests, alongside a number of local dignitaries, all of them impressively dressed. The official appearance clearly underlined the outstanding importance that the local council gave to the visit of the delegation; to me it had more resemblance to a state visit than to a school opening. The sirens, at least, clearly drew more people on to the dirt roads than they managed to keep away. The opening took its usual unspectacular course for over two hours, until the convoy departed to take the group back to Garango. When I was talking to members of the delegation after their return later that day (which took place under the same pomp and circumstance) I could not help pointing to what I felt was a dramatically overstaged event. I learnt that the German committee representatives apparently were told that the police escort was deemed necessary due to the 'generally tense and dangerous situation because of the Peul' – in other words: the escort was necessary to protect against assaults by the Fulbe. I was flabbergasted – I had not heard of any violent attack or racially or ethnically motivated incident over the past decade. The German delegation did not seem overly worried either, most never get a chance to visit a Fulbe settlement anyway, but they saw no reason to doubt the expertise of their local counterparts. The local organizing committee is an ethnically homogeneous body, largely composed of members of Garango's chiefly clan and favours infra-structural projects immediately related to either urban or agriculturally related projects. Accordingly, the Garango-Ladenburg cooperation did not fund projects that were immediately related to pastoralism or involved any Fulbe settlement (as of 2006). Having to be protected against Fulbe during their visit, probably has not raised the chances that they might do so in the near future.

So, what had really happened? Did the organizing committee, the prefect, the local chief of police conjure up a conspiracy to discredit their entire pastoral population as potential criminals – by pretending there was actually a threat of roadside attack? This seemed rather far-fetched, fierce as the competition over development and partnership resources may undoubtedly have been. The Fulbe account for a mere 10 per cent of the population and might not be in for a significant share of the funds in the first place. The local organizing committee is certainly already powerful enough to filter out project proposals and to control which villages their European counterparts will see during their stay (which is to the largest extent filled with dance perform-ances, hour-long speeches and official receptions).

(cont) that serves as a perennial water reservoir. The work of the partnership should hence not be underestimated. I also think that, despite some critical undertones in my account, the partnership has led to significant improvements in the local infrastructure.

In short, no one could have seriously requested a police patrol to protect them against a Fulbe attack. The escort was, as in so many similar cases, a mere expression of the highly official and very important character of the excursion, and local authorities would at any time be prepared to justify this in terms of the general security of the visitors, including minor road accidents. However, it offered a frame for *several* narratives and when asked, the Fulbe assault version seemed one very viable option. The committee held a quasi-monopoly in defining the image of 'the local', especially as the delegates were unlikely to get in touch with the herding population anyway. What the committee actually did by organizing the police escort and other events was to express the committee's capacity as brokers between the local and the world of the visiting delegation. By demonstrating that the committee is working with local state authorities, and that it can draw on the support of police and the local prefect, it aligns itself on the right side of order, law and civilized process and makes itself a viable and equitable counterpart of the Ladenburg council. The committee demonstrates its capacity to take care and control of the visitors, at the same manages to obfuscate other 'minor' issues, such as rumours of embezzlement, 'slow progress' of some of the projects, etc. The police patrol is an attempt to manifest an administrative culture, a 'culture de fonctionnaires', comprising committee, police and bureaucracy on the Burkinabe side along with the German delegation. The escort was at no point specifically directed against a certain part of the population; but Fulbe were, nonetheless of all, paradigmatic of the ethnic other, the antipode of a perceived global culture of 'fonctionnaires' and working bureaucracy.

Bureaucracy and the ethnic question

The case of the Ladenburg delegation is indicative of a more general pattern: it offers an example of how Fulbe communities are often marginalized in administrative practice and underprivileged in access to infrastructural resources.

Between 30 and 35 per cent of children in farmers' villages (i.e. Bisa and Mossi) attend local primary schools in rural areas[9] compared to an estimated 3 per cent of Fulbe children.[10] This can in part be ascribed to a biased administration or organizations such as the 'jumelage',

---

[9] (SAGEDECOM 2000a) In urbanized zones these numbers are significantly higher: e.g., 71% for Garango, according to the same source.

[10] This is based on my own observations and investigations in 18 Fulbe villages. It does not include Tenkodogo and Garango, where rates are expected to be higher.

which privilege farmers' villages over Fulbe communities. At the same time, however, most Fulbe families seem rather reluctant to send their children to mixed schools where, as many parents fear, farmers' children might have a 'bad influence' on their kids and do not want their sons or daughters to attend school with non-Muslim children.[11] For many state and NGO officials the Fulbe's hesitancy and reluctance has become a stereotypical ascription and part of justification rhetoric, when conversations turn to uneven distribution of infrastructural resources. Francis Jambeedo's comment in Chapter 3 on the 'nomads who have generally nothing to do with education' points in this direction.

The underprivileged access of Fulbe to development funds, schools, modern wells, etc., is owed to both endogenous and external factors. On the one hand, there is the inclination of many Fulbe communities to maintain a low profile and, on the other hand, a biased administration with a preference for Bisa, Mossi, or in more general terms, farmers' meta-ethnicity affairs. The previous section has described the endogenous dimension (of 'keeping a low profile') as a result of the herders' dilemma and the deliberate politics of small communities.

A major external factor of uneven resource access (and the resulting conflicts over the respective shares) has already been identified in the introductory episode: administration and bureaucracy often appear to have an explicit ethnic taint. Other authors have made similar observations (Zenner, 1996: 14). Wimmer and Brubaker build their argument on the assumption that ethnicized bureaucracies are a prerequisite for ethnically framed conflicts (Wimmer, 1995; 2004). The examples in this chapter, however, support these models only to a certain point: ethnicized bureaucracies are an important dimension to ethnically framed tensions in all of the cases; their ethnic bias, however, cannot necessarily be explained through an over-representation of specific groups.

The fact that the local committee in Garango was ethnically rather homogeneous certainly corresponds to Wimmer's notion of an ethnicized bureaucracy. Still, in order to take account of the complexity of cases and make the model of ethnicized bureaucracies more widely applicable, Brubaker and Wimmer's understanding of ethnicized bureaucracies appears too simplistic in the given case. The implicitly ethnic component of the administration cannot be explained in terms of recruitment policy alone. In the twin towns' example, an ethnic bias (Fulbe vs. Bisa, in this case) might have been an initial criterion in the creation and composition of the committee. In its present form,

---

[11] Or better: only 'sons'. The schooling rate of Fulbe girls is virtually zero. I have not come across a single Fulbe girl in the villages who attended school.

however, ethnicity is rather built around a perceived commonality in terms of language (French as opposed to Bisa and Fulfulde), access to and use of the same infrastructural and administrative resources, a shared ideology of modernization and the persuasion to be spearheading this development.

In the following sections I will show that the ethnicization of bureaucracy is in fact a more complex process, that does not depend on the over (or under-) representation of some ethnic groups in key administrative positions, but rather on a genuine identity and modernism ideology that prevails in bureaucratic institutions and administration. Political organization of the farming communities is often closer and more compatible with the state's territorial system of political rule. The legibility' of the social and economic landscape is a crucial factor in administration (Scott, 1998).

Accordingly, the following examples will illustrate the complexity of ethnicization and show some of the refractions of an ethnically perceived administration. The first case will engage with the argument of over-representation of ethnic groups in the administrative body and show how the ethnic affiliation of office holders plays a part in the political and juridical administrative process. It will show that ethnicization is much more a way of perceiving bureaucracy by local groups than based on factual evidence. As the local political and economic organization of some groups (notably farmers) is seen as closer to the state than others, bureaucracy can produce decisions in favour of specific ethnic groups – regardless of the ethnic background of office holders. Administrative processes are based on specific principles such as territorial organization (ibid.) which are much closer to the political and social organization of farmers, as opposed to the much more non-territorial resource management of cattle herders.

Prefectures and communes (such as Garango or Tenkodogo) are the lowest units of national administration and administered by prefects (13 in Boulgou), which are appointed by the central administration. As a result of Burkina Faso's explicitly non-ethnic policy, no data and no ethnic affiliation of public servants is recorded. It is nonetheless safe to assume that Mossi, the country's largest ethnic group, constitute the biggest block within the administrative body (Hagberg, 2004: 195–218). At the other end of the scale, few prefects are native Fulfulde speakers. It is, however, difficult to assess whether any of these groups are actually over- or under-represented in relation to the average population.[12] Prefects exert a limited degree of judicial power and are therefore the first point of call and the first level of jurisdiction in all

---

[12] Based on linguistic data, Mossi (morephones) account for about 50% of the country's population. In comparison, Fulbe constitute ca 10%, Bisa 5% of all Burkinabe.

disputes that find no immediate solution on the local level and are taken before the national authorities. A large part of conflicts that end up in the prefect's office in the Savannah provinces are ethnically framed; it is no surprise that the ethnic identity of the prefect is taken into consideration by many of the contestants. For the prefects, this is a Catch 22; being non-Fulbe, they are accused of having a bias towards the farmers' interests. If they satisfied the Fulbe herders' claims they would be considered as disloyal towards their ethnically closer farmers; a prefect of Fulbe origin on the other hand is likely to be trapped in an inverse accusation. At any rate a prefect's respective ethnic affiliation will be made an issue by either conflicting party.

The consequences are the on-going allegations of nepotism and corruption, which turn any reference to the national authorities into a threat. Farmers are aware that costs, especially for the herders, may rise exponentially once a case is brought before the authorities and they use this as a deliberate threat to maximize their compensation claims.

The haggling over compensation in Kourbila and the allegation of corruption illustrated the one-sided view of one of the litigation parties, a group of herders, and does not consider the legal grounding of the case.

Whether the allegations of corruption are true or not, however, seems almost irrelevant at this point. What is relevant in this context is the discourse of corruption and perceived uncertainty. In the present case, both parties actually lost but the costs incurred for the herders were disproportionately high. The farmer received 22.000 CFA less than originally offered; the herder ended paying almost 60.000 CFA more than claimed by the farmer.

Stories like this abound and are mostly variations of the same themes: exaggerated claims by farmers, allegations of corruption and exorbitant fines. In villages where corruption appeared to be less of a problem, the general bias of the prefect for farmers was often stressed. Fulbe herders repeatedly expressed a profound feeling of injustice, as in any conflict the herders are likely to pay irrespective of being objectively guilty – largely through the obligation to pay the fee for the pound – whereas the farmers, even if convicted of hurting or killing cattle, get away with paying only the compensation costs. The system of retaining cattle in the pounds creates a disadvantage for the herders. One herder ironically asked if 'they ever lock away the Bisa?' This practice affects all negotiations, including those that are resolved below the level of administration. Farmers, aware of the exponential costs of a convocation to the herders, use this as a means to exert pressure in negotiations over crop damage. As in the Kourbila case, herders stressed that compensation paid for crop damage tended to be higher and herders were likely to pay more than the assumed damage, knowing that the secondary costs involved in an official case may far exceed the compensations costs.

Fulbe herders especially tend to perceive administration as ethnically tainted – regardless of the respective prefect's ethnic affiliation. However, ethnicization of administration is only partly the result of overrepresentation of members of a specific ethnic or meta–ethnic group, based on similarities of economic and political organization. It is rather the dominance of members of a distinct cultural system (the 'culture des fonctionnaires'), which is defined through a shared ideology of modernism. Ethnicity mainly serves as the rhetorical frame for the local discourse over perceived injustice. This rhetoric eventually turns into a problem on a different level of social organization, when disadvantaged groups organize in order to gain recognition and claim resources vis-à-vis the state on a national level. What is perceived as ethnic exclusion on the local level must be reframed in the context of (non-ethnic) political participation and the discourse over civil society (see below for a discussion on this point.)

Another example of an ethnically relevant outcome of administrative policy is Burkina Faso's official topographic maps. Trying to determine the location of Fulbe settlements in my research, I realized that only two Fulbe settlements were distinguishable on the official map. Based on my own experience I knew that there were a lot more local Fulbe communities. Eventually and through the aid and information of the local Fulbe population I was able to subsequently pin down a total of 18 Fulbe settlements in an area of 30 by 40 km in the central north of the province. While most of the herders' hamlets and compounds were actually shown on the map as populated places, almost all of them either lacked proper names or were shown as parts ('quartiers'[13]) of neighbouring Bisa-villages (e.g., 'Pagou-Peul').

A reason for this was given by a technical director of the National Geographic Institute. Localities on maps are named first following official lists of towns and villages, which are published and updated by the ministry of the interior (MATS). These lists are the basis for all administrative decisions at provincial and departmental levels. Places that are not included in these lists (i.e. localities that do not hold the status of an official 'village administratif', but are considered parts of

---

[13] I will adopt the official (French) term 'quartier'. Administration does not recognise any vernacular terminology, as the use of French is obligatory when dealing with the bureaucracy. Referring to a place as either *ko* (Bisa) and *wuro* (Fulfulde) or 'quartier' thus has completely different connotations.

neighbouring villages) are then added to the maps on the grounds of local enquiries. IGB agents will ask locally for such quarters in the villages. This typically means inquiring from the 'chef de village' and some of the village headmen. The general tendency, on behalf of the resident farmers, to deny any cattle-herder settlement the status of a 'quartier' and simply consider it as part of the bush-land thus finds its way into the official cartographic data. When questioned, the responsible authorities clearly see this point, but lack, in their own words, any better option.

Assigning a name to a locality ('quartier' or village) is also largely considered a local affair. The name of a locality is noted by prospectors in the place itself and in two more neighbouring settlements. In case of dissent, the more frequent name is then officially registered. This makes it possible that many Fulbe settlements simply fall through the grid. Although many Fulbe settlements carry their own (Fulfulde) name, they are often merely referred to as 'the Fulbe-camp of Bisa-village (e.g.) Pagou' by the neighbouring Bisa population, which leads to the effect that Fulbe villages will be considered as Komtoega-Peul, Garango-Peul, etc., despite their inhabitants referring to them differently. As a result, Fulbe themselves often use the Bisa name for their settlements in cross-cultural communication, especially when dealing with the authorities.

The cartographic misrepresentation is only the most eye-catching. Recognition by other administrative institutions is similarly important in accessing other infrastructural resources. Development organizations draw on data supplied by the Geographic Institute and other planning authorities, such as the Ministry for Agriculture and Cattle Husbandry and the MATS, the (Ministry for Territorial Administration and Security – the home secretary). The name indicates one of the essential characteristics of MATS' work: the state defines itself as a territorial unit and builds on principles of territorial organization. A pivotal MATS planning instrument is the 'inventory of settlements', a list of villages that are recognized as administrative units by all governmental, provincial and departmental authorities. The inventory itself also serves as one of the sources for the IGB, the above geographic institute. These official villages ('villages administratifs') are the lowest and smallest unit in national administration. The recent restructuring of the national health sector and the enforcement of the 1996 land reform both helped increase the importance of those local administrative units considerably. The question of what may be called a village or not, which community can thus claim to be part of the administrative structure or not and where to set the territorial and political boundaries of such villages is of crucial importance: being a 'village

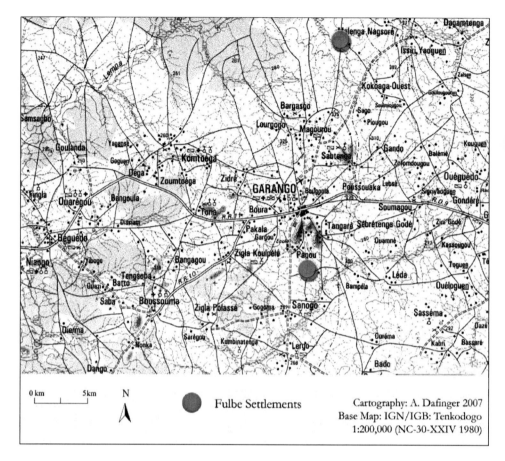

Map 8 Two Fulbe settlements on a map of Northwestern Boulgou.
(Institut Géographique National, 1980: NC–30-XXIV)

administratif' opens doors to funds and projects.

On the local level this plays out in a 'politics of size': many local communities attempt to achieve village status (as 'village administratif'), rather than being considered a 'quartier' of a neighbouring community because of the entitlements that come with being an independent unit. Many modern resources are tied to the 'village' status (as in the case of PIHVES, see below). As a consequence, settlements that are considered 'quartier' have a strong interest in becoming their own villages.

On one hand, land reform was meant to underline that all land in post-colonial Burkina Faso is officially state property. This concept, however, had not been enforced and had not affected the local practice of land distribution until recently. 'The fact that it's not their land, as a one official put it, 'has never entered the heads of those locals'. On

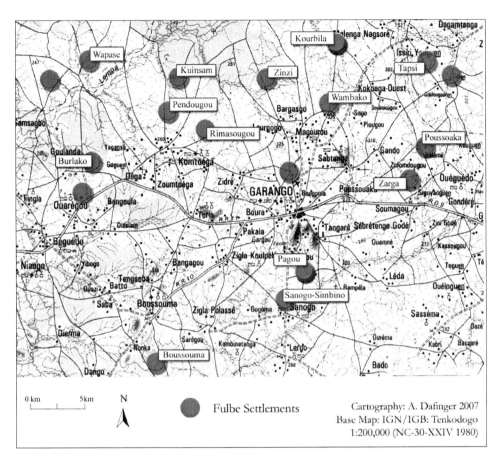

Map 9 The same map, with approximate locations of Fulbe settlements

the other hand, it has now become possible to officially assign land for individual use. Individuals, corporate groups and families, as well as village communities, may obtain titles for the permanent use of tracts of land. Village communities are assigned a privileged status in the allotment of land: major parts of village territory will be allocated to members of the autochthonous community, while only peripheral land will thereafter be assigned to other groups or individuals. This is meant to put local land rights on a firm and undisputable basis and to homogenize land rights nationwide. Therefore the question of who is rightfully to be considered a villager, autochthonous or migrant, gains considerable legal importance.

The official classification that defines a village gives general preconditions necessary to acquire the status of a village, i.e. a minimum number of inhabitants (200 individuals, or 20 families) and a minimum distance between two villages (3kms).[14] According to an official at the ministry, the physical distance was introduced to minimize, if not avoid, inter-village conflicts over territory and especially arable land – an argument that sounds only partly convincing, as the conflict potential as such is not reduced but deferred from an inter-village to an intra-village level. A corollary of this regulation is that it prevents existing villages from splitting up and reduces the overall number of villages. This was used in the past – and in some cases apparently still works – as a strategy to access resources; if one well is built per village, then being counted as two villages – instead of one with two 'quartiers' – turns out to be more profitable for the local population.

The most important prerequisite, however, is not part of the official act. In order to attain the status of a 'village administratif', a request must be made by the local (i.e. the prospective village-) community. The first and basic step in this process towards administrative recognition thus consists of a non-democratic decision process: village headmen are – almost by definition – recruited from the dominant social group (clan); village councils therefore tend to reflect the dominant socio-political order of the locality. Farmer-dominated councils may lay official claims to uncultivated bush-land as the herders living there often will have no spokesman to speak on their behalf. Since every locality that wishes to attain the status of a 'village administratif' is already part of a neighbouring village, the agreement of this village or its village council is necessary. The composition of the council which decides on the application and the administration of the future village entirely depends on local criteria. In almost all villages I visited, Fulbe occupying their own 'quartiers' (as well as any other peripheral groups) were not represented in those councils.

One more prerequisite for the creation of a 'village administratif' is not considered in the decree: that is its 'territorial dimension and the rightfulness of its land claims.' Every 'village administratif' needs to be identified through a contiguous area of land, i.e., it must occupy a definable and unique geographical area. The assessment of these issues is carried out by the local prefect, who verifies the rightfulness of the land claims, i.e., ensures that there are no other claims to the same tract of land 'in order to secure peace and prevent any uprising,' as an official characterized administrative procedures. The full process of assigning the status of a 'village administratif' to a locality thus is a combination of various national, administrative and local decision making processes. What ends with the formal recognition by the administrative body has its roots in local land rights and definitions of

---

[14] Décret présidentielle (*Décret* N° 99–3985/PRES/PM/MATS)

the landscape, which are determined almost exclusively by the local farming elite.

Administrative politics is clearly based on formal criteria that are decisively not ethnic. Nonetheless, for some ethnic groups it is easier than for others to comply with the majority of these regulations. Administrative politics is therefore often perceived as explicitly ethnic and seen as favouring specific (here: the farmers') ethnic groups.

The fact that state and NGO administrations are widely perceived by local groups as ethnically biased is in part based on factual experience and in part the consequence of a local discourse, which frames political and economic differences primarily in ethnic terms. To a considerable degree this ethnic bias is also vested in the bureaucratic machine itself.

A generally accepted line of argument concludes that once an ethnic group dominates the bureaucracy, officeholders will privilege members of their own ethnic group in filling up other administrative positions (Wimmer, 1995). However, as I suggested in Chapter 4, this approach is not particularly helpful in the given context. Although criteria of ethnicity may reinforce the boundaries and prevent members of other ethnic groups from competing over administrative resources, it is also true that ethnic exclusivity increases the competition within the privileged group. Leaving aside models that build on primordial sentiments and common descent, the argument of shared ethnicity does not carry far and neither does related criteria of a shared language account for the recruitment policy, as functionaries use their own language (official French) and largely consider the use of the vernacular backward.

Looking back at the examples given in the previous chapters, bureaucracy does indeed show ethnic components and is in many ways perceived as distinctly ethnic – largely by the marginalized population, which for several reasons finds itself precluded from major state resources.

While it would be hard to maintain that bureaucratic personnel – the functionaries – constitute an ethnic group as such, they involuntarily draw on ethnic criteria in distinguishing themselves from other parts of society: ethnic ascriptions are part of the toolbox available to most actors in this field. However, as recruitment into this circle is not based on ethnic criteria, the reasons for a distinct culture of functionaries and the quasi-ethnic identity of the administrative complex need to be sought elsewhere. The following paragraphs will look into some of the processes that determine recruitment into the bureaucracy. Having rejected the idea that ethnicity is a constitutive factor in the formation of the new administrative middle classes, the argument focuses on questions of class, language and education.

First, economic and class-oriented criteria help the members of the administration set themselves apart from the majority of the population. Being part of a formal economic system with fixed salaries, they are anxious to draw a line between themselves and their home communities. Most functionaries avoid returning to their home communities to evade the redistributive networks. Middle-class representatives complain about a general incapacity of 'the villagers' to understand the different economic and social contexts of their urban kin; less overtly, fears of witchcraft contribute to the reluctance of urban professionals to visit their relatives (see also Geschiere and Nyamnjoh, 1998). Officials avoid rather than build cross-cutting ties between administration and rural home communities, which are built around networks of solidarity and formal reciprocity (Elwert, 1980). This observation offers an alternative to constructivist approaches to ethnicity (see Chapter 4) that work on the assumption that the congruence of ethnic boundaries and class differences is a major factor in politicizing ethnicity (Hechter, 1974; Wimmer, 2004). In this case, the denial of ethnic ties leads to a politicization of ethnic groups which need to define themselves in opposition to the state bureaucracy and compete over the same political resources.

A second means of distinction is the exclusiveness of language. Burkina Faso's official language, French, is obligatory throughout administration and all officials exclusively communicate in French. While this goes almost without noticing in the administrative centres like the country's capital, in the more rural areas this is a sign of distinction of 'la culture des fonctionnaires', which sets them apart from the 'uncivilized' peasants who merely communicate in the vernacular, often employing middlemen when dealing with the administration. French helps this new middle class attach itself to the mundane elites of the capital and the international world of the development jet-set (like the Ladenburgers). As officials are transferred to new assignments every two to three years, many do not adapt to local languages and live in local francophone bubbles, adopting a trans-spatial identity.

French is also the only language used in schools, thus excluding large groups of local children from formal education, as most of these children have no prior knowledge of French: access to formal education is facilitated for children of the administrative middle class simply for reasons of language. Children of farmers' households are much less likely to attend school: the average schooling rate lies at around 30 per cent nationwide. For Fulbe children, access to education is even more precarious. As mentioned before, only about 3 per cent of the local Fulbe children in Boulgou were sent to school, with girls faring even worse than the boys. The reasons for this are manifold: Fulbe communities often do not achieve the critical mass required for schools. Attending schools in farming villages often is impracticable because of distances, especially in the newly founded settlements in the northern fringes. In the other cases, Fulbe fathers often expressed uneasiness at sending their children to schools dominated by farmer children and which have a heterogeneous religious background. Young Fulbe boys are also integrated into the household economy and work as herders from an early age onward, increasing the costs of sending these boys to school.

What remains is a visible hierarchy in terms of access to formal education: making it standard for children of administrative middle-class families, it is fairly accessible to farmers, while Fulbe children and especially girls, hardly ever enjoy primary school. The criteria for exclusion on a formal level are explicitly non-ethnic; exclusion from meeting these standards, however, is the result of local practice that segregates social groups based on ethnic criteria.

Ethnicity, to sum up this section, is not constitutive of the administrative complex. With its clearly discernible economic and social identity, however, the new administrative middle class does not act in a vacuum either and, in distinguishing itself from the local communities, positions itself as a quasi-ethnic group. It constitutes a missing link between the national and international modernization discourse and local persuasions of a hierarchy of territorial farmers and landless groups, based on degrees of being 'civilized' or 'advanced'. Non-ethnic in its set-up, administration and the development machine are perceived as ethnically biased from a local point of view. The congruence of politically defined and ethnically generated social groups, however, is to a considerable extent produced in the local arena.

NGOs AT WORK

Development projects, such as PDR, employ close to a hundred temporary and many permanent staff and have become a significant resource as a workplace for the educated youth. Jobs as 'animateurs' (campaign agents) are prestigious and much sought after by the graduates of the secondary schools in and around Tenkodogo. Working as an agent or campaign officer does not require much additional training and salaries in this sector are significantly higher than those of state employees in comparable positions: an 18-year-old high school graduate earns up to twice a teacher's salary.[15] In addition, they keep

---

[15] In 2008, entry level teachers earned around 50.000 CFA/month (~75€), the 'animateurs' made up to 100.000 CFA, even though on temporary positions.

'mobylettes' (small motor scooters) for the duration of their employment, a symbol of professional achievement that is hard to overesti-
mate.

The task of these agents is to pay day visits to villages where the
organization runs projects, to carry out surveys and to report back to
the headquarters. Others organize information campaigns to instruct
the rural population about the land reform programmes, offer sanitary
education or workshops on health-related issues. Although far from
holding executive positions, many of these young professionals quickly
develop all the symptoms of middle class-oriented urban elites. As
urban dwellers, educated, mobile and French-speaking, many of them
see it as a sacrifice to 'go out in the bush' and be talking to villagers.[16]
Although these agents are in many ways as much a target group of
the information campaigns they run, many perceive their job merely
as conveying prefabricated information and many of them show little
ambition to acquire further background knowledge of their projects'
agenda.[17]

When these 'animateurs' set out to visit a local community for a
briefing session, they will generally announce their visit a couple of
days in advance and will inform members of the community about the
purpose of their visit. When, on one occasion, I was told that one such
group was about to organize a session in one of the Fulbe settlements
north of Garango, I invited myself to take part in the gathering. The
briefing was intended to instruct the herders on the consequences of
the new amendment to the RAF, the territorial restructuring
programme, and offer an update on the extension of the existing
pastoral zones.

The day began as usual, everyone minding his or her business
around the house. The younger men were gathering their animals and
taking off for their day's pasture. As the time of the announced gathering drew closer, however, the older men, too, started to excuse themselves one by one – heading for the bush near Gando or to pursue
some other unspecified business. By the time the agents eventually
arrived at the compound, the place was half deserted and I found
myself left in the company of one older man and a small group of
women who were busy spinning cotton. Women generally take no

---

[16] Likewise, it is very difficult to motivate university students in Ouagadougou to carry out fieldwork in the rural areas. These young people, after all, study sociology, archaeology, etc, to escape the
rural backwardness.

[17] One of the campaigns meant to raise the awareness of sexually transmitted diseases and promote
the use of contraceptives. In private conversations, however, a number of the campaigners readily
admitted that they did not use condoms themselves. I found that the same was true for the
campaign on land right issues, where only few campaign workers had further reaching interest in
the implications of the 'lotissement'.

role in negotiating access rights or dealing with the administration. So the fact that virtually all the men had left was a clear sign of disrespect for, and lack of interest in, the upcoming briefing.

I knew from earlier conversations with some of the agents that this was a frequent and all too common situation that the development agents had become rather used to. To them, the indifference of the male Fulbe largely confirmed their prejudices; in their eyes, the Fulbe herders never showed any interest in political affairs, not even in questions that immediately related to their livelihood, such as the land reform programme and I was myself not surprised to see the apparent lack of interest. Meeting the agents, however, I was astonished to find that the group not only greeted us in Moré – but continued to use Moré throughout their session: none of the three visitors was Fulbe or spoke Fulfulde. This was later confirmed when I found that out of some 50 'animateurs' not one had knowledge of Fulfulde.[18] It was thought unnecessary to set up training in Fulfulde, as essentially all Fulbe spoke at least one other language – Moré in the eastern and Bisa in the western part – and that they could easily communicate with the 'animateurs' in those languages. Accordingly, the language question was not put forward as an excuse by the men who had not attended the meeting. As I caught up with some of them later that day, they acknowledged their lack of interest, stating that whatever they were supposed to hear would have no relevance to their situation in any case; anything to do with land was the business of farmers, and they, the Fulbe, did not own and were not going to own land.

The agents as well as planners in the project have no explicit intention of barring Fulbe from information and resources. Neither would most officials have vested interests in privileging farming communities because of personal ties; most, as argued before, attempt to distinguish themselves from their home communities, as the example of the Tenkodogo police had illustrated. Many officials, nonetheless, are often profoundly convinced that Fulbe are less receptive to modernization efforts and that investments in farming communities are in general more promising. By not connecting with the herding population and not actively hiring Fulbe employees, the stereotypical indifference of the herders, however, turns out to be a self-fulfilling prophecy.

One of the major developmental organizations in the region is PIHVES. It was established in 1994 with the almost exclusive aim of constructing wells and improving access to safe water in the region.

---

[18] A large number of people in Burkina Faso – if not most – are multilingual; most Bisa have a passable knowledge of Moré and often Hausa. Fulbe, almost as a rule speak Bisa and Moré. Very few Bisa, however, speak or understand Fulfulde.

It is run under the administration of the Ministère de l'environ-nement et de l'eau (MEE) and almost entirely financed through European development cooperation. PIHVES' philosophy is based on a participatory approach, i.e. on the participation of the popula-tion in decision-making and in the maintenance and management of projects. The plan was to construct 800 wells in addition to around 300 to 500 existing wells and was successfully accomplished in 2004.[19]

The construction of a new well requires the founding of a 'comité de gestion', a maintenance-committee to be elected by the village council. As these committees also play an active part in deciding the location of the new well, the question of who is represented in the village councils is most important. Here again, the village council will supply the organization's agents with a list of the village's 'quartiers'. As with the administration, only a few of the Fulbe settlements will be considered proper 'quartiers', since most are merely regarded as camps in the bush.

In order to further counterbalance potential social bias, PIHVES has set up a second, in its own terms 'objective' parameter and requires localities to be of a minimum size. This is meant to prevent sham-divisions, made to increase the number of wells in a given locality. As a side effect, this reifies existing spatial entities and affirms the domi-nance of the resident farming population. Peripheral or disadvantaged groups would encourage such fission processes in order to gain easier access to modern resources.

This 'objective parameter' requires a minimum of 300 inhabitants (significantly more than the 200 required for a 'village administratif'). The 18 Fulbe villages I documented all had less than 300 inhabitants (mostly below 200), none of them reaching the required minimum for a PDR project. While it is certainly not the intention of projects like PIHVES to systematically exclude parts of the population by setting up those parameters, it nonetheless coincides with a particu-larity of many development organizations. Working with and supporting local authorities like village headmen and village councils is a fair trade off between radically participatory approaches and the need for sustainability: 'An ideal village to work with is ethnically homogenous, has a strong internal coherence often related to intact village hierarchies and maintains friendly relationships with neigh-bouring villages' as a GTZ report put it (GTZ, 1997: 14). It seems reasonable from the point of view of these organizations to prevent separatist movements from financing projects in tiny settlements that

---

[19] C. N. d. PLAN, 1991, p. 36.

will be in constant quarrel with their new neighbours. The result, however, is that what is considered a participatory approach on paper in fact turns out to reflect and reinforce the local system of rule based on the predominance of the dominant clan.

Larger and in many respects more important than PIHVES, is another organization: the Projet du développement rural (PDR), the single biggest development agency in Boulgou. It is mainly concerned with agricultural and pastoral activities; establishing and maintaining small-scale livestock trade, veterinary support, training and education of the local herders and facilitating access to safe water are its major goals. Like PIHVES, it is mainly financed through European (namely Danish) development funds and is not considered a governmental institution – but works in close cooperation with the national authorities. Because of its strong emphasis on livestock raising and trade I expected a significantly higher share of Fulbe in the population to be affected by the projects. However, PDR's director clearly stressed the fact that the organization does not follow an 'ethnic approach' and thus could not give any breakdown of how many projects have been carried out in Fulbe or Bisa settlements. He nonetheless 'clearly remembered one "Peul" taking part in one of the garden-projects'.

Unlike the well projects described above, PDR projects do try to achieve a more or less even regional or demographic distribution, but have a rather more a community-based concept. This means that the organization itself will not establish any projects in a given locality, but rather responds to the needs brought up by certain social groups. Participatory approaches require the target group to take the initiative for the foundation of the projects themselves. Communities such as villages or 'quartiers' may apply to the organization for a local project. In real life, however, agents of the organization first visit villages and inform the population of the possibilities of projects and encourage local leaders to form local committees to formulate the application. These information gatherings are convened by the village headmen or the village council and therefore present the same problem as in the PIHVES case: peripheral groups such as the Fulbe may not be represented in these gatherings in the first place. Even if they were, the formulation of the request would have to pass through the village councils or headmen, who are in no case likely to support any such application by the Fulbe, but rather try to secure funds and resources for their own 'quartier' and population.

Still, Fulbe settlements are generally aware of PDR projects, just as information about local needs and local socio-spatial differentiation has led to a far more detailed knowledge of the region and of potential project locations on the part of the donor organization. Hardly any Fulbe settlement, however, has ever applied for one of the projects.

PDR's philosophy, just like IGB's and PIHVES' practical approaches underscore some of the leading principles of both governmental and non-governmental institutions in creating an administrative and developmental infrastructure: all institutions put a strong emphasis on the participation of the local population. Through these participatory approaches local mechanisms of inclusion and exclusion based on ethnic affiliation find their way in to the administrative and organizational level. Exclusion of parts of the population by biased definitions of 'community' is a general drawback of participatory approaches. Within donor organizations this issue is mostly identified as a problem of insufficient 'vertical' integration; in the examples given, the problem lies not as much in how deep the projects go in integrating the local population, but rather how wide 'community' is defined in terms of the spatial extensions of a local community. In the cases described, there appears to be a unanimous exclusion of the Fulbe as a peripheral group, mostly on the grounds of their spatial dissociation from the farmers' villages. The local ethnic practice – locating Fulbe at the fringes of the localities and not conceding them landed property – leads to an objective differentiation: the spatial dissociation and their minority status. In all cases, local notions of socio-spatial order seem to counteract the administration's and organizations' intention of a far-reaching implementation of their projects. Local and national notions of inclusion and exclusion seem to run along different lines: while social integration is thought of as a vertically defined process by governmental and non-governmental institutions, local communities draw on horizontal, i.e. spatial concepts: the alignment of social groups on a landed-landless scale, with differential degrees of landed entitlements. The appearance of an administrative class and modern, infrastructural resources leads to a reassessment of existing practices of ethnic division of labour and of the importance of cross-cutting ties. Both depended on the fact that members of different ethnic groups competed over the same resources only to a limited degree; pasture and fields, as outlined, could be shared over the seasonal cycles.

Modern, infrastructural resources, however, are contested equally within and between the groups as Geertz, Cohen and others had predicted (Geertz, 1963; Cohen, 1981). Pursuing strategies in which entitlements to resources based on ethnic criteria does seem to lead to a further exclusion of marginalized groups, without offering the benefits cross-cutting ties used to provide in dealing with the assets of the agropastoral economy (such as pasture, water, etc.). The motivation on the side of the farming population in these processes seems evident as it privileges them in their access to resources – the story of the 'Ladenburg convoy' offered one example. The reasons why administrative or development organizations, such as the IGB, PIHVES or PDR, show an apparent bias for some ethnic groups – non-Fulbe or non-pastoral ethnic groups – deserves a closer examination. The argument that most executive staff and directors in these organizations are themselves non-Fulbe sounds persuasive at first (Wimmer, 1995), but in fact fails to deliver convincing arguments why exactly people would privilege members of their own ethnic group (see above, Chapter 4). Concepts of practice and habitus which explain preferences for members of specific cultural subgroups, do not depend on the over-representation of any of these ethnic groups in the administrative machine (Bourdieu, 1979; Keyes, 1981). Instead, administrative staff, officials and public servants form a distinct quasi-ethnic group, as I suggested. Certain ethnic groups are more closely affiliated with the functionaries' culture than others and tend to re-join on a meta-ethnic level.

Fulbe on the local level continue to access resources through representatives of the farming community by, for example, submitting themselves to the territorial rule of the farming landowners and village representatives who are now immediate competitors over the same new resources. The following cases highlight attempts of Fulbe herders to establish themselves as political players, by-passing the dominance of the farming majority and appropriating the administrative and bureaucratic discourse.

Herders' associations: ethnicity and politics

From the late 1980s onward, Burkina Faso has seen a steady rise of state- and non-governmental development organizations. Hand in hand with this process, local organizations formed on the recipient side. Most development organizations promote local corporations as part of a democratization process and as a step towards a civil society. As a side effect, donor organizations find it easier to work with these uniform and well-structured cooperatives, instead of dealing with fuzzy and often ill-organized 'local communities'. This leads to a large-scale standardization of development work and aids the homogenization of indigenous movements across a number of developing countries: the internationalization and standardization of indigenous movements has become an essential dimension in local politics – and herders' organizations in Burkina Faso are no exception to this.

Most Fulbe organizations in Burkina Faso are based in the northern

Sahel and in the eastern parts of the country (Hagberg, 2004; Kremling, 2004). In Boulgou, except for a small unit of the herders' union
in Tenkodogo, Fulbe are not politically organized. I will also take a
look at the reasons for this absence of political engagement. Herders
associations vary in terms of size, geographic scope, their profession-
alism and internal connections. Some are explicitly local organizations
– such as the herders union in Bobo-Dioulasso; others are explicitly
international – like APESS, a Swiss-funded NGO that operates in
several West African countries. Some organizations work mainly as
lobbying institutions for their pastoral clientele (APESS, 2007; Kremling, 2004), aiming at improving the economic conditions for livestock raising and the political recognition of minority groups. Others
are organized as unions, working closer to the politically less
committed pastoral population and offering legal and administrative
assistance.

Legally, herders' associations are voluntary organizations, open to
anyone regardless of ethnic affiliation. Their by-laws stress pastoral, i.e.,
economic and ecological concerns, over any ethnic issues (APESS,
2007). They are considered essential agents in civil society, filling the
space between the overarching state and the local population and
assuming key positions in local governance regimes.

The state and most donors do not acknowledge ethnic organizations (Burkina Faso (Le Peuple Souverain), 1997). On a practical level,
however, most associations do have a distinct ethnic taint. Almost all
their members are Fulbe; only some of the associations in the northern
Sahel include smaller numbers of Tuareg (Kremling, 2004). In their
claims for international recognition many associations tend to underline the minority status of Fulbe in most national and local contexts.
In Hagberg's view, the political serves as a frame for the articulation of
ethnic issues. Leaning on Englund and Nyamnjoh's notion of the 'politics of recognition', Hagberg sees the political and ecological as indi-
visible from the ethnic; herders' associations have no alternative but to
consolidate both aspects in one single approach (Englund and
Nyamnjoh, 2004).

In an overview of East African pastoralist associations, Hodgson
describes the shift from a discourse of indigeneity to a more economically oriented definition of the organizations. In the beginning, Masai
groups had emphasized their ethnic and minority status, working
towards political recognition within the state (Hodgson, 2006). This
helped to establish them successfully on a global political map, and
awarded them international recognition as an endangered people. It
helped to secure international money and connected their leaders with
transnational networks. On the downside, it also set many associations

on a confrontational course with the national and development-oriented agenda and further marginalized Masai within the Tanzanian state. At the same time, global discourse and donors' funding policies had taken more economically defined trajectories and the herders' associations gradually adapted to access other, development-oriented funds. Today, most Masai organizations are defined in socio-economic terms as herders' corporations.

In West Africa, ethnic and economic lines of identification of pastoralists are in most cases congruent and most herders' associations are hybrid organizations, invariably addressing ethnic as well as economic and political dimensions. In order to attract followers and satisfy the expectations of their clientele, they lay a strong emphasis on the specific dimensions as Fulbe organizations. This is in itself not surprising, given that, in most of the above cases, herders tended to frame injustice in ethnic terms and feeling discriminated against not because of their specific mode of livelihood, but rather for their ethnic otherness. Even organizations such as the 'syndicat des éleveurs', with its long-standing explicit tradition of being a non-ethnic labour organization, are perceived as a 'Fulbe', i.e., as an ethnic union in the public view (Hagberg, 2004: 195–218).

However, in the national political context, the same associations do not necessarily need to act as political, economic and non-ethnic interest groups. Not only would ethnic organizations be unconstitutional and deprive themselves of public and administrative recognition, they would also be excluded from access to most financial resources, such as development funds and projects.

While, up to the 1980s, international aid had been available for groups which manage to be recognized as ethnic minorities (Hodgson), funding policies over the past 20 years favour economic associations and civil organizations that operate within – and not against – the nation state. In the case of the Fulbe, moreover, claiming minority status is a tricky affair: although Fulbe are minorities in most local settings, they still constitute Burkina Faso's second largest ethnic group – and the situation in neighbouring countries is similar.

Many organizations, such as APESS, have a leadership that is to a great extent explicitly non-Fulbe. On a membership level, however, most are homogenous ethnic organizations. APESS explicitly acknowledges its hybrid origin as a political and ethnic organization and attempts to locate itself in this discourse. It propagates a philosophy that underlines the common world view, ecological and economic ideals (by 'encourag[ing] herders to have an ideal' (APESS, 2007), promoting a meta-ethnicity that allows the incorporation of sentiments and values which are locally perceived to be part of ethnic identity and at the same time, APESS engages in the political economic rhetoric of the nation state and international development.

The shift from ethnic to ecological (in the Masai case), the oscillation between the two principles of organization (in Burkina Faso), or even their coexistence (APESS), is not only determined by the change in global development paradigms. The quandary of consolidating ethnic and economic constituents is reflected in the internal dilemma of legitimizing the associations' leadership. The leading positions in the associations are generally made up of Fulbe who are not engaged in pastoral production. This elite derives its legitimacy through stressing a common, inclusive, fictive Fulbe identity. At the same time, they aspire to be part of a political elite, the 'culture des fonctionnaires.' De Bruijn and van Dijk have pointed to the long, pre-colonial, tradition of sedentary political pastoral elites, which maintained an ideology of shared ethnicity as a means of exploiting nomadic pastoralists to better control flows of income from resources.

The elites are caught in a dilemma: of having to draw on ethnic principles to secure a following, while in the political national arena they need to act explicitly non-ethnically. This is not merely a product of a global discourse and shift of paradigms, but is also rooted in a local historical schism of Fulbe herders and Fulbe elites.

6

Conclusion

This book began by looking at the question of whether the world has seen a growth in local, small-scale conflicts over the past decades. It suggested looking instead at the increased interest in such local conflicts. The previous chapters have shown the changes in the way these conflicts are framed and perceived; defining criteria, such as ethnic stereotyping and the ethnic division of labour, are not only historically rooted categories of a local economy but also responses to a national and global discourse over ethnicity. On the one hand, strategies of accessing and controlling local resources build on the delineation of groups along ethnic lines, emphasizing the ascription of stereotypical values to a social group, and on the other, the state administration and development organizations pursue policies that are implicitly shaped by ethnic criteria. The differential treatment of Fulbe herders by the administration may simply be a case of perceived injustice and ethnic bias, as in the example of Kourbila in Chapter 4; and in other cases the exclusion of Fulbe from access to infrastructural and administrative resources can be quite real as the practice of the geographical institute and the official villages' register illustrated. The administration's policy is non-ethnic, and uneven access to resources is based on formal non-ethnic criteria. Whether certain groups meet these preconditions, however, is largely determined in a local, highly ethnicized process, as in the politics of size (Zarga) or the denial of land rights to Fulbe have shown.

Differential access to resources as a result of administrative policy that can be perceived as ethnically biased, is the result of local processes: the preconditions for entitlements to modern resources are produced through local ethnicized discourse and practice. This permits us to reassess models of ethnicized bureaucracies as driving forces in the

181

politicization of ethnicity and as a cause for (violent) ethnic conflict. Previous models argued that bureaucracies become ethnicized by preferential recruitment of one or more ethnic groups. Burkina Faso shows that this need not be the case. In fact, by decisively discarding ethnic criteria, the administration can establish itself as a distinct social group that now competes with local groups over the same or similar resources.

By rebutting ethnicity as a legitimate part of public discourse and by pretending that legal entitlements are based on purely non–ethnic conditions, the state imposes its definitions of group delineators on local relations. The state is the winner in this meta–conflict over the nature of the dispute, with the administrative middle class who act as brokers between the two frames of discourse being the main profiteers.

Herders' associations offer one alternative to the administrative exclusion of locally marginalized groups. As hybrid organizations, herders' associations acknowledge the local production of ethnicity and the existing ethnic division of labour, and assume the role of brokers between the locals and the administration. The concealment of cross–cutting ties and the economic advantages, which local Fulbe groups gain from hiding cross–cutting ties over transhumant and new–settler Fulbe are, however, a major obstacle in building an overarching Fulbe-herder identity, itself a prerequisite for strong interest groups, such as herders' unions or other lobbying institutions.

The fact that local groups employ strategies of ethnicity is part of what I have referred to in Horowitz' words as the meta-conflict (Horowitz, 1985; 1991): the struggle over defining the type of conflict and consequently over control of resource use. By stressing local principles of group formation and division of labour (ethnic groups), the representatives of landholding patriclans establish themselves as middlemen between the local population and the state and development institutions.

To take local principles of ethnicity as a form of resistance against the advancing state and development organizations, however, would not adequately represent the local elites' vested interests. Local elites are as much interested in accessing modern goods supplied by the state and development, as they are in exploiting local political and economic resources. The case of the Ladenburg visit has illustrated how local representatives manage to appropriate the space between local groups and a development jet set, and attempt to marginalize competitors by referring to ethnic categories. The administrative middle class appropriates a modernization discourse and aims to establish itself as an indispensable broker for the local population by controlling infrastructural funds. By referring to local tensions in ethnic ('Fulbe'), instead of civil, terms ('herders', or 'user-groups') the local authorities assume control over the local political landscape and establish themselves as brokers between the local and the global.

In this way they compete with the local population over the immediate developmental resources – water, health, education – but also enter into competition with administrative organizations over local political power and economic control. Administrative officials have a double allegiance: they align with the state and development against local, ethnic elites in attempting to assume political control while simultaneously standing by the local elites in controlling the flow of administrative, developmental resources. This reveals the inherent limits of anthropological approaches that envisage the ethnicization of bureaucracy as the outcome of the overrepresentation of a particular group and as ethnic nepotism. Administration, in the cases presented, cannot be reduced to 'bras longues' – extensions of local ethnic groups – since the administrative officials pursue their own vested interests.

The model of concealed economies put forward in this book accounts for the complexity and inconsistency of administrative practice. Concealment consolidates contradictions in attitude and behaviour by locating different activities in different economic and political spheres. Local farmers conceal their cross-cutting ties from members of their own ethnic group and diachronic risk management is achieved by hiding cattle behind the ethnic divide. At the same time, herders conceal their cross-cutting ties from the eyes of their fellow pastoralists to secure exclusive or privileged resource access. Conflicts, as they are perceived in the public eye, are to a large extent about maintaining this ethnic divide and the ideology of an impermeable boundary.

Moving goods and services in a sphere that is defined by its opacity, also hides political and economic transactions from the bureaucratic machine and its agents. The state and development agencies' efforts to control local conflicts are an attempt to tackle concealment and make local political and economic relations transparent and readable.

The administrative elites are similarly anxious to mask important parts of their agenda. They might not have come as 'technological assassins', as Sankara claimed (p. 5); but their infrastructural projects are nonetheless vehicles of political and social restructuring and political control comes in the shadow of the goods and services with which the state and related agents arrive.

Ethnicity plays an important role at all levels of concealment. In the local discourse it is the key argument for the division of society into two major groups – Fulbe and Bisa – and the frame in which local conflicts are embedded; ethnicity defines the boundary behind which goods and political control are hidden. The resurgence of ethnicity is part of the political and economic transformation process, in which local groups appropriate a discourse that by definition precludes the (non-ethnic) state and legitimizes the local elites as representatives of the local order. For each of the groups, the respective frame of reference serves as a means of legitimizing their specific claims to political representation and, consequently, control over material resources.

Ultimately, both aspects – the exploitation of ethnicity through over- or under-communicating ethnic differences, and the concealment of economic activities and cross-cutting ties – are strategies of dealing with economic and demographic change.

References

Acemoglu, Daron, and James A. Robinson, (2012) *Why Nations Fail: The Origins of Power, Prosperity, and Poverty* (London)

Allen, Tim, Kate Hudson, and Jean Seaton, (1996) *War, Ethnicity and the Media* (London)

Allen, Tim, and Jean Seaton, (1999) *The Media of Conflict: War Reporting and Representations of Ethnic Violence* (London)

Alonso, Ana Maria, (1994) 'The Politics of Space, Time and Substance: State Formation, Nationalism and Ethnicity', *Annual Review of Anthropology* 23, 379–405

APESS. 'La Philosophie de L'apess (L'association pour la Promotion de L'élevage Au Sahel et En Savane).' http://apess.org/philosophie .html.

Appadurai, Arjun, (1986a) 'Introduction: Commodities and the Politics of Value', *The Social Life of Things : Commodities in Cultural Perspective*, edited by Arjun Appadurai (Cambridge, UK; New York), 3–63

———, (1986b) *The Social Life of Things: Commodities in Cultural Perspective* (Cambridge, UK; New York)

———, (1998) *Modernity at Large. Cultural Dimensions of Globalization* (Minneapolis)

Ardrey, Robert, (1997) *The Territorial Imperative* (New York)

Aronoff, Myron J., ed. (1976) *Freedom and Constraint: A Memorial Tribute to Max Gluckman* (Assen)

Asche, Helmut, (1994) *Le Burkina Faso Contemporain. L'expérience D'un Auto-Dévelopment* (Paris)

Atwood, David A., (1990) 'Land Registration in Africa: The Impact on Agricultural Production', *World Development* 18, no. 5, 659–71

Baldus, Bernd, (1974) 'Social Structure and Ideology: Cognitive and Behavioral Responses to Servitude among the Machube of

Northern Dahomey', *Canadian Journal of African Studies* 8, no. 2, 355–83

Balima, Salfo-Albert, (1996) *Légendes et Histoire des Peuples du Burkina Faso* (Paris, France)

Banks, Marcus, (1996) *Ethnicity:Anthropological Constructions* (London)

Barth, Fredrik, ed. (1969a) *Ethnic Groups and Boundaries. The Social Organization of Social Differentiation* (Bergen)

———, (1969b) 'Introduction', *Ethnic Groups and Boundaries.The Social Organization of Social Differentiation* (edited by Fredrik Barth), 9–38

———, (1981) *Features of Person and Society in Swat: Collected Essays on Pathans*, Selected Essays of Fredrik Barth 2 (London)

Bassett,Thomas J., Zueli Koli, and Tiona Ouattara, (2003) 'Fire in the Savanna. Environmental Change & Land Reform', *African Savannas*, edited by Thomas J. Bassett and Donald Crummey, 53–71

Bassett,Thomas J., (1993) 'Land Use Conflicts in Pastoral Development in Northern Côte d'Ivoire', *Land in African Agrarian Systems*, edited by Thomas J. Bassett and Donald E. Crummey (Madison), 131–54

Bassett, Thomas J., and Donald E. Crummey, (1993) *Land in African Agrarian Systems* (Madison)

Beeler, Sabrina, (2006) 'Conflicts between Farmers and Herders in North-Western Mali', Issue Paper (London)

Beer, Bettina, (2001) 'Friendship', *International Encyclopedia of Social & Behavioral Sciences*, edited by Neil J. Smelser and Paul B. Baltes (Amsterdam)

Bell, Sandra, and Simon Coleman, eds, (1999) *The Anthropology of Friendship* (London)

Bentley, G. Carter, (1987) 'Ethnicity and Practice', *Comparative Studies in Society and History* 29, no. 1, 24–55

Berry, Sara, (1975) *Cocoa, Custom, and Socio-Economic Change in Rural Western Nigeria*, Oxford Studies in African Affairs (Oxford)

———, (1976) *Inequality and Underdevelopment in Africa. A Suggested Approach,* African Studies Center, Boston University: Working Papers in African Studies (Brookline)

———, (1981)*Capitalism and Underdevelopment in Africa: A Critical Essay,* African Studies Center, Boston University: Working Papers in African Studies (Brookline)

———, (1987) *Property Rights and Rural Resource Management:The Case of Tree Crops in West Africa,* African Studies Center, Boston University: Working Papers in African Studies (Brookline)

———, (1989) 'Access, Control and Use of Resources in African Agriculture: An Introduction', *Africa: Journal of the International African Institute* 59, no. 1, Access, Control and Use of Resources in African Agriculture, 1–5

———, (1989) 'Social Institutions and Access to Resources', *Africa: Journal of the International African Institute* 59, no. 1, Access, Control and Use of Resources in African Agriculture, 41–55

———, (1991) *Afrikanische Entwicklungsperspektiven. Ein Kritischer Essay*, Afrika-Hefte (Bremen)

———, (1993) *No Condition Is Permanent. The Social Dynamics of Agrarian Change in Sub-Saharan Africa* (Madison)

———, (2002) 'Debating the Land Question in Africa', *Comparative Studies in Society and History* 44, no. 4, 638–68

———, (2002) 'The Everyday Politics of Rent-Seeking: Land Allocation on the Outskirts of Kumase, Ghana', *Negotiating Property in Africa*, edited by Kristine Juul and Christian Lund (Portsmouth), 107–33

———, (2006) 'Privatization and the Politics of Belonging in West Africa', *Land and the Politics of Belonging in West Africa*, edited by Richard Kuba and Carola Lentz (Leiden, Boston), 241–63

Bierschenk, Thomas, and Georg Elwert, (1988) 'Development Aid as an Intervention in Dynamic Systems. An Introduction', *Sociologia Ruralis* 28, no. 2/3, 99–112

Bloch, Maurice, (1995) 'People into Places. The Zafimaniry Concepts of Clarity', *The Anthropology of Landscape. Perspectives on Place and Space*, edited by Eric Hirsch and Michael O'Hanlon (Oxford), 63–77

Boesen, Elisabeth, (2007) 'Pastoral Nomadism and Urban Migration. Mobility among the Fulbe-Wodaabe from Central Niger', *Cultures of Migration: African Perspectives*, edited by Hans Peter Hahn and Georg Klute (Munster, New Brunswick, USA), 32–60

Bohannan, Paul, (1959) 'The Impact of Money on an African Subsistence Economy', *The Journal of Economic History* 19, no. 4, 491–503

———, (1989) *Justice and Judgment among the Tiv* (Prospect Heights)

Bohannan, Paul, and Laura Bohannan, (1968) *Tiv Economy* (Harlow)

Bohannan, Paul, and George Dalton, (1965) *Markets in Africa. Eight Subsistence Economies in Transition*, The Natural History Library (Garden City, N.Y.)

Boissevain, Jeremy, (1974) *Friends of Friends. Networks, Manipulators and Coalitions* (Oxford)

Boissevain, Jeremy, and J. Clyde Mitchell, eds (1973) *Network Analysis: Studies in Human Interaction*, Mouton Change and Continuity in Africa Series (The Hague)

Bollig, Michael, (1998) 'Moral Economy and Self-Interest: Kinship, Friendship, and Exchange among the Pokot (N.W. Kenya)', *Kinship, Networks, and Exchange*, edited by Thomas Schweizer and Douglas White (Cambridge, UK; New York), 137–57

Bonacich, Edna, (1972) 'A Theory of Ethnic Antagonism: The Split

Labor Market', *American Sociological Review* 37, no. 5, 547–59

———, '(1973), A Theory of Middleman Minorities', *American Sociological Review* 38, no. 5 ,583–94

Bonnet, Doris, (1988) *Corps Biologique, Corps Social. Procréation et Maladies D'enfant En Pays Mossi* (Paris)

Boon, Martin. (2006) *Black Minority and Ethnic Remittance Survey*, ICM Research Report (London), http://dfid.gov.uk/pubs/files/ukremittancessurvey.pdf

Boudon, Laura E., (199) 'The 'Rectification' of the Revolution', *Political Reform in Francophone Africa*, edited by John F. Clark and David E. D.Gardinier (Boulder), 127–44

Bourdieu, Pierre, (1979) *Entwurf einer Theorie der Praxis* (Frankfurt)

———, (1999) *Outline of a Theory of Praxis* (Cambridge, UK)

Bowen, John Richard, (1996) 'The Myth of Global Ethnic Conflict', *Journal of Democracy* 7, no. 4, 3–14

Brass, Paul, (1996) 'The Politics of Ethnicity in India', *Ethnicity*, edited by John Hutchinson and Anthony D. Smith (Oxford), 301-05

Brasselle, Anne-Sophie, Frederic Gaspart, and Jean-Philippe Platteau, (2002) 'Land Tenure Security and Investment Incentives: Puzzling Evidence from Burkina Faso', *Journal of Development Economics* 67, no. 2, 373–418

Breusers, Mark, (forthcoming) 'Friendship and Spiritual Parenthood among Mossi and Fulbe in Burkina Faso', *Friendship, Descent and Alliances*, edited by Martine Guichard, Tilo Graetz and Youssouf Diallo (Oxford; New York)

Breusers, Mark, Suzanne Nederlof, and Teunis van Rheenen, (1998) 'Conflict or Symbiosis? Disentangling Farmer-Herdsman Relations: The Mossi and Fulbe of the Central Plateau, Burkina Faso', *The Journal of Modern African Studies* 36, 357–80

Brubaker, Rogers, (2000) 'Beyond "Identity"', *Theory and Society* 29, no. 1, 1–47

———, (2004) *Ethnicity without Groups* (Cambridge, MA)

Brubaker, Rogers, and David D. Laitin, 'Ethnic and Nationalist Violence', *Annual Review of Sociology* 24 (1998), 423–52

Bruijn, Mirjam de, and Han van Dijk, (1995) *Arid Ways. Cultural Understandings of Insecurity in Fulbe Society, Central Mali.* (Amsterdam)

Bruijn, Mirjam de, Rijk van Dijk, and D. Foeken, (2001) *Mobile Africa: Changing Patterns of Movement in Africa and Beyond,* (Leiden; Boston)

Bureau of African Affairs. 'Burkina Faso.' U S Department of State, http://www.state.gov/r/pa/ei/bgn/2834.htm

Burkina Faso (Le Peuple Souverain) (1996) *RAF- Loi Portant Réorganisation Agraire et Foncière* Loi n°014/96/ADP.

Burkina Faso (Le Peuple Souverain) (1997) *Constitution du Burkina Faso*

Burnham, Philip, (1999) 'Pastoralists under Pressure', *Pastoralism under Pressure? Understanding Social Change in Fulbe Society*, edited by Victor Azarya, Anneke Breedveld, Myriam de Bruijn and Han van Dijk (Leiden; Boston), 269–84

Callahan, David, (2002) 'The Enduring Challenge: Self Determination and Ethnic Conflict in the 21st Century', *Carnegie Challenge Paper* (New York)

Carrier, James G.. (1991) 'Gifts, Commodities, and Social Relations: A Maussian View of Exchange', *Sociological Forum* 6, no. 1, 119–36

Carrier, James G., (1994) 'Alienating Objects: The Emergence of Alienation in Retail Trade', *Man* 29, no. 2, 359–80

Chagnon, Napoleón A., (1968) *Yanomamö: The Fierce People*, Case Studies in Cultural Anthropology (New York)

Cleaver, Kevin M., and Götz A. Schreiber, (1994) *Reversing the Spiral: The Population, Agriculture, and Environment Nexus in Sub-Saharan Africa* (Washington, D.C.)

Cohen, Abner, (1971) 'Cultural Strategies in the Organisation of Trading Diasporas', *The Development of Indigenous Trade and Markets in West Africa*, edited by Claude Meillassoux (London), 266–81

———, (1974) 'The Lesson of Ethnicity', *Urban Ethnicity*, edited by Abner Cohen (London; New York), 9–23

———, (1974) *Two-Dimensional Man. An Essay on the Anthropology of Power and Symbolism in Complex Society* (Berkeley)

———, (1981) *The Politics of Elite Culture: Explorations in the Dramaturgy of Power in a Modern African Society* (Berkeley)

———, (2004) *Custom and Politics in Urban Africa: A Study of Hausa Migrants in Yoruba Towns*. New ed, Routledge Classic Ethnographies (London; New York)

Cohen, Ronald, (1978) 'Ethnicity: Problem and Focus in Anthropology', *Annual Review of Anthropology* 7, 379–403

Colson, Elizabeth, (1971) 'The Impact of the Colonial Period on the Definition of Land Rights', *Colonialism in Africa, 1870–1960*, edited by Victor Turner (Cambridge, UK)

Commission nationale de decentralisation, (SAGEDECOM), (2000) *Monographie de la Commune de Tenkodogo* (Ouagadougou),

Connerton, Paul, (1989) *How Societies Remember* (Cambridge, UK)

Cooper, Frederick, (1981) 'Africa and the World Economy', *African Studies Review* 24, no. 2/3, 1–86

Dafinger, Andreas, (1998) 'Parenté et Localité: Migration et Constitution des Groupes', *Frankfurter Afrikanistische Blätter* 10, 11–20

———, (1999) 'Spatial Order and Social Navigation', *Frankfurter Afrikanistische Blätter* 11, 35–50

———, (2000) 'Herrschaftsgeschichte und Konstruktion des Raums',

Zeitschrift für Ethnologie 125, 265–80

————, (2001) 'An Anthropological Case Study on the Relation between Space, Language and Social Order', *Environment and Planning A* 33, 2189–203

————, (2004) 'Integration durch Konflikt: Interethnische Beziehungen und Ressourcenmanagement im Westlichen Afrika' (Integration through Conflict: Interethnic Relations and Resource Management in Western Africa), *Yearbook 2004*, edited by Max Planck Society (Munchen)

————, (2004a)*Anthropologie des Raumes: Untersuchungen zur Beziehung Räumlicher und Sozialer Ordnung im Süden Burkina Fasos*, Studien zur Kulturkunde, 122 (Köln)

————, (2011)'Reading and Writing in Space. Bisa Architecture in Burkina Faso', *Bodies of Belonging. Inhabiting Worlds in Rural West Africa*, edited by Ann Cassiman (Leuven)

Dafinger, Andreas, and Michaela Pelican, (2002) *Land Rights and the Politics of Integration: Pastoralists' Strategies in a Comparative View*, Max Planck Institute for Social Anthropology Working Papers 48 (Halle)

————, (2006)'Sharing or Dividing the Land? Land Rights and Farmer-Herder Relations in Burkina Faso and Northwest Cameroon.', *Canadian Journal of African Studies* 1/2006 (2006), 127–51

Dafinger, Andreas, and Andrea Reikat, (1996)'Quelques aperçus Concernant la Structure et L'histoire des Concessions et des Villages dans la Région Bisa', *Communications Symposium International du Sfb 268*, 49–56

Dafinger, Andreas, and Ute Ritz-Müller, (1996) 'Les Ancêtres et les Génies. Elements pour une Histoire des Populations Mosi et Bisa dans la Province de Boulgou', *Communications Symposium International du Sfb 268*, edited by SFB 268, 211–20

Dagris. African Cotton Production. Season 2006–2007.' Dagris, http://www.farm-foundation.org/IMG/pdf/579.pdf?PHPSESSID =860f7e7a7c62e7bd18d56db8848645b8

Dalton, George,(1961) 'Economic Theory and Primitive Society', *American Anthropologist* 63, no. 1, 1–25

de Bruijn, Mirjam, and Han van Dijk, (1995) *Arid Ways. Cultural Understandings of Insecurity in Fulbe Society, Central Mali,* Ceres (Amsterdam)

de Zeeuw, Fons, (1997) 'Borrowing of Land, Security of Tenure and Sustainable Land Use in Burkina Faso', *Development and Change* 28, no. 3, 583–95

Deininger, Klaus, and Gershon Feder, (1999) 'Land Policy in Developing Countries', *Rural Development Note (The World Bank)* 3

Desai, Amit, and Evan Killick, eds. (2010) *The Ways of Friendship:*

Anthropological Perspectives (Oxford; New York)

Diallo, Salif. (2001) 'Production Agricole: Les Nouvelles …' *Sidwaya*, 16 August.

Diallo, Youssouf, (2001) 'Abgrenzung- und Assimilierungsprozesse bei den Fulbe in der Elfenbeinküste und Burkina Faso', *Integration durch Verschiedenheit: Lokale und Globale Formen Interkultureller Kommunikation*, edited by Alexander Horstmann and Günther Schlee (Bielefeld), 333–66

———, (2004) 'Viehhandel in der Elfenbeinküste', *Ethnizität und Markt*, edited by Günther Schlee (Köln), 11–34

———, (2005) *From Stability to Uncertainty. A Recent Political History of Côte d'Ivoire*, Max Planck Institute for Social Anthropology Working Papers **74** (Halle)

Downs, R. E, and Stephen P Reyna, (1988) *Land and Society in Contemporary Africa* (Hanover)

Drabo, Issa, (2002) *Monographie du Departement de Boussouma* (Province du Boulgou) (Tenkodogo, Ouagadougou)

Du Toit, (1978) Brian M., *Ethnicity in Modern Africa* (Boulder, Colo., 1978)

Dupire, Marguerite, (1996) *Peuls Nomades: Etude Descriptive des Woodaabe du Sahel Nigerien*. 2ieme ed. (Paris)

ECA, United Nations Economic Commission for Africa, *African Alternative Framework to Structural Adjustment Programmes for Socio-Economic Recovery and Transformation.* (1989) Vol. E/ECA/CM.15/6/Rev.3 (Addis Ababa)

Eibl-Eibesfeldt, Irenäus, (1974) 'The Myth of the Aggression-Free Hunter and Gatherer Society', *Primate Aggression, Territoriality, and Xenophobia. A Comparative Perspective*, edited by Ralph L. Holloway (New York), 435–58

Eliot, T. S., (1949) *Notes Towards the Definition of Culture* (New York)

Elwert, Georg, (1980) 'Die Elemente der traditionellen Solidarität. Eine Fallstudie in Westafrika', *Kölner Zeitschrift für Soziologie und Sozialpsychologie*, no. 32, 681–704

———, (1983) *Bauern und Staat in Bénin*, Sociology of Development Research Centre Working Paper **31** (Bielefeld)

———, (1999) 'Markets of Violence', *Dynamics of Violence. Processes of Escalation and De-Escalation in Violent Group Conflicts*, edited by Georg Elwert, Stephan Feuchtwang and Dieter Neubert (Berlin), 85–102

———, (2001) 'Conflict, Anthropological Perspective', *International Encyclopedia of the Social and Behavioral Sciences.*, edited by Neil Smelser and Paul Baltes (Amsterdam), 2542–47

———, (2002) 'Switching Identity Discourses: Primordial Emotions and the Social Construction of Groups', *Imagined Differences : Hatred and the Construction of Identity*, edited by Günther Schlee (Münster, New York), 33–54

Elwert, Georg, Stephan Feuchtwang, and Dieter Neubert, (1999) *Dynamics of Violence. Processes of Escalation and De-Escalation in Violent Group Conflicts*, Beihefte zu Sociologus (Berlin)

———, (2001)'The Dynamics of Collective Violence: An Introduction', *Dynamics of Violence. Processes of Escalation and De-Escalation in Violent Group Conflicts*, edited by Georg Elwert, Stephan Feuchtwang and Dieter Neubert (Berlin), 7–31

Englund, Harri, and Francis B. Nyamnjoh,(2004) *Rights and the Politics of Recognition in Africa*, Postcolonial Encounters (London; New York)

Ensminger, Jean, and Andrew Rutten, (1991)'The Political Economy of Changing Property Rights: Dismantling a Pastoral Commons', *American Ethnologist* 18, no. 4, 683–99

Eriksen, Thomas Hylland, (2002) *Ethnicity and Nationalism*. 2nd ed, Anthropology, Culture, and Society (London; Sterling, VA)

———, (2002) *Ethnicity and Nationalism: Anthropological Perspectives* (London)

Esman, Milton J., (2004) *An Introduction to Ethnic Conflict* (Cambridge, UK; Malden, MA)

Esman, Milton J., and Shibley Telhami,(1995) *International Organizations and Ethnic Conflict* (Ithaca)

Etat du Burkina Faso. Raf – Loi Portant Réorganisation Agraire et Foncière.' In Loi n°014/96/ADP, 1996)

Evans-Pritchard, Edward E., (1969) *The Nuer. A Description of the Modes of Livelihood and Political Institutions of a Nilotic People* (Oxford; New York)

Evans, Peter B., (1985) Dietrich Rueschemeyer, and Theda Skocpol, *Bringing the State Back In* (Cambridge, UK)

Fafchamps, Marcel, Christopher Udry, and Katherine Czukas, (1998) 'Drought and Saving in West Africa: Are Livestock a Buffer Stock?', *Journal of Development Economics* 55, no. 2, 273–305

Falloux, François, and Lee M. Talbot, (1993) *Crisis and Opportunity: Environment and Development in Africa* (London)

FAO, (2004) *The State of Agricultural Commodity Markets 2004* (Soco) (Rome)

Fardon, Richard, (1996) 'Covering Ethnicity? Or, Ethnicity as Coverage? 1', *Contemporary Politics* 2, no. 1, 153–58

Faure, Armelle, (1996) 'Le Pays Bissa Avant Le Barrage de Bagré'. *Anthropologie de L'espace Rural.* (Paris; Ouagadougou)

Ferguson, James, (1990) *The Anti-Politics Machine. 'Development,' Depoliti-*

cization, and Bureaucratic Power in Lesotho (Cambridge, UK)

———, (2006) *Global Shadows: Africa in the Neoliberal World Order* (Durham [N.C.])

Ferguson, James, and Akhil Gupta, (1992) 'Beyond 'Culture': Space, Identity, and the Politics of Difference', *Cultural Anthropology* 7, no. 1, Space, Identity, and the Politics of Difference (1992), 6–23

Ferguson, R. Brian, (2003) *The State, Identity and Violence: Political Disintegration in the Post-Cold War World* (London; New York)

Ferguson, R. Brian, and Neil L. Whitehead, (1992) *War in the Tribal Zone: Expanding States and Indigenous Warfare*, School of American Research Advanced Seminar Series (Sante Fe)

Firth, Raymond, (1967) *Themes in Economic Anthropology*, Asa Monographs (New York)

Fortes, Meyer, (1971)'On the Concept of the Person among the Tallensi', *La Notion de Personne En Afrique Noire*, edited by Centre National de la Recherche Scientifique (Paris), 283–320

Freidberg, Susanne, (1996) 'Contacts, Contracts, and Green Bean Schemes: Liberalisation and Agro-Entrepreneurship in Burkina Faso', *The Journal of Modern African Studies* 35, no. 1, 101–28

Gantzel, Klaus Jürgen, (1997) 'War in the Post-World War II World: Some Empirical Trends and a Theoretical Approach', *War and Ethnicity. Global Connections and Local Violence*, edited by David Turton (Rochester)

Geertz, Clifford, (1963)'The Integrative Revolution. Primordial Sentiments and Civil Politics in New States', *Old Societies and New States. The Quest for Modernity in Asia and Africa*, edited by Clifford Geertz (New York), 105–57

———, (1994) 'Primordial and Civic Ties', *Nationalism*, edited by John Hutchinson and Anthony D. Smith (Oxford; New York), 29–34

Gensler, Marlis, (2004)'Parzellierung und Geschichte: Zugang zu und Kontrolle von Bauland in einer Westafrikanischen Kleinstadt (Diébougou, Burkina Faso)', *Paideuma* 50,127–50

German Federal Ministry for Economic Cooperation and Development. 'Comments by Germany on Document Gef/Is 13 'Intersessional Work Program'.' http://www.gefweb.org/Documents/Work_Programs/IWP%20July05/GermanCommentsIntersessional.pdf.

Geschiere, Peter, (1997) *The Modernity of Witchcraft Politics and the Occult in Postcolonial Africa = Sorcellerie et Politique En Afrique: la Viande des Autres* (Charlottesville)

Geschiere, Peter, and Cyprian Fonyuy Fisiy, (1995) *Sorcellerie et Politique En Afrique la Viande des Autres*, Les Afriques: Collection Les Afriques (Paris)

Geschiere, Peter, and Francis Nyamnjoh, (1998) 'Witchcraft as an Issue in the 'Politics of Belonging': Democratization and Urban Migrants' Involvement with the Home Village', *African Studies Review* 41, no. 3, 69–91

Glazer, Nathan, Daniel Moynihan, and Corinne Schelling, (1975) *Ethnicity: Theory and Experience* (Cambridge, MA)

Gluckman, Herman Max, (1964) *Custom and Conflict in Africa* (New York)

Gluckman, Herman Max, and Philip Hugh Gulliver, (1978) *Cross-Examinations: Essays in Memory of Max Gluckman* (Leiden)

Godelier, Maurice, (1999) *The Enigma of the Gift* (Chicago)

Goody, Jack, 'Fields of Social Control among the Lodagaba', (1957) *The Journal of the Royal Anthropological Institute of Great Britain and Ireland* 87, no. 1, 75–104

————, (1976) *Production and Reproduction: A Comparative Study of the Domestic Domain* (Cambridge, UK)

————, (1980) 'Slavery in Time and Space', *Asian and African Systems of Slavery*, edited by James L. Watson (Oxford), 16–42

Grätz, Tilo, (2004) 'Friendship Ties among Young Artisanal Gold Miners in Northern Benin (West Africa)', *Africa Spectrum* 39, no. 1, 95–117

Grätz, Tilo, Barbara Meier, and Michaela Pelican, (2004) 'Freund-schaftsprozesse in Afrika aus Sozial-anthropologischer Perspektive: Eine Einführung (Processes of Friendship in Africa: Introduction)', *Africa Spectrum* 39, no. 1, 9–39

Gray, Leslie, (2003) 'Investing in Soil Quality. Farmer Responses to Land Scarcity in Southwestern Bukina Faso', *African Savannas*, edited by Thomas J Bassett and Donald Crummey (Oxford ; Portsmouth), 72–90

Gregory, Chris A., (1982) *Gifts and Commodities* (London; New York)

————, (1996) 'Cowries and Conquest: Towards a Subalternate Quality Theory of Money', *Comparative Studies in Society and History* 38, no. 2, 195–217

————, (1997) *Savage Money: The Anthropology and Politics of Commodity Exchange*. Vol. 21, Studies in Anthropology and History (Amsterdam)

Grove, Andrea, (2001) 'The Intra-National Struggle to Define 'Us': External Involvement as a Two-Way Street', *International Studies Quarterly* 45, no. 3, 357–88

GTZ, (1997) *Joint Learning for Change. Development of Innovations in Livelihood Systems around Protected Tropical Forests* (Eschborn)

Gudeman, Stephen, (1986) *Economics as Culture: Models and Metaphors of Livelihood*, International Library of Sociology (London; Boston)

Guenther, Matthias G., (1981) 'Bushman and Hunter-Gatherer Territoriality', *Zeitschrift für Ethnologie* 106,109–20

Guichard, Martine, (1996) 'So Nah und doch So Fremd. Über die
Beziehungen zwischen Fulbe und Bariba im Borgou (Nordbenin)',
107–32

———, (2000) 'L'étrangeté Comme Code de Communication Inter-
ethnique. Les Relations Entre Agropasteurs Peuls et Paysan Bariba
Au Borgu (Nord-Benin)', *L'ethnicité Peul dans des Contextes
Nouveaux*, edited by Youssouf Diallo and Günther Schlee (Paris),
93–127

———, (2007) 'Hoch Bewertet und Oft Überschätzt: Theoretische
und Empirische Einblicke in Freundschaftsbeziehungen aus Sozial-
anthropologischer Perspektive', *Freundschaft und Verwandtschaft : zur
Unterscheidung und Verflechtung Zweier Beziehungssysteme*, edited by
Johannes F. Schmidt, Martine Guichard and Peter Schuster
(Konstanz), 313–42

Gulliver, P. H., (1971) *Neighbours and Networks; the Idiom of Kinship in
Social Action among the Ndendeuli of Tanzania* (Berkeley)

Gupta, Akhil, (1995)'Blurred Boundaries: The Discourse of Corruption, the Culture of Politics, and the Imagined State', *American
Ethnologist* 22, no. 2, 375–402

———, (2001) 'Governing Population: The Integrated Child Development Services Program in India', *States of Imagination : Ethnographic Explorations of the Postcolonial State*, edited by Thomas Blom
Hansen and Finn Stepputat (Durham)

Gurr, Ted Robert, (1993) *Minorities at Risk: A Global View of Ethno-
political Conflicts* (Washington)

Gurr, Ted Robert, and Barbara Harff,(2003) *Ethnic Conflict in World
Politics*. 2nd ed. (Boulder)

Guyer, Jane I., (1993)'Wealth in People and Self-Realization in Equa-
torial Africa', *Man* 28, no. 2, 243–65

Hagberg, Sten, (1998) 'Between Peace and Justice. Dispute Settlement
between Karaboro Agriculturalists and Fulbe Agro-Pastoralists in
Burkina Faso', *Uppsala Studies in Cultural Anthropology* (Uppsala)

———, (2004) 'Ethnic Identification in Voluntary Associations: The
Politics of Development and Culture in Burkina Faso', *Rights and the
Politics of Recognition in Africa*, edited by Harri Englund and Francis
B. Nyamnjoh (London ; New York), 195–218

Hahn, Hans Peter, (2008)'The Domestication of the Mobile Phone:
Oral Society and New ICT in Burkina Faso', *Journal of Modern
African Studies* 46, no. 1

Hahn, Hans Peter, and Georg Klute, (2007) *Cultures of Migration: African
Perspectives* (Münster; New Brunswick)

Hallpike, C. R., (1973) 'Functionalist Interpretations of Primitive Warfare', *Man* 8, no. 3 (1973), 451–70

Hann, Chris, and Keith Hart, (2011) *Economic Anthropology: History, Ethnography, Critique* (Cambridge, UK)

Hansen, Thomas Blom, and Finn Stepputat, (2001) *States of Imagination: Ethnographic Explorations of the Postcolonial State*, Duke University Press Politics, History, and Culture Series (Durham)

Hardin, Garrett, (1968) 'The Tragedy of the Commons', *Science* 162, no. 3859, 1243–48

Hardin, Garrett, and John Baden, (1977) *Managing the Commons* (San Francisco, 1977)

Hardung, Christine, (1997)'Ni Vraiment Peul, Ni Vraiment Baatombu'. Le Conflit Identitaire des Gando', *Trajectoires Peules Au Bénin. Six Études Anthropologiques*, edited by Thomas Bierschenk and Pierre-Yves Le Meur (Paris), 109–38

Hart, Keith. 'Informal Economy.' http://thememorybank.co.uk/papers/informal-economy/.

Harvey, David, (2005) *A Brief History of Neoliberalism* (Oxford; New York)

Hechter, Michael, (1974) 'The Political Economy of Ethnic Change', *The American Journal of Sociology* 79, no. 5, 1151–78

———, (1976) 'Response to Cohen: Max Weber on Ethnicity and Ethnic Change', *The American Journal of Sociology* 81, no. 5, 1162–68

———, (1987) *Principles of Group Solidarity*, California Series on Social Choice and Political Economy; 11 (Berkeley)

———, (1988) 'Rational Choice Theory and the Study of Race and Ethnic Relations', *Theories of Ethnic and Race Relations*, edited by John Rex and David Mason (Cambridge), 264–79

Hechter, Michael, Debra Friedman, and Malka Appelbaum, (1982) 'A Theory of Ethnic Collective Action', *International Migration Review* 16, no. 2, Special Issue: *Theory and Methods in Migration and Ethnic Research*, 412–34

Herskovits, Melville J., (1926) 'The Cattle Complex in East Africa', *American Anthropologist* 28, no. 1, 230–72

Hill, Hamner (1987) 'A Functional Taxonomy of Normative Conflict', *Law and Philosophy* 6, no. 2, 227–47

Hirschfeld, Lawrence A., (1995) 'The Inheritability of Identity: Children's Understanding of the Cultural Biology of Race', *Child Development* 66, no. 5, 1418–37

Hirschman, Albert O., (1970) Exit, Voice, and Loyalty: Responses to Decline in Firms, Organizations, and States (Cambridge, MA)

Hobbes, Thomas, (1968 [1651]) *Leviathan*. Edited by C. B. Macpherson (Baltimore)

Hodgson, Dorothy L. (2008) 'Cosmopolitics, Neoliberalism, and the State: The Indigenous Rights Movement in Africa.' In Pnina Werbner, ed. *Anthropology and the New Cosmopolitanism: Rooted, Feminist and Vernacular Perspectives* (New York)

Hopkins, Terence K., and Immanuel M. Wallerstein, (1982) *World-Systems Analysis: Theory and Methodology*, Explorations in the World-Economy ; V. 1 (Beverly Hills, Calif.)

Horowitz, Donald L., (1985) *Ethnic Groups in Conflict* (Berkeley)

———, (1991) 'A Democratic South Africa?: Constitutional Engineering in a Divided Society.' Vol. 46, *Perspectives on Southern Africa* (Berkeley)

Houis, Maurice, (1963) *Les Noms Individuels Chez les Mosi* (Dakar)

Huntington, Samuel P., (1996) *The Clash of Civilizations and the Remaking of World Order* (New York)

Hutchinson, Sharon, (1992) 'The Cattle of Money and the Cattle of Girls among the Nuer, 1930–83', *American Ethnologist* 19, no. 2 , 294–316

INSD, (2010) Institut national de la statistique et de la démographie. 'La Région du Centre-Est.' edited by Ministere de l'economie et des finances. (Ouagadougou)

———, 'Indicateurs Clé.' http://www.insd.bf/fr/.

Izard, Michel, (1970) 'Introduction a L'histoire des Royaumes Mossi', *Recherches Voltaïques* (Paris)

Jenkins, Richard, (1997) *Rethinking Ethnicity. Arguments and Explorations* (London; Thousand Oaks, California)

Juul, Kristine, and Christian Lund, (2002) *Negotiating Property in Africa* (Portsmouth)

Kagone, Hamade, and S.G. Reynolds. 'Profil Fourrager Burkina Faso, Grassland and Pasture Crops.' FAO, http://www.fao.org/ag/agp/agpc/doc/counprof/burkinafeng.htm

Kapferer, Bruce, (1988) *Legends of People, Myths of State: Violence, Intolerance and Political Culture in Sri Lanka and Australia* (Washington; London)

Kaplan, Robert D., (1993) *Balkan Ghosts: A Journey through History*. 1st ed. (New York)

Keuthmann, Klaus, (1998) 'L'îlot Linguistique Bisa. Considerations Sous L'angle Ethnolinguistique.', *Les Bisa du Burkina Faso. Contributions À L'étude D'un Peuple Mandé*, edited by Klaus Keuthmann, Andrea Reikat and Hans Jürgen Sturm (Köln)

Keuthmann, Klaus, Andrea Reikat, and Hans Jürgen Sturm, (1998) *Les Bisa du Burkina Faso. Contributions À L'étude D'un Peuple Mandé*, Frankfurter Afrikanistische Blätter (Köln)

Kevane, Michael, (1997) 'Land Tenure and Rental in Western Sudan',

Land Use Policy 14, no. 4, 295–310

Keyes, Charles, (1981)'The Dialectics of Ethnic Change', *Ethnic Change*, edited by Charles Keyes (Seattle), 3–30

Kintz, D., (1982) 'Pastoralisme, Agro-Pastoralisme et Organisation Foncière: Le Cas des Peuls', *Enjeux Fonciers En Afrique Noire*, edited by Emile Le Bris, Etienne Le Roy and F. Leimdorfer (Paris)

Klare, Michael T., (2001) *Resource Wars: The New Landscape of Global Conflict* (New York)

Klute, Georg, (2011) 'From Friends to Enemies: Negotiating Nationalism, Tribal Identities, and Kinship in the Fratricidal War of the Malian Tuareg', *L'Année du Maghreb*, no. VII

Kopytoff, Igor, (1986) 'The Cultural Biography of Things: Commoditization as Process', *The Social Life of Things : Commodities in Cultural Perspective*, edited by Arjun Appadurai (Cambridge, UK), 64–91

———, (1987) ed. *The African Frontier: The Reproduction of Traditional African Societies* (Bloomington)

———, (1987) 'The Internal African Frontier. The Making of African Political Culture.', *The African Frontier: The Reproduction of Traditional African Societies*, edited by Igor Kopytoff (Bloomington), 3–84

———, (1999) 'The Internal African Frontier: Cultural Conservatism and Ethnic Innovation', edited by Michael Rösler and Tobias Wendl (Frankfurt), 31–44

Kremling, Verena, (2004) *Zu Kalt Um Aufzustehen? Einflüsse von Identität und Weltbild Auf die Entwicklungszusammmenarbeit Mit Fulbe Viehhaltern im Liptako (Burkina Faso)* (Herbolzheim)

Lahuec, Jean-Paul, (1979) 'Le Peuplement et L'abandon de la Vallée de la Volta Blanche En Pays Bissa', *Mobilite et Peuplement Bissa et Mossi*, edited by Jean-Paul Lahuec and J.Y. Marchal (Paris)

———, (1983) 'Contraintes Historiques et Onchocercose: une Explication des Faits de Peuplement dans la Sous-Préfecture de Garango, Nord Pays Bissa', *De L'épidémiologie à la Géographie Humaine* (Paris), 253–58

Laidlaw, James, (2000)'A Free Gift Makes No Friends', *The Journal of the Royal Anthropological Institute* 6, no. 4, 617–34

Leach, Edmund Ronald, (1954) *Political Systems of Highland Burma. A Study of Kachin Social Structure* (London)

Lemarchand, René, (1996) *Burundi: Ethnic Conflict and Genocide*, Woodrow Wilson Center Series (Cambridge; New York)

Lentz, Carola, (1995) 'Tribalismus und Ethnizität in Afrika – Ein Forschungsüberblick', *Leviathan* 23, 115–45

———, (1998) *Die Konstruktion von Ethnizität Eine Politische Geschichte Nord-West Ghanas, 1870–1990*, Studien zur Kulturkunde (Köln)

———, (2006) *Ethnicity and the Making of History in Northern Ghana*,

International African Library (Edinburgh)

Lentz, Carola, and Paul Nugent, (1999) *Ethnicity in Ghana: The Limits of Invention* (Basingstoke)

LeVine, Robert A., (1961) 'Anthropology and the Study of of Conflict: An Introduction', *The Journal of Conflict Resolution* 5, no. 1, The Anthropology of Conflict, 3–15

Lichbach, Mark Irving, (1995) *The Rebel's Dilemma*, University of Michigan Press Economics, Cognition, and Society Series (Ann Arbor)

———, (1998) 'Contending Theories of Contentious Politics and the Structure-Action Problem of Social Order', *Annual Review of Political Science* 1, no. 1, 401–24

Lorenz, Konrad, (1966) *On Aggression* (London)

Lund, Christian, (2001) 'Questioning Some Assumptions About Land Tenure', *Politics, Property and Production in the West African Sahel. Understanding Natural Resources Management*, edited by Tor A. Benjaminsen and Christian Lund (Uppsala), 144–62

Malinowski, Bronislaw, (1926) *Crime and Custom in Savage Society*, The International Library of Psychology, Philosophy and Scientific Methods (London)

———, (1967) *A Diary in the Strict Sense of the Term* (London)

Mamdani, Mahmood, (2001) *When Victims Become Killers: Colonialism, Nativism, and the Genocide in Rwanda* (Princeton)

Mauss, Marcel, (1954 [1925]) *The Gift; Forms and Functions of Exchange in Archaic Societies* (Glencoe, Ill)

McMillan, Della E., (1995) *Sahel Visions: Planned Settlement and River Blindness Control in Burkina Faso* (Tucson)

Ministère des ressources animales (MRA) (2008) 'Les Statistiques du Secteur de L'élevage Au Burkina Faso.' (Ouagadougou)

Mitchell, T., 2002, *Rule of Experts: Egypt, Techno-Politics, Modernity* (Berkeley)

Moll, Henk, and Nico Heerink. 'Price Adjustments and the Cattle Sub-Sector in Central West Africa.' http://www.fao.org/wairdocs/LEAD/X6138E/X6138E00.htm.

Moore, Sally Falk, (1998) 'Changing African Land Tenure: Reflections on the Incapacities of the State', *European Journal of Development Research* 10, no. 2, 33–49

Moritz, Mark. (2011 [2003]) 'Commoditization and the Pursuit of Piety. The Transformation of an African Pastoral System'. (London)

Mutume, Gumisai, (2005) 'Workers' Remittances: A Boon to Development', *Africa Renewal (UN Dept. for Public Information)* 19, no. 3, 10

Nugent, Paul, (2008) 'Putting the History Back into Ethnicity: Enslavement, Religion, and Cultural Brokerage in the Construction of Mandinka/Jola and Ewe/Agotime Identities in West Africa, C. 1650–1930', *Comparative Studies in Society and History* 50, no. 4, 920–48

Oksen, Peter. (1996) *Intensification and Agricultural Development in the Boulgou Province, Burkina Faso.* SEREIN Working Paper **20** (Copenhagen)

———, (2001)'Agricultural Expansion and Animal Husbandry in a West African Savannah Environment', *Politics, Property and Production in the West African Sahel. Understanding Natural Resources Management.*, edited by Tor A. Benjaminsen and Christian Lund (Uppsala), 303–31

Oksen, Peter, Mark Breusers, Suzanne Nederlof, and Teunis van Rheenen, (2000) 'Disentanglements: A Comment on 'Conflict or Symbiosis', *The Journal of Modern African Studies* 38, no. 1, 121–24

Olivier de Sardan, Jean-Pierre, (1988) 'Peasant Logics and Development Projects Logics', *Sociologia Ruralis* 28, no. 2/3, 216–26

Ortner, Sherry B., (1984) 'Theory in Anthropology since the Sixties', *Comparative Studies in Society and History* 26, no. 1, 126–66

Ouedraogo, H., (ed.) (2001) 'La Raf: Objectifs Politiques, Économiques et Contenu', *La Réorganisation Agraire et Foncière et L'aménagement Agro-Sylvo-Pastoral de la Vallée de la Nouhao* (Ouagadougou)

Pare, Ernest, and Jerome Yameogo, (2001) *Monographie de la Province du Boulgou.* (Ouagadougou)

Parry, Jonathan, (1986) 'The Gift, the Indian Gift and the "Indian Gift"', *Man* 21, no. 3, 453–73

Parry, Jonathan, and Maurice Bloch, (1989) *Money and the Morality of Exchange* (Cambridge, UK; New York)

Patterson, Orlando, (1975) 'Context and Choice in Ethnic Allegiance: A Theoretical Framework and Caribean Case Study', *Ethnicity : Theory and Experience*, edited by Nathan Glazer, Daniel Moynihan and Corinne Schelling (Cambridge, MA), 305–49

Peel, John, (1989) 'The Cultural Work of Yoruba Ethnogenesis', *History and Ethnicity*, edited by Elizabeth Tonkin, Malcolm Chapman and Maryon McDonald (London ; New York), ix, 270 p.

Peters, Pauline E., (2007) *Challenges in Land Tenure and Land Reform in Africa: An Anthropological Perspective.* Cid Working Paper 141(Cambridge, MA)

Piot, Charles D.,'Of Persons and Things: Some Reflections on African Spheres of Exchange', *Man* 26, no. 3 (1991), 405–24

PLAN, (1991) Conseil National du, *Deuxième Plan Quinquennal de Développement Populaire 1991–1995* (Ouagadougou)

Polanyi, Karl, (1944) *The Great Transformation* (New York; Toronto)

———, (1975 [1944] *The Great Transformation* (New York)

Polanyi, Karl, and Harry W. Pearson, (1997) *The Livelihood of Man, Studies in Social Discontinuity* (New York)

Prost, André, (1950) *La Langue Bisa. Grammaire et Dictionnaire* (Ouagadougou, 1950)

Ratha, Dilip, and Sanket Mohapatra, (2011) *Remittance Markets in Africa.* (Washington: World Bank)

Reenberg, Anette. (1997) *Agricultural Land Use in Silmiogou – Boulgou Province. The Spatial Allocation of Land at Household and Village Levels*, SEREIN Working Papers 35 (Copenhagen)

Richards, Paul, and Bernhard Helander, (2005) *No Peace, No War: An Anthropology of Contemporary Armed Conflicts* (Athens; Oxford)

Ross, Marc Howard, (1986) 'The Limits to Social Structure: Social Structural and Psychocultural Explanations for Political Conflict and Violence', *Anthropological Quarterly* 59, no. 4, Culture and Aggression, 171–76+200-04–171–76+200-04

———, (2007) *Cultural Contestation in Ethnic Conflict*, Cambridge Studies in Comparative Politics (Cambridge, UK; New York)

Rubinstein, Robert A., (1994) 'Collective Violence and Common Security', *Companion Encyclopedia of Anthropology: Humanity, Culture and Social Life*, edited by Tim Ingold (Cambridge), 983–1009

Sahlins, Marshall D., (1961) 'The Segmentary Lineage: An Organization of Predatory Expansion', *American Anthropologist* 63, no. 2, Part 1, 322–45

———, (1972) *Stone Age Economics* (Chicago)

Saul, Mahir, 'Development of the Grain Market and Merchants in Burkina Faso', *The Journal of Modern African Studies* 24, no. 1 (Mar 1986, 127–53)

Sawadogo, Jean-Pierre, and Volker Stamm, (2000) 'Local Perceptions of Indigenous Land Tenure Systems: Views of Peasants, Women and Dignitaries in a Rural Province of Burkina Faso', *Journal of Modern African Studies* 38, no. 2, 279–94

Scherrer, Christian, (1994) 'Ethnische Strukturierung und Politische Mobilisierung in Äthiopien', *Ethnische Dynamik in der Aussereuropäischen Welt*, edited by Hans-Peter Müller (Zürich), 133–206

Schlee, Günther, (1997) *Ethnicities in New Contexts : Urban and Pastoral Nomadic Migrants (Burkina Faso, Ivory Coast, Benin, Cameroon, Sudan).* Universität Bielefeld, Forschungsschwerpunkt Entwicklungssoziologie Working Paper **282** (Bielefeld)

———, (1998) 'Gada Systems on the Meta-Ethnic Level. Gabbra/Boran/Garre Interactions in the Kenyan/Ethiopian Borderland.', 121–46

———, (1999) 'Cross-Cutting Ties. Grenzen, Raub und Krieg', 315–32

————, (2002) *Imagined Differences: Hatred and the Construction of Identity*, Market, Culture, and Society 5 (Münster; New York)

————, (2004) ed. *Ethnizität und Markt*, Vol. 4, Topics in African Studies (Köln)

————, (2004) 'Taking Sides and Constructing Identities: Reflections on Conflict Theory', *The Journal of the Royal Anthropological Institute* 10, no. 1, 135–56

————, (2006) *Wie Feindbilder Entstehen. Eine Theorie religiöser und ethnischer Konflikte* (München)

Schmidt, Heike, (1999) 'Neither War nor Peace', *Dynamics of Violence. Processes of Escalation and De-Escalation in Violent Group Conflicts*, edited by Georg Elwert, Stephan Feuchtwang and Dieter Neubert (Berlin), 211–25

Schmidt, Johannes F., Martine Guichard, Peter Schuster, and Fritz Trillmich, eds. (2007) *Freundschaft und Verwandtschaft: zur Unterscheidung und Verflechtung Zweier Beziehungssysteme* (Konstanz)

Schneider, Harold K., (1979) *Livestock and Equality in East Africa: The Economic Basis for Social Structure* (Bloomington)

Schweizer, Thomas, and Douglas White, eds (1998) *Kinship, Networks, and Exchange*, Structural Analysis in the Social Sciences (Cambridge, UK; New York)

Scott, James C, (1998) *Seeing Like a State. How Certain Schemes to Improve the Human Condition Have Failed*, Yale Agrarian Studies (New Haven)

Seabright, Paul, (2000) *The Vanishing Rouble: Barter Networks and Non-Monetary Transactions in Post-Soviet Societies* (Cambridge, UK; New York)

Seligman, Adam B., (1997) *The Problem of Trust* (Princeton)

Shipton, Parker MacDonald, (1989) *Bitter Money. Cultural Economy and Some African Meanings of Forbidden Commodities*, American Ethnological Society Monograph Series (Washington)

Shipton, Parker MacDonald, and Mitzi Goheen, (1992a) 'Introduction. Understanding African Land-Holding: Power, Wealth, and Meaning', *Africa: Journal of the International African Institute* 62, no. 3 (Rights over Land: Categories and Controversies)

————, (1992b) 'Understanding African Land Holding. Power, Wealth and Meaning.', *Africa* 62, no. 3, 307–25

Spencer, Jonathan, (1990) 'Collective Violence and Everyday Practice in Sri Lanka', *Modern Asian Studies* 24, no. 3, 603–23

————, (1997) 'Post-Colonialism and the Political Imagination', *The Journal of the Royal Anthropological Institute* no. 3, 11–19

Stamm, Volker, (2004) 'The World Bank on Land Policies: A West African Look at the World Bank Policy Research Report.', *Africa* 74, no. 4, 670–78

Strathern, Marilyn, (1988) 'The Gender of the Gift: Problems with Women and Problems with Society in Melanesia', *Studies in Melanesian Anthropology* ; 6 (Berkeley)

Swinton, S., (1987) 'Drought Survival Tactics of Subsistence Farmers in Niger', *Human Ecology* 1, no. 2

Tambiah, Stanley Jeyaraja, (1986) *Sri Lanka: Ethnic Fratricide and the Dismantling of Democracy* (Chicago)

Thorsen, Dorte, (2007) 'Junior-Senior Linkages. Youngster's Perceptions of Migration in Burkina Faso', *Cultures of Migration: African Perspectives*, edited by Hans Peter Hahn and Georg Klute (Münster; New Brunswick), 175–99

Turton, David, *War and Ethnicity. Global Connections and Local Violence, Studies on the Nature of War* (Rochester)

UNCTAD. 'Cotton | Price Developments.' http://unctad.org/infocomm/anglais/cotton/prices.htm.

United Nations (UNDP). 'Human Development Report (HDR) 2009' http://hdr.undp.org/en/reports/global/hdr2009/.

United Nations (UNDP), and Government of Burkina Faso (2006). 'Country Partnership Programme on Sustainable Land Management in Burkina Faso (CPP).'

United Nations Development Programme (UNDP). 'Poverty Reduction: Macro and Structural Policies.' http://www.undp.org/poverty/macro.htm.

van den Bergh, Govaert, (1996) 'Property Versus Ownership', *The Role of Law in Natural Resource Management*, edited by Joep Spiertz and Melanie Wiber (s-Gravenhage), 167–76

van den Brink, R., Daniel W. Bromley, and J.-P. Chavas, (1995) 'The Economics of Cain and Abel', *The Journal of Development Studies* 31, 371–99

van Dijk, Han, (2000) 'Livestock Transfers and Social Security in Fulbe Society in Hayre, Central Mali.', *Focaal,* 97–111

Voßen, Rainer, (1998)'Les Bisa du Burkina Faso. Contributions À L'étude D'un Peuple Mandé', *La Situation Dialecto-Géographique dans Le Bisa (Mandé Oriental): les Données Lexicales.*, edited by Klaus Keuthmann, Andrea Reikat and Hans-Jürgen Sturm (Köln), 99–117

Wallerstein, Immanuel M., (1974) *The Modern World-System* (New York, 1974)

———, (1976) 'A World-System Perspective on the Social Sciences', *The British Journal of Sociology* 27, no. 3, Special Issue. History and Sociology, 343–52

———, (1984) 'The Development of the Concept of Development', *Sociological Theory* 2, 102–16

————, (2004) *The Modern World-System in the Longue Durée* (Boulder)

————, (2004) *World-Systems Analysis* (Durham)

Weber, Max, (1961) 'Ethnic Groups', *Theories of Society*, edited by E. Shils, T. Parsons, K. D. Naegele, J. Pitts (New York), 305–8

————, (1968) *Economy and Society; an Outline of Interpretive Sociology.* 3 vols (New York)

————, (1978) [1922], Guenther Roth, and Claus Wittich, *Economy and Society: An Outline of Interpretive Sociology.* 2 vols (Berkeley)

Weiß, Roland, (1986), *Wir haben mehr Geld – aber es geht uns schlechter'. Über die Folgen der Entwicklungshilfe Am Beispiel Burkina Faso* (Saarbrücken)

Whitehead, Neil L., (2000) 'A History of Research on Warfare in Anthropology: Reply to Keith Otterbein', *American Anthropologist* 102, no. 4, 834–37

Wilson, Bryan R., (1973) *Magic and the Millenium: A Sociological Study of Religious Movements of Protest among Tribal and 3rd World Peoples* (New York)

Wimmer, Andreas, (1995) 'Interethnische Konflikte', *Kölner Zeitschrift für Soziologie und Sozialpsychologie* 47, no. 3, 464–93

————, (2004) *Facing Ethnic Conflicts: Toward a New Realism* (Lanham, MD)

Wodon, Quentin, D Echevin, and C. Tsimpo, (2006) 'Migration, Remittances, and Poverty in Senegal', in *Migration, Remittances, and Poverty: Case Studies from West Africa* edited by Quentin Wodon (Washington, DC) 139–54

Wolf, Eric R., (1982) *Europe and the People without History* (Berkeley)

World Bank. (2006) 'Burkina Faso Data Profile.'

World Bank. 'World Development Indicators | Data.' http://data.worldbank.org/data-catalog/world-development-indicators?cid=GPD_WDI.

————, 'Gdp Per Capita | Data | Table.' http://data.worldbank.org/indicator/NY.GDP.PCAP.CD.

World Bank. (2011a) 'World Development Indicators | Data.' http://data.worldbank.org/data-catalog/world-development-indicators?cid=GPD_WDI.

————, (2011b) 'Gdp Per Capita' http://data.worldbank.org/indicator/NY.GDP.PCAP.CD.

Zenner, Walter, (1996) 'Middlemen Minorities', *Ethnicity*, edited by John Hutchinson and Anthony D. Smith (Oxford), 179–88

Index